WIGAN & LEIGH

Advertising and Promotion

Chris Hackley, PhD, is Professor of Marketing at the School of Management, Royal Holloway University of London. He has published research on advertising, consumer research and marketing communication in many leading journals including *Journal of Advertising Research, International Journal of Advertising, Admap* and *Journal of Business Ethics*.

Advertising and Promotion

Communicating Brands

Chris Hackley

SAGE Publications
London ● Thousand Oaks ● New Delhi

SAGE Publications
1 Oliver's Yard
55 City Road
London EC1Y 1SP

SAGE Publications Inc
2455 Teller Road
Thousand Oaks, California 91320

SAGE Publications India Pvt Ltd
B-42, Panchsheel Enclave
Post Box 4109
New Delhi 110 017

Library of Congress Control Number: 2004114267

A catalogue record for this book is available from the British Library

ISBN 0 7619 4153 3
ISBN 0 7619 4154 1 (pbk)

Typeset by Selective Minds Infotech Pvt Ltd, Mohali, India
Printed and bound in Great Britain by Athenaeum Press, Gateshead

This book is dedicated to
Suzanne, Michael, James and Nicholas.

Contents

Acknowledgements

I am grateful to the advertising agencies in the UK, USA and Thailand which have kindly answered my calls and taken the time to talk to me. I have referred to many UK Institute of Practitioners in Advertising (IPA) award-winning cases which have been published in full by WARC in the IPA's series of books *Advertising Works*.

This book has evolved from my teaching and benefits from countless conversations with colleagues, postgraduate and undergraduate students from many countries at the Universities of Birmingham, Aston and Oxford Brookes. Several students whose research dissertations I have supervised are cited in the text. They include PhD student Rungpaka (Amy) Tiwsakul who contributed to the sections on product placement and Thai advertising in Chapters 6 and 7. Professor Arthur Kover, former editor of the *Journal of Advertising Research*, and David Brent, former Unilever researcher and pioneer of the account planning discipline in Australia, kindly contributed case vignettes. My thanks also to Delia Martinez Alfonso of SAGE Publications and Chris Blackburn of Oxford Brookes University.

I also offer my thanks to the following for kind permission to use or adapt copyright material: the IPA, Roderick White at *Admap*, Mary Hilton at the the American Advertising Federation (AAF), Publicis Thailand and St Luke's, Dentsu Thailand for generously providing material that I have adapted in the case of their successful campaign for the Tourism Authority of Thailand, many people at DDB London (formerly BMP DDB) for kindly granting me interviews and access to case material over some eight years, and Harrison Troughton Wunderman of London for permission to adapt their award-winning M&G case material. I have also referred to numerous practical examples drawn from websites and print sources which I have cited in the text. Where reproducing or adapting copyright material I have made every effort to obtain permission from the appropriate source. However, if any copyright owners have not been located and contacted at the time of publication, the publishers will be pleased to make the necessary arrangements at the first opportunity.

Introducing Advertising and Promotion

Chapter Outline

Few topics in management or social studies attract such fascinated attention, or elicit such wide disagreement, as advertising and promotion. This opening chapter sets a course through this complex area. It explains the book's intended audiences, aims and main assumptions. The subtitle 'Communicating brands' is explained in terms of the book's pre-eminent, though not exclusive, emphasis on the role of advertising and promotion in the marketing of branded goods and services. The chapter draws on many practical illustrations as the foundation of a theoretically informed study of contemporary advertising and promotion practice.

BOX 1.0 Communicating Brands: Advertising, Communication and The Social Power of Brands

The meaning of a brand is not necessarily limited to the functionality of the product or service it represents. Advertising is central to the creation and maintenance of the wider meaning. Brands such as Marlboro, Mercedes-Benz, Gucci, Prada and Rolls-Royce have powerful significance for non-consumers as well as for consumers. For many consumers branded items carry a promise of quality and value. But the symbolic meaning the brand may have for friends, acquaintances and strangers cannot be discounted as a factor in its appeal. For example, a simple item of clothing such as a shirt will sell in far greater numbers if it is bedecked with a logo that confers a symbolic meaning on that item. Wearing a Tommy Hilfiger branded shirt is said to confer prestige on the wearer because of the values of affluence and social privilege the brand represents (Schor, 1998: 47, cited in Szmigin, 2003: 139).

Anthropologists have long noted the importance of ownership and display of prized items for signifying social identity and status in non-consumer societies. In economically advanced societies brands take this role as a 'cultural resource' (Holt, 2002: 87; see also Belk, 1988; Elliott and Wattanasuwan, 1998; McCracken, 1988) that enables and extends social communication. The influence of brands is such that even resistance to brands has become a defining social position. The 'social power' of brands (Feldwick, 2002: 11) refers to the meaning that goes beyond functionality and is a symbolic reference point among consumers and non-consumers alike. This symbolic meaning is powerfully framed by advertising and sustained through other forms of communication such as word-of-mouth, public relations, product and brand placement in entertainment media, sponsorship and package design.

Aims of the Book

Advertising and promotion: Communicating brands is written primarily for those studying advertising, promotion and related topics, such as brand marketing, as part of taught academic programmes at advanced undergraduate and postgraduate level. The book introduces intellectual perspectives on advertising and promotion from cultural and social studies within a detailed account of how and why contemporary advertising is created. Many cultural studies of advertising focus on the textual analysis of ads: in other words, they look at the consumption of advertising while giving less attention to the material conditions that give rise to its production. But many managerial texts offer accounts of the marketing context for advertising and promotional campaigns while giving only arm's-length treatment to the ways in which these campaigns are understood and consumed. This book offers a basis for an intellectually informed treatment of advertising and promotion that builds on an inside view of the management practices in the field.

Advertising and promotion: Communicating brands will also be of interest to the general reader. Prior knowledge of advertising and marketing is not assumed but some acquaintance with marketing basics will be useful for readers who are interested in the management perspective. Those readers not acquainted with the field should, in any case, soon grasp the concepts of **positioning, targeting** and **segmentation** that are central to understanding the way advertising is used to accomplish brand marketing ends. To aid study important concepts are highlighted (in bold type) in each chapter and explained in a glossary at its end. Review exercises, questions and short cases are provided as material for reinforcement and reflection. There are also explanatory notes and references for those wishing to acquire deeper knowledge of particular topics through more specific reading. The book uses many international examples to illustrate particular aspects of practice. Underlying its practical perspective is a strong sense of how advertising can be understood in intellectually viable ways that connect management practice, consumer experience and other fields of social study.

Outline of the Book

Chapter 1 sets the scene for the academic study of advertising and promotion and explains the major assumptions the book makes. For convenience, the practical descriptions of how the promotional communication industry does its work usually adopt the perspective of the full-service advertising agency. Full-service agencies, as the phrase suggests, provide any marketing communications service a client requires. They are pretty self-sufficient in all communications and related disciplines (research, strategic planning, media, art production). The self-sufficiency of such agencies can, however, be illusory because of the extent of sub-contracting that goes on,[1] especially on big accounts. However, the major advertising agencies remain hugely influential as umbrella organizations operating at the centre of marketing, corporate and brand communications practice. As the book explains, the dominance of the traditional advertising agency over the marketing communications industry is being challenged by media agencies, and direct and other below-the-line marketing agencies, as integrated communications solutions are increasingly required by clients. Chapter 2 introduces the theoretical themes that are drawn on throughout to understand the engagement between advertising and its audiences. The book begins its detailed consideration of the advertising and promotion business in Chapter 3, which explains the management context for marketing communication by describing its influential role in brand marketing. Chapter 4 describes the personalities, roles and processes of a typical agency. Chapter 5 describes the media planning task and reflects on the rapid changes that have taken place in the media infrastructure. Chapter 6 develops some of the implications these changes have had for media strategy in advertising and promotion and discusses the evolution of hybrid forms of promotion such as sponsorship and brand placement in entertainment communications.

Many of the practical illustrations in the book are international in scope but the cultural and commercial importance of international promotion in brand marketing justifies the dedicated examination of the topic in Chapter 7.

Chapter 8 explores some of the many contrasting arguments in the contentious and complex topic of advertising ethics. While the ethics of advertising is a major concern for many consumers and other groups, within the advertising industry the role of research creates far more heated argument. Chapter 9 describes the main kinds of research and indicates why advertising professionals feel so strongly about what kinds of research are deployed and how research findings are used. Chapter 10 draws the book's theoretical themes together and synthesizes the various levels of theory.

Advertising and promotion: Communicating brands seeks to promote a greater understanding of the subject area both as a managerial discipline and as (arguably) one of the most far-reaching cultural forces of our time. To this end the book offers a thorough descriptive account of how advertising and promotional campaigns are devised and executed and the role they play for international brand marketing and other forms of organization such as charities and government agencies.[2] This managerial perspective is used as a point of departure from which to better understand how advertising comes to have its persuasive effect on individuals and its pervasive influence on individual and collective cultural lives. The managerial perspective on advertising is framed within a conceptual account of the nature of the engagement between consumers and advertising.

BOX 1.1   Advertising and Cultural Change: Gender Representations in UK Alcohol Advertising

In many cultures, cigarette smoking by females was once considered to be unacceptable and outrageous behaviour. From the 1940s advertising popularized cigarette smoking and, in particular, made smoking acceptable for females in images that implied female smoking was a progressive move for gender relations. Similarly, more recent portrayals of alcohol consumption in advertising have encouraged and reflected a profound change in the culture of alcohol consumption in the UK. In the 1970s, UK advertisements for Courage beer brands such as John Smith's portrayed drinkers as exclusively male, fond only of the company of other males and continually devising strategies to escape domestic imprisonment (and the nagging wife) for the liberation and companionship of the (male-dominated) 'pub'. In the 1980s advertising campaigns for beer brands such as Hofmeister and Castlemaine XXXX portrayed the male drinker in a radically different light, as a streetwise 'jack the lad', much more image-conscious and flirtatious than the bluff, blazer-wearing rugby hearty of the 1970s.

Why Study Advertising and Promotion as an Academic Field?

Advertising and Consumption

Advertising has, perhaps, lagged somewhat behind the broader field of consumption as a focus for social research. (Advertising is, though, an 'integral part of twentieth-century consumption' and an 'important form of representation in the contemporary world' (Nava et al., 1997: 3–4).) As a form of representation, advertising takes signs and meanings extant in non-advertising culture and transforms them, creating new representations in juxtaposition with marketed brands. Advertisements can be seen as 'dynamic and sensuous representations of cultural values' (Lears, 1994, in Richards et al., 2000: 1). The ways in which we consumers interpret advertisements can reflect our own culturally-derived values and our culturally-learned fantasies and aspirations.

In expressing opinions about advertising we can indicate 'our personality, or our social and ideological position' (Cook, 2001: 1). Our attitudes to advertising can express values that connect us to a desired peer group, especially if we are young (Ritson and Elliott, 1999). Life in economically advanced societies is saturated with marketing communication. Advertising in all its forms offers a vast and dynamic vocabulary of cultural meanings from which we can select a personally tailored ensemble of brands that reflects and communicates our sense of social positioning. There is no need to conflate consumption, advertising and marketing to exaggerate the importance of either field for social study. While marketing, in important respects, is communication (Schultz et al., 1993; Wells, 1975: 197), there are clear areas that demarcate each field from the other. What we can say is that advertising, as the super-ordinate category embracing all forms of marketing communication, carries great importance both reflecting and informing marketing and consumption. Advertising has been cited as a force for cultural change of many kinds. Changes in the portrayals of brand consumption in advertisements both reflect and legitimize changes in the social world beyond advertising.

Today's alcohol culture in the UK seems far removed from these dated advertising representations. Box 1.1 shows that there has been a proliferation of alcohol brands (especially 'alco-pops') mixed with fruit flavours and targeted at younger consumers. Along with the reduction in the age profile of targeted consumers there has been a reversal of gender roles in advertising, with the female now often portrayed as smarter and more inclined to risk-taking than the male in TV ads for alcohol brands such as Archer's and Bacardi. This kind of advertising has raised concern among pressure groups because of rises in alcohol-related illness among young British women.

The space between the portrayals of social life in advertising, and social life as it is acted out in non-advertising social settings, reveals tensions and contradictions that are of direct concern for health, social and economic policy. (Recent alcohol ads have been overtly sexualized, causing public concern[3] that alcohol brand advertising is promoting high-risk behaviour.) The public concern is matched by official concern at the influence of alcohol advertising: the World Health Organization made alcohol advertising a key priority in their anti-alcohol campaigns (WHO, 1988, in Nelson and Young, 2001). The fact that people now make the connection between advertising and social behaviour so readily reflects the cultural influence that advertising is seen to have.

Advertising and Management Studies

Alongside its importance as a field of cultural and consumer studies, advertising is a major field of management studies. It has assumed particular significance as the major element of brand marketing. Marketing communications in general and advertising in particular are now seen as a major, and possibly *the* major source of competitive advantage in consumer markets (Shimp, 1997). As the brand image has come to represent a dynamic and enduring source of consumer interest (and company revenue), the ways in which brands can be portrayed and their image controlled have become central to the concerns of brand management. Advertising alone does not make the brand but the successful consumer brand is, nevertheless, inseparable from its portrayal in advertising and other marketing communications media. The multiplication of media channels through new technology and regulatory change has meant that most aspects of brand marketing management have become tinged with a concern for the potential impact on brand communications and the integrity of the brand personality. Decisions on pricing, design, packaging, distribution outlet and even raw materials are taken with one eye on the brand's core values and how these might be perceived in the light of media coverage of the brand. It is mistaken to argue that communication is all there is to brand marketing (but see Schultz et al., 1993; Wells, 1975), and it is a truism that advertising and marketing communications have assumed a key importance in the destiny of brands and their producing organizations. Advertising, and the work of advertising agencies, lie at the centre of this rapidly evolving integrated marketing communications field.

Marketing communications do not simply portray brands: they constitute those brands in the sense that the meaning of the brand cannot be properly understood in separation from its brand name, logo, advertising and other communications associated with it. Whether brand *a* is better designed, more attractive, easier to use, or more useful than brand *b* is rarely something that can be decided finally and objectively. It is usually to some degree a matter of opinion. This is where advertising acquires its suggestive power. It occupies a realm in which consumers are actively seeking suggestions to layer consumption with new social significance.

Advertisers offer us material to engage our imagination and open up new possibilities for consumption experiences. Consumers are not passive dupes being sold on exaggerated claims. Advertising is so powerful because, as consumers, we are actively complicit in our own exploitation.

To put this another way, in a decidedly non-trivial sense, advertising gives us what we want. Both damning advertising as lies and puffery and defending it as an essential economic function oversimplify the complexities of understanding advertising. Advertising communication frames the way consumers engage with and understand marketed brands. It is the advertising, rather than the more tangible aspects of marketing management, that symbolically realize the marketing ideal of giving the consumers what we (think we) want.

Another important reason why advertising is a useful subject of study is because it lends itself to examination from many differing disciplinary perspectives and therefore offers means of linking those perspectives through multidisciplinary studies. The boom in the quantity of advertising to which we are exposed on a daily basis and the intriguing sophistication of many creative executions have generated lively popular interest. In its most high-profile manifestations advertising has almost become a branch of showbiz, with ostentatious televised award shows for the best ads, lavish conferences in Cannes and, for the most innovative film producers, frequent career movement between the advertising and movie businesses. Through this profile and exposure advertising intrudes frequently on typical personal experience, which offers a point of departure for the wider study of the topic both as a management discipline and as a subject of consumer and cultural studies.

The edgy tone of many advertisements, the popular attention advertising attracts in national press and TV media and the massive budgets allocated to it by brand marketing organizations make it a topic of intense interest among many commentators. In fact, advertising is typically treated as a subject of controversy. In the following section we will try to elaborate on the theatre of advertising by outlining some of the many contradictory views that are held about this modern enigma.

What is Advertising and How Can We Understand It?

Defining Advertising

In marketing management texts advertising is conventionally regarded as one element of the **promotional mix**, a management tool defined by its explicitly promotional, mediated and paid-for character, and differentiated from other marketing communications disciplines such as public relations, personal selling, corporate communications, sales promotion and so on. In turn, promotion is regarded as one sub-category of the marketing management mix of price, product (design) and distribution. The advertising industry often pays little regard to such hierarchical sub-divisions, preferring to see all marketing elements as interacting parts of a whole. This view cuts across communications disciplines and acknowledges the interlocking and symbiotic relation of the elements of marketing. Advertising man Bill Bernbach's reputed comment that 'Nothing kills a bad product faster than good advertising' illustrates well the pitfalls of taking a compartmentalized view of marketing activities. Marketing operations and marketing communication are interdependent in important respects.

The ingenuity of advertisers and the flexibility of advertising as a communication form often render attempts to define it in one sentence trite or tautologous. Advertising often sells something, but often does not, as with much political, public-service or charities advertising. Advertising is often an impersonal communication, distinguishing it from personal selling, but there are many ads that are eye-to-eye sales pitches delivered by actors or celebrity endorsers in a mediated imitation of a personal sales encounter. Advertising often comprises stereotypical elements that set it apart from other forms of mediated communication. Overheated sales pitches from improbably coiffed spokespersons, happy housewives singing irritatingly catchy jingles at the kitchen sink, unfeasibly attractive models unreasonably excited by chocolate confections all spring to mind as advertising clichés. But then again, many advertisements contradict advertising stereotypes. The use of hybrid forms of promotions such as product placement, sponsorship and public relations make categorization still more problematic.

Industry professionals tend to regard advertising as a powerful marketing tool, a means of persuasively communicating with millions of customers. Advertising's ability to sell tends to be overplayed: its ability to persuade consumers to think in terms of brands is the source of its economic power. A narrow definition of what advertising is obscures consideration of what advertising does. We might categorize a given piece of communication as an advertisement in terms of its parallels with a vague and fuzzy mental prototype of what an ad should look or sound like, perhaps in line with the stereotypes mentioned above (Rosch, 1977, cited in Cook, 2001: 13), but the marketing industry itself has a vested interested in challenging its own norms. Advertising may be a communication that at some level has a promotional motive, but this hardly prepares us for all the kinds of promotional messages we are likely to encounter. Neither can it prepare us for the subtlety of motive that underlies many hybrid promotional forms. A post-match interview with a logo-wearing sporting star, a free movie character toy in a fast-food meal, a 'courtesy' phone call from your bank can each be regarded as promotional forms at some level. They stretch beyond the conventional definitions of advertising but, nevertheless, typify the integrated and multi-channel trends of much contemporary promotional activity. A realistic study of advertising and promotion cannot hope to put the parts neatly in a labelled box. Advertising takes the enquirer on a journey that is all the more fascinating because it defies boundaries.

The Experience of Advertising

Take a moment to think about the advertisements you have seen or heard this week. At whom were they aimed? What, exactly, were they trying to communicate? How did they make you feel? Did you rush to buy the brand? Which medium conveyed the ads? Did you see them on a passing vehicle, on outdoor poster sites, on the television, hear them on the radio, read them in the press? Did you see other forms of promotion on your clothing, smell them in a promotionally enhanced shopping environment, see them on packaging, on an air balloon in the sky or on the back of a bus ticket? It is difficult to remember more than a few of all the hundreds of promotions you see every week. Advertising has become such a feature of daily life in developed market economies that sometimes it seems as if we hardly notice it. Advertising pervades our cultural landscape, especially in urban settings, and we carry on our lives taking it for granted, as if it were as natural as grass or trees.[4]

 We are struck, then, when particular ads become topics of general conversation or objects of public disapproval. It is then that we realize how taken for granted much advertising is and we wonder how this paradox occurs. Advertising is, of course, so powerful precisely because it is taken for granted. There are frequent press features that reflect our puzzled fascination with the latest iconic or controversial ad. The TV show dedicated to the funniest or most outlandish ads has become a mainstay of popular TV programming in many countries. Advertising's crossing over into mainstream entertainment and the uses mainstream entertainment media make of advertising styles and techniques reflect another aspect of advertising's dynamic character. It is evolving into forms that are increasingly difficult to categorize. The hard-sell ads remain but there are also new narrative forms of ever greater subtlety.

Contrasting Views of Advertising

The Management Perspective

Among professional managers there is a wide diversity of opinion on the uses of advertising. Some feel that it is a necessary part of getting a brand noticed, remembered and bought. Others are more sceptical about the claims made for advertising and resent allocating large budgets to advertising agencies to squander (as they see it) on unaccountable creativity. Many in the marketing business feel that they do not know how advertising works

BOX 1.2   New Narrative Forms of Advertising: Adidas and
            Celebrity Sportsmen

In the UK in late 2003 a series of TV ads for the Adidas
sportswear brand featured the soccer star David Beckham with the
England rugby football star Johnny Wilkinson. The ads are edited
vignettes of a contrived kick-about session in which each tests the
other's skill at their respective sports. There is no backing-track or
voice-over. There is nothing to indicate that it is an ad, apart from
the appearance of the Adidas name in small type at the end of each
ad. There is no need for Adidas to labour the point: these
superstars of sport represent all the values the brand would wish to
be associated with. The campaign has merged the marketing
communications genres of sponsorship, celebrity endorsement and
advertising by producing a hybrid form that does not easily fit into
any of these categories. The ads are presented simply as
entertainments. They attracted press coverage in the UK even
before they were aired and generated widespread interest and
attention from sports fans. Adidas adopted a similar approach in
New Zealand to try to contrive a sense of sporting authenticity for
the brand: TV ads featured the New Zealand All Blacks rugby
football team, revered as sporting heroes in their homeland.

but cannot take the risk of not advertising their product or service in case
they suffer a disadvantage compared with their competitors. Even amid
this scepticism and doubt, there is an acknowledgement that the world's
major brands would be inconceivable without it. Neither can it be doubt-
ed that the commercial fortunes of some brands, and in some cases the
shape of entire markets, have been transformed through powerful and
creatively compelling advertising campaigns. For example, the famous
'Laundrette' ad that John Hegarty of the agency Bartle Bogle Hegarty
created in the 1982 campaign for Levi's 501s used American provenance
to revolutionize the denim jeans market in general and sales of Levi's in
particular for the following decade. It has been said that the ads increased
sales of denim jeans by some 600 per cent.

More recently, popular ads for Budweiser beer increased market share
for the brand and earned valuable free publicity simply because they
added a word ('Whassup') to the vernacular of American English (and
even earned a listing in Longman's *Dictionary*).[5] Campaigns for Gold
Blend coffee and for the Renault Clio in the 1990s earned similar fame in
the UK and provided valuable PR benefits for those brands. A survey of
senior executives in US corporations revealed the view that a powerful ad
campaign for a brand can have significant effects on the share price,

profitability and long-term financial stability of the entire corporation (see the section on the *American Advertising Federation* survey in Chapter 2). Even so, many of the same executives are chary of increasing their advertising budget and suspicious of advertising agencies.

The Consumer/Citizen Perspective

Advertising tends to be blamed for many social evils, from eating disorders to the decline in public manners. Yet, paradoxically, advertising is also widely regarded as trivial. It occupies a lowly status in our cultural hierarchy. Popular art, literature, movies, even stand-up comedy performers are discussed, critiqued and analysed in the Sunday supplements as aspects of aesthetic culture. But advertising is typically criticized. Yet its lowly cultural status is belied by our fascination with it. We enjoy TV shows about the funniest ads and we often talk about the latest ads in our daily conversations. Cook (2001) notes this duality about advertising's cultural status. It is regarded as both trivial and powerful, banal and sinister, amusing and degrading. Advertising is historically a relatively recent development in communication and we still struggle to come to terms with its apparent force.

Although the level of popular interest in advertising is great, there is little consensus about its role in society. Some argue that it corrupts cultural life with its insistent, hectoring presence cajoling us to buy ever greater quantities of goods and services. Organized consumer resistance to advertising has taken the form of vandalism, such as a French anti-advertising group spray-painting '*le pub tue*' or '*le pub pue*' on all the advertising posters in the Paris metro, the RATP.[6] Advertising intrudes into ever more social spaces. Many schools, especially in the USA, now accept fees to give exclusive rights to commercial organisations to advertise and sell their goods on campus. It was reported that one student was suspended for wearing a Pepsi T-shirt on his school's 'Coke Day'.[7] Even religious observance is not immune from advertising's influence. Advertising-style slogans in brash colours promoting religious observance can be seen outside many places of worship. Evidently, advertising discourse influences the very culture from which it draws.

But while some have a political objection to advertising in all its forms, many people are irritated not by advertising in general but by what they see as its excesses. Even acknowledging advertising's unique ideological force promoting consumerism, legitimizing capitalism and framing every-day experience (Elliott and Ritson, 1997) does not necessarily imply an anti-advertising stance. Few can deny that advertising is intrinsic to the creation of wealth and many would argue that it has a role in the free and untrammelled expression of ideas, a socially progressive exchange of 'ideas for living', to adapt John Stuart Mill's phrase.[8]

For many who accept the economic inevitability of advertising, its forms and styles provide particular sources of irritation. Pop-up ads and email spam are a continuing irritation for many internet users; unwanted junk direct advertising mail annoys millions of householders daily. Our favourite TV shows are frequently interrupted by lengthy commercial breaks. Some TV shows even break the narrative to make space for contrived brand references within the plot. Roadside poster sites are sometimes accused of polluting the urban environment or even of distracting drivers and causing road accidents. Organizations are often accused of using advertising unethically for commercial advantage. The national press in the UK has recently run features criticizing aspects of advertising,[9] particularly its alleged influence over health and children's development. The rise of 'pester power' as a marketing technique and the distortion of childhood values into those of adults[10] are two of the trends that ad agencies have been accused of initiating, or at least exploiting. All these issues reflect concern with the social responsibility, ethics and regulation of advertising (discussed in detail in Chapter 8).

The Organizational Perspective

Organizations survive by returning value to shareholders and other stakeholders. They do what they must within regulatory frameworks and laws governing advertising standards that seem, to them, to be excessively restrictive. Manufacturers and advertisers will argue that, given the competitive pressures under which they operate, the level of integrity in advertising and marketing is remarkably high. In advanced economies there are industry regulations and legal strictures that give consumers considerable redress if they can show that an advertiser's promise was literally untrue or that their product was dangerous. For advertisers, finding a creative execution that is within the bounds of regulations and gets their brand noticed at all is a major challenge. From an advertiser's point of view, the brand is responsible for the livelihoods of many people: a successful brand creates jobs and generates wealth for employees, shareholders and suppliers. Successful brands are a mainstay of economic growth. In advanced economies, poverty of the scale and severity of the previous century is no longer known. Advertising has played its part in this wealth creation as an engine of economic growth, maintaining competition by communicating offers, and by collectively promoting an ethos of consumption.

Advertising's persuasiveness is not only used in profit generation. Social advertising is a genre that has informed the public on social issues and in some cases even changed behaviour. Many public services or charities use advertising campaigns to try to promote their causes or to change social behaviour with respect to, for example, alcohol consumption, safer driving, sexual practice, domestic violence or social prejudice towards disability or ethnicity. Social advertising has developed such that it even shouts louder than brand advertising. As we will see in Chapter 8, many social campaigns are allowed by regulatory authorities to push the boundaries of tasteful depiction further than brand advertisers because of their ostensibly virtuous motives.

Advertising is regarded by many as inherently deceitful. Yet considering the tenaciousness with which corporations pursue profits, remarkably few ads tell literal untruths. Of course, some do, but most advertising satisfies typical social conventions of truthfulness. The interaction of consumers with communications which have a marketing subtext is usually too complex and subtle to be thought of as, simply, a matter of either fact or fiction. If an ad implies that a man's sexual attractiveness and social status will be enhanced by using a Gillette razor, surely this is merely preposterous rather than untrue? To be sure, consumer perceptions and beliefs about brands are self-sustaining to some degree: we believe what we want to believe, sometimes in the face of contradictory evidence. Do smokers really cough less using low-tar cigarettes? Are we slimmer because we put calorie-free sugar substitute in our coffee? It can hardly be denied that there is an important element of wish fulfilment in what we choose to believe in advertising.

A peculiarity of advertising is that we are expected to be able to distinguish between untruth and humorous hyperbole, but the advertisers make very little effort to blur this distinction. This is just one reason why this sophisticated communication form is rightfully a part of academic study: advertising performs an essential economic function in capitalist economies but for it to perform its economic function well it demands a sophisticated level of discernment from consumers. Advertising, strangely, is rarely a significant part of the school curriculum even though negotiating a way through the advertising landscape is essential to the economic and social competence of citizens.

Advertising and Promotional Culture

The diversity of views advertising attracts reflects its role at the centre of what Wernick (1991) called 'promotional culture'. In developed market economies we are experiencing a revolution in public communication. Broadcasting deregulation, vertical and lateral mergers in the media industry and technological advances in communication are creating a promotional environment that has no precedent in modern history. The ethos, language and aesthetic forms of promotion have become parts of everyday experience that are taken for granted. As we have seen, even churches advertise heaven in a world that has become a heaven for advertisers.

Within promotional culture we grow accustomed to spending significant sums of money on items that are not essential for survival. We associate happiness with consumption, indeed, in many ways we define our existence in terms of consumption. As advertising and communication make continuous consumption of branded items a culturally normal practice, other competing cultural values that encourage abstention from consumption are relatively reduced in status. Today in the Western developed economies over-indulgence is the norm and waste is everywhere. Changes in cultural norms and practices of consumption (such as the move towards eating fast food and away from the family-based social ritual of the home-cooked meal) to some extent reflect the influence of promotional culture. Deeply held values and practices are undermined and finally overthrown under the influence of advertising. Advertising's apparent triviality as a sub-category of popular art should not distract us from this powerful cultural influence in framing and changing, as well as reflecting, the way we live.

In linking the study of advertising's cultural influence with its study as a management discipline this book takes a new broad and inclusive approach to its subject. The remainder of Chapter 1 sets the terms of engagement with its topic by explaining how such a broad scope reflects contemporary practice in the field.

Advertising Management and This Book

Strategy, Integration and Research

This book's standpoint on advertising practice reflects a concern with three main concepts: strategy, integration and research. The strategic

---

BOX 1.3   Advertising and Truthfulness: 'Lynx' Ads Make Fun of Themselves

'Lynx'-branded male grooming products are marketed with expensively produced TV ads that show male users becoming unexpectedly irresistible to beautiful women. The ads assume that the viewer will understand that it is all just a joke: the plots are clearly intended to be funny. Lynx is pointing at the narrative conventions of male grooming brands and laughing at them with the viewer. But the high production standards of the ads show viewers that in fact the marketing campaign is deadly serious. Viewers agree – Lynx is the leading brand in several male grooming product segments. Could it be that knowing the ads are not serious strengthens rather than weakens the message, that using Lynx deodorant might just make the user more sexually alluring to the woman of his dreams?

perspective on advertising and promotion implies a purposive, pragmatic, medium-to-long-term approach to communication, driven by marketing imperatives and commanding significant resources. An important part of the strategic perspective for brand communications is the need for an underlying purpose to inform and guide management action. This marketing rationality is intended to bring coherence and unity of purpose to the various marketing communications activities. The integration of creative themes and media channels is often considered to have an important role in sustaining this coherence.

Integrated Marketing Communications

The phrase '**Integrated Marketing Communications**' (Schultz et al., 1993) reflects managerial interest in co-ordinating different media channels to optimize the effectiveness of marketing communications programmes. If brand communications reflect implied values and imagery that are consistent throughout differing media channels, then clearly these channels act in a mutually reinforcing way with each successive consumer engagement. Interest in IMC has developed because of the view that marketing communication offers the 'only sustainable competitive advantage of marketing organizations' (Schultz et al., 1993: 47). Consequently, all points of contact between an organization and its audience can be utilized as possible communications channels through which all forms of communication may be used. The end goal is to influence the behaviour of targeted audiences (Shimp, 1997: 13).

Although advertising agencies consider traditional advertising to be their core activity, the larger, full-service agencies are increasingly finding that clients expect them to offer expertise across the marketing communication disciplines. Consumers, moreover, do not make a strong distinction between the differing media that carry advertising. As Percy et al. point out, 'people generally look at all marketing communications as "advertising"' (2001: v). The rise of brand marketing makes the advertising medium secondary to the brand personality, an entity that can be expressed through many differing forms of creative execution and communicated through different media. Indeed, it is recognized that an explicit, paid-for advertisement placed in a mass medium may have no greater impact for a brand than a carefully integrated product placement in a movie or a high-profile sports sponsorship deal. It is no longer unusual for public relations or direct mail to be used as the main, strategic arm of marketing communications effort. Integrated advertising campaigns utilize the qualities of different media in a communications onslaught designed to project consistent brand values regardless of whatever communication source the consumer encounters.

This blurring of the lines between marketing communications disciplines is part of a radical change in the media infrastructure coming from developments in electronic communications technology and the rise of global business. Global brands now cross borders and resonate with the consumers of many countries. Mass media, above-the-line advertising is often regarded as the strategic element of marketing communications, the one communication technique that can transform the fortunes of corporations, create brands and change entire markets. Although there are still good reasons for holding this view, there is also a strong case for managers to consider advertising from a strategic and integrated perspective which acknowledges that the rationale for brand communications drives the pragmatic development of integrated creative executions and media strategies.

Research

Research is another key theme reflecting this book's practical perspective. In order to create consistently successful advertising, advertisers have to understand the business of their clients, the markets in which they operate and the consumers with whom they wish to communicate. Research for advertising can take many forms which will be explained in Chapter 9. At this point the role and importance of research need to be emphasized because of a common misconception, which is that research, with its connotations of statistics and mass questionnaire surveys, has no role in the creative world of advertising. In fact research conceived broadly to include qualitative and informal insights into consumers is central to the advertising communication task.

The advertising legend David Ogilvy (1983) pointed out that research has played a central role in successful advertising for decades, although the type of research conducted and the way it is integrated into the creative development of advertising may differ from case to case. Research can inspire and direct creative work by offering an insight into the market or the consumer that provides a hook of reality on which to hang the fantasy of advertising. It can also help to prejudge the way a given creative execution might be received by consumers or to measure the changes in attitude as a result of a given campaign. As we see in Chapter 9, the rightful role of research in advertising and also the question of who should be responsible for it are subject to strong disagreement in the advertising industry. In some agencies research is the responsibility of a specialist labelled 'the account planner', as it was in the Edgell Potato Whip case described below. The account planning ethos or philosophy, though, is not adopted throughout the industry and is subject to a degree of controversy puzzling to those outside the relatively closed circle of ad agencies (Hackley, 2003a).

The tension, often a fruitful one, surrounding the role of research in advertising practice is also reflected in a similar tension in academic research into advertising. The assumption of this book is that the academic and practitioner perspectives need not be mutually exclusive, although we

BOX 1.4   Integrating Research, Advertising and Marketing Strategy: Smashing the Instant Potato Market in Australia

TV ads for Cadbury's Smash instant dried mashed potato created a mass appeal for the product and occupy a legendary status (the Smash laughing 'Martians') in the UK advertising industry. In Australia the Edgell Canned Foods company used carefully conceived consumer research to market a successful rival that significantly outsold the Cadbury's brand even though the two products were almost identical in taste and composition. Former Unilever researcher David Brent carried out qualitative focus groups with Australian consumers on preparing and eating both real and instant mashed potato. They also tested consumer preferences on a ring-pull can. Both Cadbury's Smash and the market leader, Unilever's Deb brand, used a sachet. Further research used in-home and in-store sampling. Finally, other brand names were tested against the soon-to-be-launched Smash and other competitors. Smash came a poor last in the ratings, indicating that the Cadbury's product might run into consumer resistance in Australia because of its brand name.

Edgell Potato Whip (a name deriving from qualitative research in which housewives' used the analogy of whipping the product into a light mash) was launched with a TV ad that used the authority of an Irish family as experts in potato-eating. After 18 months the Edgell brand had taken almost 50 per cent of the market from market leader Deb. Cadbury's Smash, launched around the same time using the theme that had been a runaway success in the UK, failed in Australia and was delisted.

The success of Edgell's Potato Whip in Australia was attributed to the agency's account planning approach that integrated research findings into advertising strategy and creative development. In addition, the company allowed the agency to influence their overall marketing strategy.[11]

acknowledge below that C.P. Snow's 'two cultures', art and science, find powerfully opposing expressions among advertising managers (Hackley, 2003b).

Brands and Marketing Signification

One final point needs to be made to underline the broad perspective this book takes on promotional and marketing communications. We have already suggested that marketing and communication cannot be easily separated. We now need to draw out the implications of this point of view and to explain exactly what is meant by it. **Signification** is a concept that will be useful in this task. The term is used here in a broad sense to refer to signs that communicate a message that carries meaning (or, as we shall see, meanings). More will be mentioned about different kinds of signification in Chapter 2; for the present we wish simply to highlight the communicative dimension of marketing activity as a whole.

Brands signify in the sense that they are signs or combinations of signs (words, music, colours, logos, packaging design, and so on) that communicate values or ideas to various **consumer communities**. We have noted above that consumers often regard all marketing and promotion, colloquially, as advertising. For consumers, the world of marketing is a kaleidoscope of communication, the component parts of which are impossible to disentangle. There are many dimensions to communication in relation to brand marketing. Marketing management cannot be reduced to advertising and communication, since it is a complex set of substantive activities in its own right. Nonetheless, when commentators say that marketing and communications are inseparable (Leiss et al., 1997; Shimp, 1997: 4; Schultz et al., 1994: 46), they are making an important point. Every aspect of marketing management (price, distribution, product design) can carry powerfully suggestive signification.

Marketing is replete with signification in many forms. Marketing activities of all kinds can be seen to combine signs that resonate with cultural meanings (Barthes, 1972; Umiker-Sebeok, 1997; Williamson, 1978). The futuristic design of a Dyson vacuum cleaner or the clean, sweeping lines of a Mazda MX5 sports car have the powerful appeal of implied values that are very important to the consumer. A Rolex watch might be a well-made jewellery item with time-keeping utility but the Rolex brand is best known as a symbol of ostentatious, perhaps extravagant, wealth. Rodeo Drive in Beverly Hills, California, Madison Avenue, New York, and Knightsbridge, London are home to many designer stores because these locations have become culturally identified with prestige retail outlets. The location, as well as the price, carries a powerful message about the products.

Many other aspects of organizational activity not usually categorized as communication can carry powerful signification: that is, they can be interpreted in terms of particular meanings. Perhaps the most visible aspects of organizational communication for consumers are advertisements placed in above-the-line media such as TV, outdoors, the press or commercial radio. But organizations know that consumers' experience of brands is integrated in a powerful sense: consumers will not normally distinguish between different communication channels when they think of a brand or an organization. So organizations need to be conscious of the way that their various communications can be interpreted and of how consistent these interpretations may be with those from other communication sources.

When the UK airline corporation British Airways redesigned the livery on its airplanes at great expense the aim was to offer a stronger and more contemporary corporate image to support other communications and marketing activities. As consumers encounter corporate communications through vehicle liveries, and also through letterhead design, corporate advertising, staff uniforms, telephone conversations with organizational staff and press coverage of the organization's activities, they will assimilate these experiences into their overall understanding of the brand. Corporate identity is a distinct field of research and practice (Melewar and Wooldridge, 2001) but much if its importance lies in the connection consumers make between corporations and their brands in an integrated marketing communications landscape. More broadly still, in advanced economies marketing activity can be responsible for a huge majority of the images we see and the ways in which we interpret, understand and use them are central to our experience of marketing and consumption (Schroeder, 2004).

There are yet more subtle dimensions of communication to consider. In the Veblen effect (Veblen, [1899] 1970), demand for a product reacts inversely with price changes. Price signifies the quality positioning of the brand and this can be an important influence on demand for very expensive, prestige items. Although it is anti-competitive for manufacturers to enforce prices on retailers, nonetheless many brand owners do not like to have their product discounted because of the potential threat to consumers' perceptions of quality. The high price of prestige brands is an essential part of their brand positioning. Such brands are seldom discounted because of the fear that such an action will dilute the brand appeal and damage its market positioning.

As we have already noted, the location of the retail outlet (for example, in a prestige development) signifies that the brand is acceptable together with an ensemble of similarly positioned brands. The architecture and floor design of retail stores can also carry heavy signification. In the early 1900s US department store retailers were well aware of the power of impressive architecture in creating environments that inspired consumers to consume (Marchand, 1998). The interior design of retail outlets is also a powerful signifier in the marketing process. Retail organizations often commission detailed research into in-store consumer behaviour in order to help the design to cohere with the brand image of the store and to enhance sales per square foot of floorspace.

Consumers, then, understand brands holistically by assimilating messages about that brand from many diverse channels of communication. Media editorial, direct mail shots, customer service encounters, television and press advertising and retail store displays, brand logos, product design and price relative to competition all converge to form the consumer's understanding of a given brand. Include word-of-mouth and personal experience of brand usage, and it becomes clear that consumers cannot normally remember which particular communication or experience was significant in forming their enduring impression of a brand. Furthermore, many consumers do not distinguish the elements of marketing at all when they think of a specific brand.

Brands, then, subsist symbolically as a nebulous and mutable, yet enduring, memory of many kinds of consumer experience. Brands have a tangible, concrete reality, of course; they are created through human and production processes, they require resources and usually (though not always, as in the case of virtual corporations) occupy office or factory space. But, most importantly, a brand also has a secret life as an abstraction. This abstraction, the brand image or personality, acts in concert with its more tangible dimensions to frame and support the consumer's overall idea of that brand. Many brand marketing organizations try to integrate the various communications channels they use so that they act in harmony and, together, carry coherent and consistent messages about the brand. Doing this makes possible synergy effects by which each medium can leverage the influence of the others, enhancing marketing effectiveness by projecting the brand values and personality more powerfully.

The integrated perspective of this book does not conflate disciplines or media channels that are, rightly, considered by managers to be separate and distinct. Rather, it acknowledges the blurring and convergence of communications media sources in consumers' outlook. It also acknowledges that communications act interdependently: there are synergies that, in the new global media infrastructure, can be exploited by marketing organizations. The assimilation of brand advertising and marketing into mainstream entertainment media, discussed in detail in Chapter 6, is perhaps the most powerful indication of this integrative synergy (Hackley, 2003c).

This book describes the context for the production of contemporary advertising and promotion and frames it within a theoretical consideration of advertising consumption, introduced in Chapter 2.

Review Exercises

1. Make a list of all the forms of advertising and promotion that you have encountered or heard of in the last month. Does the list surprise you? Can you think of any social spaces or media that have not yet been exploited by advertisers?
2. After reading this chapter, has your view of advertising's social role changed? Make a list of arguments in favour of advertising and contrast it with a list of arguments against advertising. Convene a study group to discuss their implications: can the opposing viewpoints be reconciled?

3. List all the communication sources you can think of that might potentially influence your perception of a brand. Can you think of ways in which your perception of three brands has been so influenced? In your view, which communications channel was most influential in forming your impression of the brand? Why was this?
4. What is the role of signification in marketing? Gather all the promotional material you can for two brands. What meanings do you feel are implied by the imagery, the typography and the other features of these promotions? Could the meanings be interpreted differently by different people?
5. Think of two advertising campaigns that generated public debate. Can you say what their strategic marketing purpose was? Can you say why they generated public debate?

CASE Tourism Authority of Thailand

For many years Thailand has been one of the most popular tourist destinations in South-east Asia, attracting visitors from all over the world. It is famed for the natural beauty of its beaches and countryside, the luxury of its hotels, the friendliness of its people and its world-class food. This attraction is enhanced by the low cost of living in Thailand. All categories of tourists, from student back-packers to well-heeled travellers, seek luxury and comfort in Thailand's exotic setting. The SARS outbreak and the Iraq war had a very adverse effect on tourism across Asia. Many destinations reacted by discounting to win back tourist confidence and branding to try to differentiate their country's appeal from others.

The TAT (Tourism Authority of Thailand) engaged Dentsu Thailand as their agency. Their marketing objectives were to:

1. increase the number of tourist arrivals;
2. increase average daily spending rates of tourists;
3. raise the profile of Thailand by targeting prestige market segments.

Dentsu's approach to strategic campaign planning entails a focus on consumer orientation, perception change and integration, all linked under the overarching concept of the brand. Their four-phase approach begins with analysis, in which they consider the branding and marketing issues and generate communications strategies and ideas. The second phase entails strategic planning of integrated media solutions. In the third phase the campaign is executed, and the fourth phase involves monitoring the brand health and marketing objectives in the context of the campaign's execution.

Thailand is a rapidly growing economy, reflected in having the largest domestic advertising expenditure in the region. Total advertising spend grew some 15.5 per cent overall between 2001 and 2002 in spite of adverse economic conditions, according to AC Nielson Adquest. Urban Thailand has growing and highly brand-conscious consumer markets that attract major promotional investment from global manufacturers such as Unilever, P&G, Toyota and Sony, to name just a few.

Dentsu Global Research found that Thailand's image abroad did not always reflect the reality of an economically sophisticated and culturally complex country. Very positive perceptions were recorded of Thailand's warmth, friendliness, value-for-money and exotic and beautiful natural resources. Of its regional competitors, Singapore was regarded as a place for excellent shopping, commerce and entertainment, and Hong Kong was rated highly for educational opportunities, business and investment. Thailand's exotic appeal was rated more highly than India, China and Egypt, and its hospitality to visitors was rated more highly than that of the USA, Australia and Mexico. Thailand's image problem seemed to be that tourists' perceptions of its prostitution and poverty were sometimes pre-eminent, overshadowing those regarding food, natural resources, culture and other virtues.

Dentsu agreed a set of communication objectives to 'reveal the richness that is Thailand' and to 'appeal to up-market tourists'. In achieving these objectives a related aim was to 'create even more differentiation from competitive countries'.

The communication message was: 'Thailand: It's not just what you see … It's how it makes you feel'. The creative concept developed the theme that Thailand talks to you (the tourist) in many different ways, for example in the way that Thais greet you, in the gentle beauty of the Buddhist way of life, in the food, the natural beauty and the reverence for flowers. Print and TV executions were linked by the focus on language and the ways in which Thailand speaks to you.

Case Exercises

1. In a study group, explore the group members' perceptions of Thailand. Contrast these perceptions with three other countries. Develop a **perception matrix** with the four countries contrasted along two suitable axes. Discuss what has formed or influenced these perceptions. What kinds of promotional or communication activity might be powerful in changing these perceptions?
2. Consider Thailand's tourism situation. What do you think of Dentsu's creative solution? Can you think of other creative themes that you feel would be effective?

▶
3. Take a country of your choice and construct a scenario similar to that described above. Present your promotional plan and explain its rationale.

Further Reading

General managerial texts on advertising and promotion
Pickton, D. and Broderick, A. (2003) *Integrated Marketing Communications*. London: Pitman Publishing.
Shimp, T.A. (1997) *Advertising, Promotion and Integrated Aspects of Marketing Communications*. Florida and Texas: Dryden Press.

Managerial introductions to advertising
Jones, J.P. (1999) *The Advertising Business*. New York: Sage.
Wilmshurst, J. and Mackay, A. (1999) *The Fundamentals of Advertising*. Oxford: Butterworth Heinemann, ISBA.

Cultural and historical studies on advertising
McFall, L. (2004) *Advertising: A Cultural Economy*. London: Sage.
Nava, M., Blake, A., MacRury, I. and Richards, B. (eds) *Buy This Book*. London: Routledge.

Studies of consumption
McCracken, G. (1990) *Culture and Consumption: New Approaches to the Symbolic Character of Consumer Goods and Activities*. Bloomington, IN; Indiana University Press.
Szmigin, I. (2003) *Understanding The Consumer*. London: Sage.

Studies of marketing and signification
Barthes, R. (2000) *Mythologies* (Translation Jonathan Cape, 1972). London: Vintage.
Umiker-Sebeok, J. (ed.) (1997) *Marketing and Semiotics*. Amsterdam: Mouton de Gruyter.

Useful Web Resources

Duke University US advertising history site: www.scriptorium.lib.duke.edu/eaa
Advertising Age magazine: www.adage.com
UK Advertising Association: www.adassoc.org.uk
Campaign magazine website: www.brandrepublic.com
University of Texas teaching resource: http://advertising.utexas.edu

Notes

1 In this context sub-contracting refers to advertising agencies' buying in specialist expertise (such as creative hot shops, media specialists, production houses or research specialists) to assist on larger accounts while acting as the single strategic co-ordinator and point of contact for the client.

2 Although this book is mainly concerned with consumer brand marketing communication it draws examples from all sectors of practice including non-profit and government campaigns and therefore the word 'organization' is used throughout in preference to 'company' or 'firm'.

3 See UK *Sunday Times*, 17 August, 2003: 'Alcohol lads' ads to be sexed down'.

4 It maybe a mistake to suggest that grass is somehow more natural than advertising. The rolling lawns of golf course fairways or hotel grounds are often featured in advertisements and have been designed partly for their visual appeal: fans of televised sports are used to the pristine green swathes of the sporting field being turned into advertising by the technique of superimposing a giant sponsor's logo or club crest on the field during coverage.

5 'Whassup' interj. American slang word meaning "Hello", from "What's up?" used especially as a greeting to someone you know well', in Longman's *Dictionary of Contemporary English*, 2001, cited in (2003) *DDB London Works*, p. 23; published in Oxfordshire by World Advertising Research Centre.

6 *'Le pub tue'* ('ads kill') and *'Le pub pue'* ('ads stink'): see report in UK newspaper *The Independent*, Thursday, 11 March 2004: 23, 'French charge 62 activists over war on "brainless ads"'.

7 Described in Michael Moore's book, *Stupid White Men*, Penguin Books, 2002: 111.

8 John Stuart Mill, *On Liberty*, Penguin Books, 1982.

9 UK *Sunday Times*, 6 July 2003, '"Unhealthy" food ads for young face ban'. UK *Sunday Times*, 31 August, 2003, 'Junk food ads face children's TV ban'.

10 Described on a UK BBC2 TV show, 'Little Women', broadcast on 29 March 2001.

11 With thanks to David Brent, Brand Plan Pty Ltd, Sydney, Australia for this vignette.

12 My thanks to Marc Davies of Dentsu, Thailand, for discussions on this case.

Theorizing Advertising and Promotion

2

Chapter Outline

Before the book develops its descriptive account of the advertising business and its role in marketing, this chapter introduces some theoretical concepts for understanding the nature of the engagement between advertising and its audiences. 'Theory' is, in this chapter, a word used to indicate ways of articulating the everyday experience of advertising. The chapter particularly stresses the practical and theoretical inadequacy of conceiving an advertisement as a univocal message and discusses other intellectually richer possibilities.

BOX 2.0   The Role of Intertextuality in Understanding Advertisements

Advertising is 'parasitic'[1] (Cook, 2001) in the sense that it draws from, and refers to, other **discourse** forms. Intertextual references evince other ads or other genres. Early ads often evoked inter-generic genres of, say, scientific reports (with a white-coated, male actor as 'objective' spokesman for the proven qualities of the brand), the sales pitch (delivered by a man in a loud tie and check jacket) and the confidential piece of advice from the older woman experienced in household management to the younger (examples are taken from Cook, 2001: 194). Intra-generic intertextual references to other ads have become more common in ads since the 1950s.

In research with young British consumers, O'Donohoe (1997) has shown how these intertextual references frame and form the way ads are understood. Many creative executions use intertextuality deliberately to engage their audience or to **connote** certain values by

▶

linking the brand with the discourses of, say, sport or movies. For example, ads for Fosters lager parodied the Australian Mad Max movies (and ads for Carling Black Label lager parodied the Foster's ads parodying the Mad Max movies).[2] Other ads evince analogies of TV quiz shows, news announcements, fashion photographs, courtroom dialogue and TV situation comedies. In many cases ads deploying intertextual references are then featured on compilation TV shows of funniest ads, completing the circle by drawing ads into mainstream entertainment.

Creative professionals may use intertextuality as a tactic to try to engage consumers with points of shared cultural reference. Intertextual references are often used in a spirit of parody to break down consumer resistance to advertising appeals. In such cases the marketing message is predicated on the target consumers getting the reference and appreciating the wit. In one example a car chase from the movie 'Bullett' was reproduced with the car digitally replaced with a Ford Puma, driven by the laconic star Steve McQueen. The ad mocked the sporty pretensions of the Puma but in a way that might be appreciated by its audience, since it broke the advertising cliché of earnestness about the brand. Ads that make parodic intra-generic intertextual reference to advertising as a genre have become common. There is no sales message as such, merely an assumption that consumers will understand that the self-mockery is as insincere as the earnestness of stereotypical advertising. The marketing aim is not to make a sales pitch but to endear the desired group of consumers to the brand.

Why Theorize Advertising and Promotion?

Business people, marketing and advertising professionals included, rarely have much time for theory. Theory is popularly understood as a synonym for complex, esoteric, abstract. The term 'in theory' is often used in a pejorative sense to refer to ideas that are seen as irrelevant, impractical or obscure. But theory can be seen in another, more constructive way. It can be viewed as a form of everyday understanding that allows us a sense of control over our world and, sometimes, helps us to predict outcomes based on previous experience. Rudimentary theories allow us to understand our world in ways that are not possible if we are solely concerned with concrete experience. We all live by implicit theories: knowing that rain gets you wet therefore you should put on a coat before you leave the house may strike you as obvious, but it involves an abstraction from particular experiences of getting wet and it informs our behaviour. It may not be as complex as a theory of relativity but it is the kind of theorizing that most of us are more familiar with.

Practical theory guides behaviour and action in the workplace even though it may be implicit rather than explicit. In one study (Kover, 1995) creative professionals in advertising worked to differing implicit theories of communication, which guided their approach to addressing creative briefs and solving communications problems. In another study (Hackley, 2003d) account team professionals worked to differing implicit models of the consumer. These models implied quite different ways of understanding, and therefore of communicating with, consumers. Advertising people hold their own theories of advertising communication and of consumers, which guide the assumptions they make when solving practical problems at work.

Intellectually, theorizing allows us to use our imagination to move from the concrete to the abstract. We can compare and combine ideas and speculate on new ways of understanding the world. Our understanding of any social phenomenon requires some theoretical dimension in order to raise it beyond the trivial. One can say without fear of vehement contra-diction that books are made up of words, but to compare different books and to offer views on their qualities one has to invoke implicit theories of, say, prose style ('this book is well-written') theories of narrative ('the plot was exciting') or theories of dramatic characterization ('the characters were not believable'). We have an opinion of what constitutes good writing or effective characterization even though we may not be at all familiar with intellectual traditions of literary criticism. Advertising is a field par-ticularly concerned with human communication, thought and behaviour. Advertising professionals are practical people who develop experience in particular areas and know what works for them in given situations, but advertising as a category can hardly be spoken of at all without some basic theoretical assumptions to guide us. In this book, then, theory is not considered a byword for obscurity. At a rudimentary but decidedly non-trivial level it simply allows us to articulate the world in ways that go beyond the unimportant or the obvious.

How Can We Theorize Advertising and Promotion?

Models of Advertising Effects

The research fields of mass communications, artificial intelligence and cognitive psychology, social psychology, sociology and anthropology have all influenced advertising research in differing ways and degrees. We will not offer a detailed history or critique of communications research in relation to advertising here, but will outline some major themes in order to set the foregoing discussion in a broader context.

Linear Communication and the Hierarchy of Effects

What we will call the **linear information processing theories of communication** and persuasion have been highly influential in both advertising and marketing communications textbooks (Buttle, 1994) and also in professional practice (for a discussion see Crosier, 1999). These theories generally reflect the methods and assumptions of cognitive psychology. In particular, they draw an analogy between the information processing of computers and that of humans. These research traditions have been drawn on by advertising and communications theorists to develop 'hierarchy-of-effects' models of advertising persuasion (review in Barry and Howard, 1990; also see Lavidge and Steiner, 1961; Rossiter et al., 1991; Vaughn, 1986). In the **hierarchy-of-effects** theoretical tradition the consumer is seen as an individual entity who is resistant to marketing communication until the accumulated weight of persuasive messages finally results in acquiescence (that is, in purchase). The consumer's resistance, so to speak, is broken by an accumulation of advertising effects, hence the expression 'hierarchy-of-effects'. The consumer, like a computer, is assumed to process information sequentially, according to rules.

Hierarchy-of-effects models of advertising persuasion tend to be variations on Strong's (1925) AIDA (Awareness, Interest, Desire, Action) sequence in which the consumer is moved along a linear continuum of internal states from unawareness to awareness, then interest is elicited and desire (for the brand) aroused. Finally, the consumer is stirred into action in the form of a purchase (hence the acronym AIDA). The 'hierarchy-of-effect' represents 'compounding probabilities' (Percy et al., 2001: 36), as each step in the process is a necessary condition for the subsequent step. This ever popular model of persuasive communication has been criticized for its main virtue: for enthusiasts it is succinct, for detractors it is simplistic. It is also criticized on the grounds that it conceives of advertising consumption as an essentially dyadic process, transmitted through a media channel to an individual viewer and consumed in social isolation. A further criticism is that it represents only **high-involvement** purchases: many or most purchases are more spontaneous and do not engage consumers in this sort of rational processing.

Other approaches have argued that, in contrast, advertising consumption should be properly understood as an ineluctably social process (Ritson and Elliott, 1999). We do not generally view ads in an experimental booth – our interpretation of them is normally framed by the social context in which we encounter them. A further criticism of linear models of advertising persuasion is that they risk overplaying the role of economic rationality in the consumption of advertising[3]. Subsequent models have incorporated stronger elements of consumer emotionality into the persuasion process (Elliott, 1998; Holbrook and Hirschman, 1982) to reflect the often irrational and quirky motivations behind consumer behaviour (review in Dermody, 1999).

Of course, this implies that promotional communication may not be particularly effective as a persuasive sales pitch, a point made forcefully by research that emphasizes the 'weak' theory of advertising effect (see p. 34).

One well-known generic model incorporated emotionality into purchase decisions by using a three-stage conceptualization: cognitive, affective and conative (known colloquially as think-feel-do. For discussions see Bagozzi, 1979; Barnard and Ehrenberg, 1997; Lutz, 1997). Cognition (thinking) refers to the rational appeal of advertising as, for example, a motor-car ad which includes data on engine performance or utility features such as fold-away seating. The affective stage refers to the emotional response of the consumer to an ad. Not only does the ad seek to engage with the consumer on a rational level by emphasizing product benefits: it also tries to elicit a positive emotional response with aesthetically pleasing imagery and alluring symbolism. Motor-car ads, for example, usually feature the engine and other product data within a carefully shot picture of the car and its occupants in a pleasing setting, perhaps an attractive and affluent family laughing gaily as they travel along a coastal highway. The emotional response is desire, triggered by identification. Finally, conation refers to action: the combination of rational and emotional appeal in the same ad might then act persuasively and motivate a purchase response.

The think-feel-do hierarchy is a commonsense (or self-evident) conceptualization which tells us that many ads combine rational with emotional appeals. It cannot tell us which of those appeals will prove more powerful or what the right balance of rational-emotional appeal should be. Neither can the model explain to us which aspect of the appeal is rational or emotional. For some motor-car ad consumers, small-print text describing the brake horsepower of a car has an emotional appeal if they are excited by the idea of a very powerful engine. For others, such technical data are less than exciting. The appropriate degree of balance between the two kinds of appeal is neither fixed nor clear. Intrinsic product virtues can be implied rather than stated, while symbolic references can be highlighted or hinted at.

Häagen-Dazs ice cream is one good example of how a whole product category was re-energized through an overtly stylized brand advertising (and PR) initiative which used overt intertextual references to sex and celebrity while also implying through the pricing and packaging that the product itself is intrinsically of high quality. An appeal on the basis of the dairy wholesomeness of Häagen Dazs ice-cream (like the UK Wall's ice-cream ads of the 1960s) would hardly have had the same impact. Levi's 501s and Benetton are, similarly, brands that have eschewed the rational appeals sometimes characteristic of those product categories (hard-wearing, colour-fast, well-made) in favour of intertextual visual, musical and linguistic references that draw more complex meanings into the ad and the brand. Picking apart the rational from the emotional in such communications is a task of detailed and somewhat subjective analysis.

The Linear Model of Communication

The linear theory of communication, so-called because it suggests that communication can be modelled as a linear sequence of events, has been another influential feature in advertising theory. It is closely associated with Schramm's (1948) work on mass communication and has been influential in other communications research (Katz and Larzarsfeld, 1955; Larzarsfeld, 1941; Lasswell, 1948).

An advertisement can be said to communicate a message to receivers. A message is said to have a source, the sender of the message. The sender has to encode the message into a form that will carry the desired meaning. Encoding will put the message into a form in which communication is possible, such as words, pictures, gestures, music or a combination of all of these. The receiver has to decode the message in order to retrieve the meaning intended. The surrounding environment may have noise of various forms that distracts from the message. Noise can be construed metaphorically as anything that might disrupt the communication by, say, distracting the attention of the receiver. In an aural communication it may be literal noise that disrupts the communicative process. With visual communications such as roadside advertising poster sites, noise may be all the activities of an urban road that might distract a person's attention from the poster, such as pedestrians, cars, shops, stray dogs or whatever.

This simple conceptualization has many descriptive uses. It has been a mainstay of marketing communications and advertising texts because of its economy and descriptive scope. It can be applied to almost any communications scenario and will have a degree of applicability. But all conceptual models have their limitations. A model is no more than a textual representation

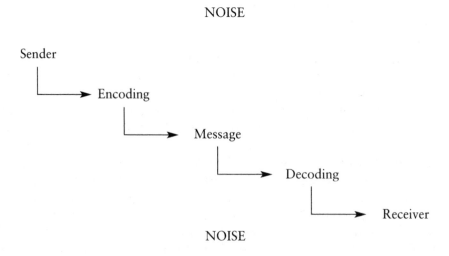

Figure 2.1　A Linear Model of Communication.

that captures by analogy some, but by no means all, of the features of the phenomenon it purports to represent. In other words, models as theoretical representations have weaknesses.

Some Limitations of the Linear Model of Communication

One weakness of the linear model of communication is that it is easy to interpret in such a way that meaning and message are understood to be synonymous. This risks misconstruing the interpretive possibilities that subsist within a given promotional communication. Cultural and linguistic studies of advertising have noted that advertisements often deploy ambiguity as a virtue (Forceville, 1996: 102, citing Pateman, 1983). The openness of the advertising text can draw consumers into a deeper engagement as they ponder on the possible meanings of the ad. In the UK, many cigarette ads have used cryptic visual metaphors, such as when the Silk Cut brand deployed a poster of a cut silk sheet with no supporting copy. The poster carried no meaning as such, and indeed no message, but merely winked a knowing eye at consumers who were already familiar with the brand name. Constructs such as message, and indeed meaning, seem ill-suited to cryptic ads such as this.

The construct message may be a convenient shorthand for whatever meaning (or meanings) that may emerge from a communication, but creative professionals know very well that encapsulating a preconceived message into a given communication in such a way that it will be similarly interpreted by culturally heterogeneous consumers is a complex challenge. It is telling that advertising agency professionals seldom use the term 'message', preferring to speak of 'advertising strategy' to express the communication theme they wish to capture in the ad. 'Strategy' (discussed in more detail in Chapters 3 and 4) is less precise a term than 'message' and allows both creative professionals and consumers some scope of interpretation while maintaining a focus on a theme that will support the client's marketing objective.

The linear model, then, risks oversimplifying the consumer's cognitive engagement with advertising by emphasizing a singular message that has one, unproblematic meaning. The use of linearity itself in social research has been attacked. In artificial intelligence research, for example, the linear processing that is said to characterize computer data processing has given way to the notion of parallel processing. In other words, the assumption that computers (and human brains) can only process one bit of data at a time has been challenged by more complex models which indicate that information (data) can be processed by more than one channel simultaneously. Clearly, this has implications for understanding how consumers engage with advertising in environments which are full of competing advertising messages. It may suggest, for example, that just because we do not pay explicit attention to an ad it does not necessarily mean that we are not conscious of the ad or that it has no effect on us. Conventional linear models of advertising effect

BOX 2.1   Miscommunication in Advertising

In an oft-told story of advertising miscommunication, a 1950s cigarette brand was advertised in the UK with cinema ads. The ads featured an actor alone on London Bridge at night, mock heroically lighting up a Strand cigarette to the accompanying strapline, 'You're never alone with a Strand'. The brand failed to sell and it transpired that cinema audiences felt that the user was a lonely soul who couldn't find friends. To ad agency types familiar with Hollywood movie heroes such as Humphrey Bogart, it seemed inconceivable that cigarette smoking could be seen as anything but the act of a streetwise tough guy whose heroic destiny was to be alone. The audience decoded a different meaning from the one the agency had planned to encode into the message. The reason for the miscommunication was not known: it may have been the actor was unconvincing as a hero, the clothes, the set or the props – all may have undermined the intended effect. Today such a mistake would be unlikely to happen. Most major advertising campaigns are carefully pre-tested on trial audiences before launch. The story reveals the subtlety of meaning in advertising communication.

imply that ads must get our explicit attention in order to be effective, and furthermore that we filter most ads out of our field of attention because they do not pass our criterion of interest. But if we are conscious of advertising to which we are not paying express attention, it suggests that advertising works in quite a different way from a personal sales encounter.

The linear model of communication with its sequential processing translates conveniently into a model of persuasion if the sequential stages are replaced with attitudinal or behavioural states (awareness, interest, desire and action). Much experimental and survey research effort in advertising is invested in measuring these psychological states on the assumption that they indicate the likelihood of purchase and therefore are indicative of the success (or otherwise) of an ad campaign. These intermediate states may be a necessary condition for advertising to accomplish its marketing aims, but they may not be a sufficient condition. A further problem is that they may not predict the outcome of an advert-ing campaign, because consumers may be aware of and like an ad without buying the product. However, even though most ads no doubt fall into this category for many consumers, an ad that is liked but not acted upon may not have failed as a marketing device, as we shall see.

In some cases, and in some cultures, the direct sales appeal has greater relevance. For example, as a generalization, much US advertising contrasts with that of Europe, Australasia and Asia in the direct style of its sales appeal. US consumers may be simply more accustomed to this style of advertising and, perhaps, more receptive to its method. The 'strong' or 'weak' advertising appeal may not be mutually exclusive. Even though the sales appeal may be direct, the ad can still carry important values and connotations that contribute to long-term brand-building and maintaining the communications objective. And ads with an indirect appeal may often coincide with contiguous purchase behaviour that immediately follows exposure to the ad.

Strong and Weak Theories of Advertising Effect

Strong Theories

The hierarchy-of-effects traditions have influenced theories of how advertising works (for a review see Vakratsas and Ambler, 1999). The verb 'works' can be construed in different ways: for many clients, a campaign only

BOX 2.2   'Strong' or 'Weak' Advertising Appeals[4]

Many contemporary ads eschew the 'strong' sales pitch format in favour of a more tenuous brand reference (Ehrenberg et al., 2002). Since short-term memory only accommodates six or seven pieces of information, consumer choice sets are limited. Brands have to ensure that they have a place in this choice set by reminding consumers that the brand remains salient and relevant to their lifestyle. Many car brand ads for, say, BMW or Mercedes-Benz, evince general brand values because consumers may only buy that car brand once or twice in a lifetime. They need to be consistently reminded of the brand's relevance and values for the time when they might be in a position to buy. Where a brand has built a sense of prestige through its advertising, and this prestige is acknowledged among stakeholder groups such as employees, shareholders and the non-consuming public, this can translate to indirect but tangible market benefits such as share price, positive PR and word-of-mouth approval. Many consumer purchases are, like cars, infrequent. A new suit, a holiday, life insurance, a house, a new watch are relatively rare purchases for most people. Brand advertising must be persistent and enduring to have any effect on the purchasing behaviour of such people. When one considers that there are around 60 million people in the UK, over 200 million in the USA and 1000 million in China, we can see that being an infrequently purchased item for each individual translates into a huge potential market because of the number of such individuals that can be accessed by advertising.

works if the sales graph spears upwards within a few days of the campaign launch. This direct, causal relationship between advertising and sales is often what is implied in the metaphor. Campaigns do often result in sales increases but the causal link can never be proven, even though the circumstantial evidence that advertising caused the sales increase may seem compelling. There will always be other possible causal variables influencing purchase patterns, such as seasonality, changes in disposable income and topical events.

The hierarchy-of-effects theories of persuasion clearly assume that advertising works in a directly persuasive way (or 'strong' way (Ambler, 1998)) on individuals. The best attempts to demonstrate advertising's effect on purchasing trends are where multivariate statistical analysis isolates a number of variables so that it becomes reasonable to assume that advertising was a causal factor in the sales pattern. Many advertising case histories have done this. Even in such studies, the results are not beyond dispute and only offer reasonable grounds, rather than proof, for suggesting that the advertising caused a given sales pattern. **'Split-run' studies** can offer interesting evidence by measuring sales in regions with similar demographic characteristics but showing slightly different ads. The sales difference might be attributed to variations in the ad design or to how frequently it is aired. Nonetheless, evidence remains inconclusive and an inadequate basis for generalization.

Weak Theories

Weak theories of advertising assume that the advertising cause and the sales effect are far less directly linked than strong theories. The link is, nevertheless, powerful and enduring. Ads may often exercise influence over long periods of time, they may be designed to influence parties other than buyers or potential buyers (such as shareholders or employees) and they may be intended simply to remind consumers that the brand is still around and still relevant. In many consumer markets the only way a brand can hope to compete is to match competitors' advertising expenditure (or adspend). If they do not, the consumer might infer that their brand is somehow second-rate or less serious than the more heavily advertised brands.

An important function of branding is that it is a badge of reassurance for the consumer. Consumers are often insecure about making difficult purchase decisions. None of us wants to get our purchase home to find that it is defective in any way or that our peers regard it with disdain. Brand names offer reassurance for the consumer that the purchase we have made is safe in the sense that the brand is credible and the quality good. Brand advertising, then, supports this sense of reassurance by reminding consumers that the brand is current, relevant and successful.

In other words, the advertising supports the brand by creating and maintaining a favourable consumer predisposition towards it over long periods.

There is rarely, then, a specified point at which a given ad clinches a sale. The power and the limitations of ads need to be understood in terms of the intrinsic limitation of mediated communication to directly persuade. Individual consumers seldom leave their living-room immediately after seeing an ad to buy the product at the nearest store. Advertising simply places a brand in the consumer's awareness in association with certain contrived values and qualities. In this weak role, advertising may portray brands in persuasive ways but their main task is not persuasive: it is to provide reassurance.

This weak, reminding role is important since advertising does not engage with consumers singly but collectively. Advertising is a social experience (Ritson and Elliott, 1999) in many senses. It draws on cultural reference points that subsist in interactive social contexts. Large numbers of consumers are exposed to ads, of whom it is statistically likely that a proportion may be thinking of purchasing a particular category of product or service. The brand then has a positive presence in the consumer's set of choices when next in a position to buy that product category. Given that the short-term memory of humans is estimated at about seven chunks of

---

BOX 2.3   Whassup with Weak Advertising Appeals?

Anheuser-Busch has used various creative approaches to promote their Budweiser beer brand, for instance ads that emphasized the brewing process and highlighted the intrinsic quality of the beer ('King of Beers'). They have also drawn on American provenance to position the brand in an heroic light. More recent campaigns have shifted the positioning somewhat to broaden the appeal. One campaign placed the beer as a minor set prop in a narrative form that appeared to be more like a movie clip than a TV ad. One execution had a set of apparently Afro-American friends going about their domestic business and greeting each other with an increasingly loud cry of 'Whassup?!' (see colour insert). The characters are in a variety of situations familiar in TV domestic dramas or situation comedies: watching TV, working at a computer, bringing shopping home (a bag of Budweiser), talking to a lover on the telephone. The brand was implicated in the plot as the choice of working professionals of any ethnic origin but with an authenticity coming from their use of street slang, street clothes and love of TV sport. The ads hinted that the brand itself had the same authenticity as the characters ('Budweiser. True').

▶

'Whassup' became a popular catchword attracting much media comment and coverage, extending the audience for the brand.

A website was set up to exploit the popularity of the advertising and to allow people to download ads and screensavers. While beer ads generally seek out an audience of 18–50-year-old males, the creative appeal of these particular ads clearly included but reached beyond beer drinkers. They showed an awareness that a brand is a social construction in the sense that it has a cultural meaning which is not confined to its target audience, but is informed by the ideas and associations brought to the brand by non-consuming social groups.

information, the buying set from which we choose for most purchases is relatively small. Simply being in the recalled buying set of several million consumers is useful, and indeed necessary, for a consumer brand in a competitive situation.

Self-evidently, there must be some occasions when an individual ad informs and persuades a particular consumer to purchase the brand. Weak theories of advertising effect hold that such occasions are relatively rare and that the majority of purchase decisions are made by default. In other words, most consumer purchases are influenced by brand perceptions that are formed and sustained over long periods. Advertising is only one of many possible sources of brand perceptions, but it is an important source because of its high public profile, persuasive authority and huge reach in developed economies. The interpretive theories that this book draws upon to conceptualize the consumer–advertising relation are perhaps most compatible with weak theories of how advertising works.

'Weak' Theories of Advertising and Ambiguity of Meaning in Communication

(Sperber and Wilson (1986, cited in Forceville, 1996) noted that all non-verbal communication can be seen as 'weak' communication) By weak communication they mean that the meaning of the communication can never be precisely ascertained, there will always be room for alternative interpretations. Many conceptualizations of advertising link the notion of advertising message with advertising effect without fully exploring why these links can be assumed. The point of view held in this book is that a univocal notion of advertising meaning conceived in a social vacuum, decoded by an individual receiver and understood independently from both the sending and receiving contexts, cannot adequately capture the complexity of the communicative engagement between ad and consumer.

In the rest of this chapter a number of interpretive constructs will be introduced.

The Social Context of Advertising and Promotion

The Social Constructionist Standpoint on Advertising

Most theorizing contributes something to our understanding of the world. Constructs deriving from cognitive psychology such as memory and attitude are self-evidently relevant, in some way, in the communicative engagement between ad and consumer. Such constructs are, as we have seen, conceived as intermediate states in the communication-purchase sequence. But in and of themselves they only permit a superficial understanding of this engagement. What we remember of ads and what we express as attitudes to brands in response to questionnaires have no necessary connection with the meaning that ads and brands have for us in our lives as consumers and citizens. If you are asked to fill in a consumer questionnaire concerning household goods, you may well express opinions on brands which you have heard of but have never purchased. There may be some value for brand marketing organizations in establishing the attitudes of non-consumers to particular brands. There are also limits to the usefulness of such information in strategy formulations.

Developments in cultural psychology have suggested that constructs such as memory and attitude cannot be understood only at an individual level (Potter and Wetherell, 1987). Our cognitive understanding of the social world is not only private: it is inherently social. Our preferences and attitudes are culturally primed, and we choose them from a range of possibilities presented to us in our own cultural field. Consumers do not typically engage with advertising in experimental viewing booths. We understand advertising as part of our cultural landscape. It is simply there, like road signs, newspapers and TV shows, and conversations in bars. All are normal parts of our social world. As a normal feature of social life advertising reflects and reveals values and social practices in this world. The ways we interpret advertising, and the attitudes we form of the brands portrayed, are not only our own: they are views borrowed from the social worlds which we encounter.

If a brand is popular, such as Nike or BMW, its consumers are well aware that they are not the only people to favour this brand. Indeed, they will very likely have an idea of the kind of other person who likes the brand. They may well have gained this impression from advertising. Our senses of discernment and preference are not fixed or given by nature. They are culturally learned in interaction with our social worlds.

Advertising seeks to create meanings that will resonate in some way with our sense of social identity and our culturally derived values, aspirations and fantasies.

Advertising as Commodity

Advertising is not merely a force acting upon us. We actively use it in our own social lives. Research studies have drawn attention to the ways advertising is actively used in social life (O'Donohoe, 1994) as well as being passively consumed in some contexts. Advertising research often emphasizes the individual encounter with an individual ad (McCracken, 1986) when, in fact, we usually consume ads socially in the sense that we often view them in the company of others and we discuss our interpretation of them and modify it in the light of other views. Ritson and Elliott (1999) showed how important advertising can be in the everyday conversation of adolescents. By expressing preferences and finding certain ads funny or enjoyable the researchers found that the adolescents were also expressing their sense of social identity and group membership.

Brand Advertising and Social Construction

Advertising's meaning draws on the cultural environment within which it is framed. Our understanding of ads and the brands they promote is formed in the light of the social contexts within which such communications subsist. This inherently social aspect of human understanding reflects a broader concern with the socially constructed character of social reality (Berger and Luckman, 1966) and the socially constructed nature of individual psychology (for introductions see Burr, 1995; Nightingale and Cromby, 1999). In important respects we maintain that brands and their advertising cannot be properly understood simply as self-evident entities. They must also be understood as entities that exist in the realm of social interaction, sustained through the way they are talked about and used. In other words, brands can be seen as social constructions.

A great deal of marketing activity can be seen to have a socially constructed character (Hirschman, 1986, cited in Hackley, 2001: 47) in the sense that it has an existence that is sustained in the social world beyond the tangible realities of product features, packaging and price. A brand's meaning as portrayed or implied in advertising subsists in the social space between the organization, the advertising and its interpretive communities of consumers.

Social constructionism is sometimes identified with the extreme idealism of the philosopher Bishop Berkeley, but unlike it, social constructionist theory does not contend that the mental is all that is real and

BOX 2.4   Nike as Social Construction

The Nike sportswear brand was developed through its proprietor Phil Knight's obsession with designing running shoes. Knight's original running shoes were endorsed by track star Steve Prefontaine. The brand acquired another dimension when it became fashionable street wear in Los Angeles. What had been a brand associated with sporting excellence and promoted through a policy of personal endorsement by sports stars acquired new connotations of street authenticity, toughness and resistance to conformity. The Nike 'Swoosh' is one of the most universally recognized icons of twenty-first-century culture. Although its connotations are controlled by Nike, to some extent there are elements that are beyond control because a brand within public discourse has a self-sustaining momentum. Nike became a feature of urban culture as well as a marketed brand: the values and connotations inspired by its association with sporting performance have become inseparable from those of street coolness and opposition to authority. The brand's marketing has been able to exploit its street authenticity, but arguably it did not create that authenticity. It is a good example of a brand as a social construction, since its cultural meaning is bound up with wider discourses (in this case, those of class, ethnicity, urban identity and the American sense of individuality).

Brands as social constructions are then no more or less than what we as consumers think they are. If Volvo is seen as safe, Rolex as prestigious, Marlboro as tough, Body Shop as environmentally conscious, such perceptions are produced by consumers in interaction with each other. Brand marketing organizations try to influence this brand discourse through their brand and communications policies.

---

the material world is a chimera. Rather, it maintains that the social and material worlds co-exist but do not share the same rules (Hackley, 1998). Social constructionism is not really a metaphysical position at all but a psychological one. It acknowledges that it is in the nature of human communication that meanings can be produced that are self-sustaining, because in talking to each other we generate new meanings. It is this human tendency to reify or to treat the abstract (the socially constructed) as if it were real that brand marketing exploits. Consumers know very well that wearing Nike sports shoes does not make them any more likely to be a winner nor does it make them into a street-smart urban survivor. They do know that these very connotations are embodied in the brand

and they know that others know it too. The brand's socially constructed meaning is part of the communication game we play with each other in negotiating our social identity.

Marketing executives and advertising and communications professionals are all interested in what advertisements mean to consumers. They use different vocabularies to articulate their views, reflecting the theoretical traditions which they draw upon (Cook and Kover, 1998). This book takes the view that in order to adequately theorize communication within advertising, it is necessary not only to ask what ads mean. It is important also to ask how ads mean. The interpretive intellectual traditions assert this very question. Interpretive traditions of social research (outlined in, for example, Burrell and Morgan, 1979 and developed in Easterby-Smith et al., 2002) have been adopted by many academic researchers in advertising and consumer research (Hirschman, 1986; Stern, 1998) as viable alternatives to the **positivistic** and **managerialist** traditions of articulating marketing phenomena.

Interpretive Concepts for Advertising

Advertising as Discourse

We have referred to advertising as a form of **discourse** (following Cook, 2001). Discourse is described in cultural theory in various ways. It is a way of seeing the world, a way of describing things and a thing that can be described. The term is often used in conjunction with 'social text'. A text in cultural studies is a linguistic and/or orthographic (written) description of any event or entity whatsoever. It is anything that can be described in words, that is, converted to text. Particular discourses may be groups of social texts that usually conform to certain rules and conventions, such as the discourse of advertising, of medical consultation, of literary appreciation or of marketing management. These discourses are comprised of accepted conventions of speech, manner, subject and tone. As we have seen, many ads refer to non-advertising discourses in order to enhance the resonance of their meaning for consumers.

The conventions of a given discourse form can be very difficult to ascertain under conditions of normal social interaction. If, say, a medical consultation was recited in iambic pentameters, or shouted, or if the medical professional told the patient jokes rather than diagnosing the problem, the interaction would seem odd and socially inappropriate. These examples are less outlandish than they seem: the social conventions of speech and manner that govern acceptable behaviour in given contexts are often noticeable only when they are broken. We tend to take them for granted within the cultures with which we are familiar. Many advertisers have won our attention by challenging our ideas of what conventions an ad should conform to. Direct mail ads for charities are sometimes printed in a child's handwriting to give the emotional appeal an extra resonance; TV ads are sometimes filmed in a documentary or newscast style.

The accepted conventions and practices of advertising discourse are not given or obvious to the uninitiated. They have to be learned, and they vary between different cultures and eras. TV or press ads from the 1950s now seem odd and funny, or sexist and inappropriate to a young viewer in 2003. Many alcohol ads of today would seem deeply inappropriate to a viewer in the 1950s. Indeed, many contemporary ads would be unrecognizable as ads if they had been shown to viewers in 1950 because those consumers would not recognize the intertextual references in much contemporary advertising. The textual conventions of advertising discourse have, perhaps, changed in the intervening years. Discourse, then, refers to the sets of communication conventions and practices that characterize a particular kind of social phenomenon (such as advertising) in a given context. These practices and conventions are constantly in negotiation. One of the ways in which ad agencies have kept the discourse form of advertising fresh and novel has been to continually challenge those conventions by appropriating new textual forms.

Advertising Text and Context

Discourses consist of texts in context. Advertising acquires meaning not only by its content but also its context.

Appreciating the context of communication is an important part of understanding the way meaning is construed. For Cook (2001) the contexts of advertising (that is, marketing communication) discourse include the following:

- the physical material or medium which carries the text (such as the cathode ray tube, newsprint or radio waves); the music and pictures that may accompany the text
- the gestures, facial expressions and typography that constitute the 'paralanguage' of the text (in the UK, TV ads for Nescafé Gold Blend instant coffee featured romantically linked characters who created a sexually charged atmosphere, while interacting in settings that suggested affluence and social poise)
- the location of the text in time and space, on an outdoor poster site, in a magazine or during a commercial TV break
- the other texts that connect to that text such as the other ads in the same magazine or the other brands appearing or mentioned in a TV show
- the connections with other social discourses implied in the ads (for example intertextuality)
- the participants, that is, the intended audience, the apparent originator or sender of the ad and their respective assumptions, intentions and communicative idiom (Cook, 2001: 2) (ads sometimes have a particular

BOX 2.5   Advertisement Context and Advertising Regulation

A good illustration of the importance of the context of advertising for the meaning we construe from it can be found in a UK campaign for a perfume brand. A magazine ad for Yves St Laurent's Opium perfume featuring model Sophie Dahl, apparently naked, elicited little comment. Such ads are common in lifestyle and fashion magazines. When the print ad was blown up into a poster and featured on roadside billboards it elicited the largest number of complains the UK Advertising Standards Authority (ASA)[5] had ever received for a single ad, along with outraged press features and comment on British TV. The magazine ad was, presumably, seen as sensuous and witty in the context of many such ads for perfume in fashion and lifestyle magazines. The same ad on posters was widely considered to be obscene. The complaints to the ASA were predominantly from young women, exactly the readers of the magazines in which the press ad had featured. The meanings we impute to ads are, it seems, highly influenced by the interpretive context in which the ad is placed.

'voice' designed to give it authority with its audience, such as when ads for children's toys feature adults speaking the voice-over in the tone and patois of children).

Clearly, this list of the contexts of advertising implies that research studies which analyse the recall and attitude of an individual consumer to a single promotion by exposing the consumer to the ad in a viewing booth risk ignoring some of the most powerful influences on how ads are interpreted and understood. Given the many features of communication which impinge on the consumption of advertising and promotion, it is not surprising that advertising professionals have learned to exploit the persuasive potential of this complexity. Ads that have no evident meaning, or ads that seem to carry numerous potential meanings, are far from uncommon. Ads that have no determinate meaning can be useful because (as noted above) they can draw consumers into a communicative engagement as they try to puzzle out the enigma of the ad. Just what is it saying? Similarly, ads that have many potential interpretations can exploit this **polysemy** to create consumer interest and enhance communication.

Polysemy in Advertisements

Polysemy refers to the potential of a social text such as an ad to have many possible meanings. This perspective, of course, is not really compatible with the linear model of communication and its implied emphasis on a single, unequivocal message. The meaning of some ads is indeterminate: none of the polysemic meanings is prior to or stronger than the others. This opens up an interpretive space through which consumers can engage creatively with the ad. This gives advertising a particular power. It is us, the audience for advertising, who impose particular meanings on a given ad, helped, of course, by the cues placed in the ad by the creative people. This freedom to interpret advertising and to use it creatively in our own lives gives advertising a dynamic character as communication. Advertising agencies, far from being limited by the complexity of advertising meaning, exploit the ambiguity of advertising (Pateman, 1983, in Forceville, 1996) to create an intimate and personal engagement with consumers.

The polysemic potential of ads was striking in the famous (and infamous) Benetton campaigns. In some cases the same ad that won awards for creativity in Europe was the cause of consumer boycotts in the USA (for example, the visual image of a black-skinned woman's breasts suckling a white Caucasian baby). The Benetton ads exploited polysemy to generate a powerful and high-profile debate about their meaning, particularly concerning whether they should be construed as offensive or socially worthy. The brand's management of this polysemic creative strategy came unstuck when the negative interpretations of ads began to have commercial consequences (discussed in Chapter 8).

Ads that are deliberately obscure can seem inaccessible to older consumers and, by implication, aimed at younger consumers. Ambiguity of meaning in ads can, as we have noted above, be used as a deliberate strategy. In addition, carefully coded ads can create a sense of conspiracy by communicating in a way that excludes non-targeted groups. One way of signalling the desired market segment in an ad is to be seen to be excluding other segments. A TV ad campaign for Frizzell insurance in the UK (see p. 71) deliberately deployed a creative execution that would mainly be of interest to older viewers because they wanted to signal that younger consumers were not the primary desired market segment.

BOX 2.6   Diesel Ads Exploit Polysemy

A series of print ads for the Diesel clothing brand throughout the 1990s made use of both polysemy and intertextuality to try to draw the consumer into a deeper engagement, and at the same time to signal the quirky, witty, but irreverent values of the brand. One ad featured an enigmatic scene of bodybuilders wearing white sailor caps and bathing briefs. The scene included scientific equipment and puzzled spectators viewing the scene from behind a red rope, as if they were at an exhibition or performance.

The only direct reference to the brand was a brand name logo in small type in the corner. The ads were visually intriguing because they challenged our preconceptions about images and visual context. The viewer wanted to make connections between the images: humans actively try to makes sense of sense data, imposing sense even where there is little to be made. Perception is subject to a Gestalt impulse whereby humans try to complete visual cues to form a coherent whole. In polysemic ads that mix visual cues drawn from unconnected discourses this impulse draws us into the ad as we try to make the visual cues into a coherent whole.

A long series of similar Diesel print ads used bizarre visual intertextual references drawing on cultural texts as diverse as museum attendance, public health advertising, educational announcements, British seaside beauty contests, soccer reports, shoot-'em-up movies and news reportage of war zones. Short, inappropriate passages of copy were imprinted on the posters to make the scene even more puzzling. The effect was to provide an entertaining visual puzzle which consumers could try to figure out. Of course, there was no definitive answer to the meaning of these ads. The creative people at the agency were just having fun in the interests of the brand, playing with cultural meaning. Underlying the apparently incoherent images was a clear advertising strategy. Viewers were expected to infer that the Diesel brand, like the ads, challenged convention in a quirky, youthful and irreverent yet cool way.

Interpretive Communities

Saying that an ad carries many possible meanings does not imply that advertising is a hit-or-miss marketing communication device. The possible meanings it carries are only arbitrary to unintended audiences or in poorly designed ads. Effective advertisements are designed through a detailed understanding of the kinds of meaning a given group of consumers may impute to a given advertisement. This is why advertising development is a complex and painstaking exercise. Understanding the cultural and linguistic idiom of a given consumer group is the key to designing creative strategies that will resonate. The term 'interpretive community' refers to an identifiable group that shares a sense of common meaning with regard to some area of consumption practice. For some interpretive communities, polysemic ads make intertextual references to postmodernist themes in films and literature to which they are accustomed. This familiarity with polysemy (and intertextuality) creates a sense of the ad being an in-joke that excludes outsiders (or other interpretive communities).

An interpretive community may have little in common apart from its mutual interest in one particular consumption category. 'Brand communities' is an expression used by some advertising agencies to try to capture the apparent connection between consumers of different ages, sex and nationalities who appear to have one interest that transcends all other cultural boundaries, that is, their common interest in the brand. The concept of interpretive communities can be useful to marketing strategists where there is a range of communicative practices that characterize a given consumption practice. Agencies can find out the favoured values and vocabulary of a group and use this insight to make their own advertising resonate with meaning for those specific people (see also discussion of consumer communities in Chapter 1).

Ostensive and Covert Meaning in Advertising and Promotion

Much interpretive theory has been devoted to understanding the process whereby consumers read meaning into advertising. The levels of possible meaning in a given ad can be theorized in a number of ways. Forceville (1996: 105) refers to a distinction made by Tanaka (1994: 41) between ostensive communication and covert communication in advertising. This distinction allows us to theorize what is implied in ads as opposed to what is clearly and unambiguously claimed. The ostensive communicator makes the intention of the communication clear. The covert communicator does not. Many ads make clear and unambiguous claims but they are strictly constrained by law and industry regulation from making claims that are

BOX 2.7   The Community of Soccer Fans Get Extra Value

Young soccer fans joining Manchester United's membership scheme in 2003 receive a mock front page of the *Manchester Evening News* newspaper. It carries the new fan's name in the headline followed by 'signs for champions'. Some UK soccer clubs just give young members a plastic card. This promotional innovation is exciting for the new members and generates goodwill from their parents or guardians. The involvement of the *Manchester Evening News* makes the mock front page more authentic while incidentally publicizing the newspaper as belonging to United's multinational fan base. Manchester United has one of the largest global followings of any soccer team. Followers are avid consumers of club merchandise and television coverage of games but have no demographic in common other than their enthusiasm for Manchester United.

untrue or preposterous. They get around this inconvenience by implying covertly those claims that could be seen as ridiculous or would open them up to criticism if they were made explicitly.

Advertising cannot compel us to believe particular claims or to accept that certain values are embodied in a given brand. Rather, advertising suggests, implies and hints. It places images and words in suggestive juxtaposition to imply that consuming a given brand will symbolically confer certain qualities and values. If you use a Gillette razor you are enjoying 'The Best A Man Can Get' (at least, according to the ads) and you might even acquire some of the characteristics and lifestyle of the actor in the ads. Driving a prestigious motor-car brand such as a Toyota Avensis will (we are invited to infer from the TV ads), confer a symbolic social status on us that reflects our success and desire. The ads don't actually say these things: they merely imply them, hoping that viewers will read the desired implication.

Ads frequently imply that consumers will be more sexually attractive, more powerful or will appear more materially successful if they consume a given brand. Much advertising acquires its motivational force through its non-explicit suggestions rather than through its explicit claims. Where branded products are juxtaposed with images of attractive, happy and successful people, the link between the two is implied but not stated. Most importantly, it is not necessary for the advertising audience to believe these implied suggestions for the theory of covert communication to hold. It is only necessary that the audience can retrieve the meaning implied. We can see what ads are suggesting even where we neither trust the advertiser nor believe the covert implications. We know that a deodorant brand will not make us sexually attractive. We also know that the ads are implying that it will.

Covert meaning is often conveyed in advertising though pictorial, auditory or linguistic metaphor. If a branded bottle of alcoholic drink is pictured juxtaposed with scenes of fit, young, affluent people, then the metaphoric link is clear. For example, Martini used to be advertised in the UK as a drink enjoyed by swimsuited young men and women diving from a yacht moored at a tropical island. The juxtaposition of a branded alcohol drink with apparent wealth, attractiveness and physical fitness is exactly the opposite of what one might reasonably expect, since alcohol drinking is quite likely to make exponents fat and unfit, and may also make them poor if they drink enough. The covert communication in this campaign was preposterous but was nevertheless clear. The Martini brand was used as a metaphor for sexual attractiveness and the good life. It matters little that the drink may often be consumed in social contexts that are, on the face of it, as far from the good life as one might wish to be.

Recent Bacardi rum TV campaigns in the UK have featured the rough-hewn charm of a certain professional footballer turned movie star flirting with beautiful women in a scenario that has the brand as the hero.

The ad is set in a wildly partying bar scene with a Latin theme. The campaign, which has drawn criticism for contributing to the sexualization of alcohol advertising, implies covertly that consumption of the brand opens a door for the user to a semi-illicit world in which excitement and sexual allure are normal parts. A British woman ordering a Bacardi and soda in a terrace pub on a rainy Monday night in Doncaster will not, of course, be transported, even in her imagination, to a scene of elegant bacchanalia in downtown Havana. The Bacardi brand, nevertheless, features in the drinker's set of buying choices because of the powerfully evocative advertising.

Ads as Visual Rhetoric

Another way of understanding the levels of advertising meaning theoretically is to view ads as visual rhetoric. Visual consumption (Shroeder, 2002) is a powerful aspect of advertising's influence. We not only consume advertising and promotional images, we seek to understand their persuasive intent: we wonder what they are saying to us. Promotional communication has a persuasive motive, so the analogy with linguistic rhetoric is telling. In rhetoric, what is not said but left implicit is often considered to be as significant, or more significant, than what is explicitly said (Billig, 1987, 1991). In advertising it is the implication, rather than the overt (or ostensive) claim that is often the most potent and persuasive element of communication.

The underlying or suggested meanings in ads can also be theorized as **sub-texts** subsisting beneath the level of the ostensive text. The advertising text might tell a story of brand value and product quality. The sub-text might tell a slightly different story by, for example, suggesting by pictorial juxtaposition that consumers of this brand may assume some of the qualities and lifestyle of the actors who feature in the ad. The advertising text may be a quite prosaic 'buy this brand' appeal while the suggested and implied sub-textual meanings are more complex, subtle and, to the viewer, more interesting.

Many perfume ads in lifestyle and fashion magazines make no direct reference to the odour: instead, they juxtapose sensuous images with an enigmatic strapline or slogan that evinces some abstract notion of the brand. The visual organization of image and copy is carefully designed to rhetorically support the implicit claims made about the brand. A UK press ad for an Estée Lauder perfume portrayed a woman with flowing hair against images of waves, scattered flowers and sunlight with the copy 'Introducing the new fantasy in fragrance' and 'Beyond paradise' with the explanation that it offers 'an intoxication of the senses'. The ad had visual impact: it made a striking image when placed in a double-page section[6] immediately inside the magazine cover. By its size and page location the ad was rhetorically declaring that its subject matter was important, more important, perhaps, than the magazine's editorial. The woman's face engages the reader eye to eye with a questioning and provocative expression that seems to be asking 'Dare you join me in paradise?' The face rhetorically supports the idea that this brand transports the ordinary woman from the everyday to a different world in which she can be free to be any self she chooses. The French brand name draws on the cultural idiom of style and sophistication to imply that the perfume has those qualities and so, by association, will the reader who buys the brand. Of course, consumers will decide if they like the odour, but the odour is designed to be pleasant. Once again, the powerfully suggestive aspect of this ad is not only in its message but in its creativity. The ad is rhetorically organized to support certain implied meanings.

The visual rhetoric of ads is not, then, confined to the copy. An ad is an argument, a persuasive communication. Every part of it must support the main argument, must be persuasively suggestive. A press ad for Retinol Activ Pur face cream used a clever visual metaphor to support a claim that the cream reduced facial wrinkles. The ad featured two juxtaposed images of a beautiful (Caucasian) woman. She was wearing what seemed to be a white robe, folded over one shoulder like a Roman toga. In the background was a pure blue sky and a suggestion of white pillars, of the kind in a Greek temple. One picture was cracked, like the surface of an old oil painting. The other was smooth. The metaphoric reference was clear: the cracks suggested wrinkles, but in an elegant way that was complimentary, not demeaning, to age. Old paintings are things of classical beauty but the paint does tend to crack with age. The ad was designed to draw the eye across aesthetically appealing images while giving the reader heavy hints about the classic beauty they might aspire to if they were to consume the brand.

However the levels of meaning in advertisements are theorized, acknowledging their presence lends a new dimension to the analysis of advertising as persuasive communication. It brings to light some of the subtlety and complexity of advertising design while also allowing us to draw an intellectual connection between the various artificially differentiated categories of marketing communication.

In principle, then, any communication is open to varied interpretations since meaning itself is rooted in culturally-based forms of understanding. Once the incorrigibility of meaning is acknowledged, the complexity of the task facing marketing communications specialists can be understood. Creative professionals in advertising overcome the problem of the indeterminacy (or polysemy) of meaning in advertising by hinting through suggestive juxtaposition that certain values are associated with certain brands, rather than by making claims which, if taken literally, would seem ridiculous. More importantly, advertising agencies put up claims that, if they were made explicit, would open them up to criticism or censure. It is a measure of poor general understanding that advertising regulation and legislation focus on the ostensive content of ads and ignore the far more significant implied or covert meanings that ads carry. Guinness ads make no claims at all as such but imply that the brand is a major global player, with the connotations of glamour that this entails.

The polysemy of meaning in advertising creates the space for consumers of advertising to use some licence in reinterpreting ads creatively according to their own cultural reference points and reflecting their own sense of identity. The text of advertising, its *prima facie* meaning, can sometimes be its least interesting aspect because consumers may reject marketing strategies that seem too contrived or obvious. They may, however, use advertising and the brands that are advertised in ways that subvert the marketing text but reflect the consumers' own values and social strategies. For example, UK consumers once mocked ads for the Skoda car by inventing jokes at the brand's expense. Skoda improved the quality of their products and then exploited the fact that their brand had become so well known by creating ads that referred to its poor public image with

BOX 2.8   Guinness Rides the Waves of Ambiguity

Guinness advertisements are often media events in themselves. The brand has created a strong tradition of creatively flamboyant and often expensive advertising that does not carry a sales message as such. The famous 'White Horses' ad produced by a large UK agency, AMV BBDO, portrays a group of middle-aged beach bums on an exotic island waiting for and finding their perfect surfing wave. The creative strategy exploited the frustrating fact that ordering a pint of Guinness in a bar entails a fairly long wait while the beer settles. The voice-over states that 'he waits, and he waits ...' until the perfect wave arrives. There is no explicit (or ostensive) marketing message, other than a brief shot of a pint of stout to help those completely in the dark about the manufacturer generously funding this lavish entertainment. Guinness (or the brand owners, Diageo) is well aware that its famous stout is an unusual, acquired taste. They are, it seems, content that their off-the-wall advertising tradition keeps the brand in the public domain and lends it a mystique which, when you think about it, is quite an achievement considering the prosaic origins of the product they have to work with. A quirky local beverage with a history of being the tipple of choice of working-class Irish men does not, on the face of it, have great potential as a global brand. The prominence of the brand can be attributed in no small part to its tradition of creatively striking, intriguingly entertaining and deeply ambiguous advertising.

straplines such as 'It's a Skoda – honest'. Consumers knew that the brand was mocking their poor (and flawed) perception of it, but the manufacturer gambled that consumers would enjoy the joke at their expense and understand that the joke had a serious point: that Skoda cars were much improved.

Marketing organizations can use the inderterminacy of advertising meaning to play games with consumers, second-guessing their interpretation with ironic or self-deprecating ads. In this way, for example, brands may be regarded as 'cool' if they appear to subvert the establishment discourse of brand advertising by producing self-consciously bad, outrageous or uncomfortably frank ads. Some brands (such as Skoda or Marmite) even use a self-deprecating creative strategy, gambling that the consumers' advertising literacy is of such sophistication that they will not take the self-deprecation at face value and will understand that it is meant to be ironic.

Advertising and Semiotics

Semiotics deserves a brief mention because of its influence in studies of advertising. Semiotics is the study of signs and their meaning. American influence (particularly that of Charles Sanders Peirce) has broadened the field from the study of linguistic signs, also called semiology (Saussure, 1974) to include the study of any signs whatsoever (Peirce, 1958; introductions in Danesi, 1994; Hackley, 1999a). Advertising and marketing have attracted much attention from semioticians (Barthes, 1972; Williamson, 1978). Ads are seen by semioticians as 'strings of signs' (Umiker Sebeok, 1997), assemblages of collections of signs in the service of the brand. Such signs (copy, typeface, soundtrack, positioning, image, colour, objects) rhetorically support the sub-textual or covert meanings that are central to the persuasive force of advertising. The meaning of a given sign depends on the context, the receiver and the communication codes that form the cultural expectations of the sender and receiver.

The message, if one can be discerned among the cacophony of signification in many ads, is only one part of the complex process of communication that is going on when a consumer engages with an ad and attempts to interpret its meaning. In an example used above press ads for Diesel clothing were described to illustrate their use of intertextual cultural references. Another way of analysing these ads is to look at the signification properties of each part of the ad, the visual images, the copy, the relation of images to each other and so on. Semiotics seeks to recover the communicative codes through which we receive messages from word, visual, auditory or other signs. A crucial aspect of the communicative power of promotional communication is that humans actively seek meaning by completing a Gestalt whole from even incoherent visual or other cues.

Cleverly designed marketing communication can allow consumers licence to play with meaning in an interpretive space that reflects the brand's personality and values.

Marketing as a whole is a rich source of signification (Sawchuck, 1995) that reaches into the most intimate areas of our lives to transform the meaning of everyday signs. The acts of shaving, washing, even personal cleanliness are superimposed with marketed values (is your toilet tissue extra-soft?). Advertising lies at the fulcrum of marketing's semiotic mechanism, symbolically articulating the brand values contrived by the strategists.

We will return to some of these concepts as the book progresses through its account of the advertising and promotion field. It is hoped that readers will bear in mind these concepts when they are reading how particular campaigns came about or how consumers reacted to given promotions.

Review Exercises

1. Choose three print advertisements and three TV ads. For each, construct descriptions that distinguish the covert from the ostensive meanings in the ad. Compare your interpretations with colleagues: do they differ?
2. What is polysemy? What is its importance in the work of advertising agencies? Collect several magazines: can you find ads that appear to be polysemic?
3. Choose one print ad and form a group with three collaborators. Try to pick out all the individual signs that might carry meaning in the ad. These might include the copy (the words, the position of the copy in the visual and the typeface or font that is used), the models, the props in the set, the background, the relation of objects and bodies to each other, the gestures, the quality of paper and use of colour and the other brands advertised in the magazine.
4. What is a message? To what extent is meaning carried unequivocally within an advertisement? Compare three ads to discuss this.
5. Using any promotional communications that you have collected as a basis for discussion, describe intertextuality and examine its use in contemporary advertising. How can intertextuality be of use to advertisers?

CASE St Luke's Prickly Heat Powder

In South-east Asian countries the extreme heat can be uncomfortable. A product that would be described as talcum powder in the UK is marketed because of its cooling effect on the skin. In Thailand the brand leader is St Luke's 'Prickly Heat Powder'.

It is a popular remedy for the discomfort that can be experienced in very hot weather. The client asked the agency Publicis Thailand[7] to develop a creative execution that could energize its marketing, maintaining its brand awareness and market-leading position.

Publicis Thailand apply a consumer insight tool they call 'Streetsmart' to their advertising development. They encourage the whole account team to gain a consumer's-eye-view of the client's brand category. In many cases this means taking the account team to consume the brand in typical settings. Their aim is to ground their advertising development in an intimate understanding of the consumer. If the whole account team shares this understanding, then the problem of having one function persuade another of its point of view is avoided. The consumer insight that drives creative development is considered to be self-evident, since all the team have experienced it first-hand.

Thai consumers are discerning. They are highly brand-conscious and love to be amused and intrigued by advertising. In the case of St Luke's (like many Asian brands, the brand name is displayed in English on the packaging) the challenge was to create a succinct visual image that won the consumer's attention and at the same time clearly indicated the brand's utility. If the creative solution could be amusing as well, then so much the better.

The award-winning creative solution involved a simple visual metaphor portrayed in high-quality photography. Three print ads were created that featured the product packaging metamorphosed into a fire extinguisher, a refrigerator and an ice-cream. The ads' visual metaphor succinctly reinforced the product's utility while doing so in a way that would amuse (see also colour insert). The client's marketing objectives were accomplished.

Case Exercises

1. Using a visual metaphor to indicate brand functionality may seem a simple solution to a communications challenge.
   Can you guess what prior cultural knowledge would be required for a consumer to fully understand the communication in the St Luke's campaign?
2. Collect examples of five ads that deploy visual metaphors. Do they all use them in the same way? Can you think of any product categories or markets in which visual metaphors would not be useful? Why?
3. Some of the most troubling challenges facing account teams

concern mundane products with a largely functional appeal. In what ways was this agency able to invest brand values in the product through its choice of creative execution?

Further Reading

Introductions to interpretive concepts and methods

Elliott, R.H. and Beckmann, S. (eds) (2001) *Interpretive Consumer Research: Paradigms, Methodologies and Applications*. Copenhagen: Copenhagen Business School Press.

Hackley, C. (2003e) *Doing Research Projects in Marketing, Management and Consumer Research*. London: Routledge.

Advertising as discourse, from an applied linguistics perspective

Cook, G. (2001) *The Discourse of Advertising*, 2nd edn. London: Routledge.

Semiotics

Eco, U. (1976) *A Theory of Semiotics*. Bloomington, IN: Indiana University Press.

Eco, U. (1984) *Semiotics and Philosophy of Language*. London: Macmillan.

Reviews of advertising effects research

Kitchen, P.J. (ed.) (1999) *Marketing Communications – Principles and Practice*. London: Thompson.

Wells, W.D. (ed.) (1997) *Measuring Advertising Effectiveness*. Hillsidale, NJ: Lawrence Erlbaum Associates.

Some useful academic journals

These can normally be obtained through academic libraries and electronic databases.

Advances in Consumer Research *(Proceedings of the Association of Consumer Research: downloads are available at www.vancouver.wsu.edu/acr/home.htm)*

European Journal of Marketing

International Journal of Advertising

Journal of Advertising

Journal of Advertising Research

Journal of Business Research

Journal of Consumer Research

Journal of Current Issues and Research in Advertising

Journal of Economic Psychology

Journal of Marketing

Journal of Marketing Research

Psychology and Marketing

Notes

1 Cook (2001) maintains that advertising is no different in its 'parasitic' character from any other discourse form. Intertextuality can be discerned in culturally valued discourse forms such as classical art, drama and literature, as well as in 'low' or popular cultural forms such as movies, comic books and popular theatre, as well as advertising.

2 The examples were referred to by O'Donohoe (1997).

3 The consumption metaphor here is extended to consuming (viewing, reading, thinking about) advertising itself.

4 Jones, J.P. (1990) 'Advertising: Strong Force or Weak Force? Two Views an Ocean Apart', International Journal of Advertising, 9: 233–46.

5 The Advertising Standards Authority is the industry body responsible for the voluntary regulation of British press and poster advertising (www.asa.org.uk).

6 In Hello! magazine No. 781, 9 September, 2003.

7 My thanks to Publicis Thailand.

Advertising and Promotion's Role in Brand Marketing

Chapter Outline

This chapter begins the book's description of the managerial practices of brand advertising and promotion. It uses many case examples[1] to illustrate the flexibility and precision of advertising in supporting and promoting a wide variety of marketing objectives in a range of market conditions. The chapter sets this influence within a brief historical outline of advertising's evolution before drawing attention to its collective influence in promotional culture. Advertising and promotion of all kinds constitute a mutually reinforcing system promoting consumption of brands. The emphasis of this chapter falls on the careful planning required to turn advertising's collective persuasive power to the service of specific brands.

BOX 3.0   The Effectiveness of Creativity in Building Brands

Speaking to the UK advertising industry as president of the IPA[2] John Bartle of Bartle Bogle Hegarty pointed out that many advertising campaigns that win awards for creativity are also demonstrably effective in supporting brand marketing objectives. He cited campaigns for Wonderbra that won six creative awards in two years and also coincided with an average 41 per cent per week increase in sales year on year. British Airways was another campaign that created a stir for its creativity and yielded market share growth estimated at £7.8 billion for a worldwide advertising investment of £400 million. Other brands cited included BMW, Boddington's beer and Peperami snacks. Bartle did not argue that the values of creativity necessarily equate with marketing effectiveness. He simply drew attention to the compelling evidence that there is no inherent contradiction between advertising creativity and effectiveness. Creative excellence can, in a carefully conceived communications strategy, be highly effective in supporting the sales, revenue and market share objectives of brands.

The Strategic Role of Advertising

Advertising's role as a feature of marketing strategy is often under-emphasized. It is easy to see why. Advertising and promotion are, too often, the very last things marketing or brand managers think about, after product development, market testing, business analysis, production planning, material sourcing, distribution and so on. Yet it is a mistake to assume that the sequence of managerial activities involved in bringing a market offering to the consuming public reflects their relative importance. Advertising and other forms of marketing communication are not in themselves sufficient for successful consumer brand marketing. But in most cases they are necessary to the success of the venture.

From a managerial perspective advertising and promotion are the final step in bringing an offering to market. From a consumer perspective advertising is often the only step that they see before consumption. Advertising is the typical consumer's point of entry into the long chain of brand marketing planning and co-ordination. The advertising helps to establish a set of assumptions that the consumer will bring to all other aspects of their engagement with a given brand. Advertising is also important for the confidence and morale of other parties who have a stake in the success of a brand, such as shareholders, sales staff and other employees, and suppliers. Advertising provides tangible evidence of the financial credibility and competitive presence of an organization. Corporate communication is a distinct discipline in itself. But in a broader sense every ad is a reflection on the corporation that sponsored it because of the cumulative influence on its commercial credibility. Tangible benefits from this credibility might include longer supplier credit periods, greater influence over suppliers' prices, better employee retention and more effective recruitment, and greater confidence among stockmarket players. Advertising's corporate influence can spread far beyond the brand.

Advertising's Collective Influence

On a wider scale, it can be argued that advertising and other forms of promotional communication collectively create the cultural preconditions that lead to consumers' acceptance of advertising's legitimacy. This legitimacy in turn supports consumption as an end in itself. Of course, marketing communications managers and brand managers are interested only in the efficacy of advertising for their particular brands. However, in order to fully understand advertising's specific effects it is necessary to also appreciate its collective influence. Advertising is seen collectively as an engine of economic growth by economists. Tables tracking advertising expenditure as a proportion of a country's GDP show a striking relationship between these two economic variables.[3] Of course, the fluctuations in a country's GDP may also cause fluctuations in advertising expenditure, rather than the other way round. Nevertheless, it is reasonable to assume some relationship between the variables: advertising, after all, promotes consumption and consumer-led economic growth is a well-established phenomenon. Advertising plays an important economic role, driving consumption in the cycle of consumer expenditure, jobs and investment.

There is another sense in which advertising has a collective effect. It is a form of communication which consumers have to learn. There is a level of cultural understanding that is a precondition for interpreting ads (Scott, 1994a, cited in Hackley, 2002). Once we are acculturated to reading advertising texts, experiencing new forms of advertising modifies our understanding of subsequent ads. Advertising and promotion within promotional culture constitute a self-generating system of signs that frames our experience as consumers and places our sense of social identity and economic relations within a consumption-based sign system.

By being exposed to different kinds of advertising text over time, consumers are educated to understand advertising in all its complexity

BOX 3.1   Learning to Read Irony in Advertising

Advertising man Bill Bernbach is sometimes credited with the introduction of irony in advertising in 1960s VW commercials. Today a great deal of advertising is replete with ironic references. Consumers have by and large learned to read such ads because of their increasing familiarity. Even self-deprecation has become acceptable in advertising texts. Campaigns in the UK for Walker's Crisps have featured a sporting hero, Gary Lineker, stealing a little boy's bag of crisps. Some clients might think this a dangerous plot since they may feel that they want positive associations from the celebrity to feed into positive associations about the brand. The agency (DDB London) was able to persuade the client that British advertising audiences would understand the humorously ironic script and would, in fact, like the celebrity even more for making fun of his own 'nice guy' public image (self-deprecation being considered a virtue in the UK, if nowhere else).

> The Walker's brand has become, according to some reports, the second most well-known brand in the UK after Coca-Cola. This campaign has been another commercial success, reflecting the advertising literacy of many consumers.

and variety, which masks the fact that at one level all advertising promotes the same thing – consumption.

Taking one further aspect of advertising's collective influence, there is a sense in which advertisers who fund a successful high-profile campaign can be said to be subsidizing their competitors. A creatively striking TV ad for, say the Ford convertible Street Ka may do much for the brand. However, it cannot help but glamorize driving and car ownership in general. Ads for branded goods and services always carry the sub-text that consumption as an end in itself is exciting, fun and important. Furthermore, if one TV ad in ten is creatively striking, it will act as an incentive to viewers to sit and watch the other nine less interesting ads just in case a good one follows. In a sense, perhaps the great ads create space for the majority of less inspired ones.

Advertising and Brand Presence

Advertising has helped to develop an international presence for the world's most well-known brands. If one tries to think of an internationally known brand, names like Sony, Marlboro, McDonald's, Levi Strauss, Nike, Disney, Kodak, Gillette, Mercedes-Benz and Coca-Cola are likely to come up. Advertising was not solely responsible for the success of these brands, since brand management is more complex and substantial than mere advertising. But it is hard to deny that the brands' status is inconceivable without advertising, in its various forms. Indeed, for a great majority of people the advertising supplies the only knowledge of the brand they will ever have. Millions of consumers have never owned a Mercedes, do not smoke cigarettes, rarely drink carbonated beverages and are indifferent to the brand of film in their camera. Nevertheless, if asked, many of these consumers could offer a fairly detailed description of the values and ideas they associate with Mercedes-Benz, Marlboro, Coca-Cola and Kodak. Even brand names such as Prada, Gucci and Yves St Laurent are well-known among consumers who have never owned them.

The influence that advertising and promotion wield over non-consumers of brands is not trivial or incidental. Advertising that conveys the brand's values, presence and personality to non-consumers is far from wasted.

BOX 3.2   Advertising as Publicity

In the above argument there is an implicit theory of how advertising works. Advertising in the context of consumer brand markets may be important not as a series of mediated sales encounters with individual consumers but, rather, in a much more general sense, as publicity (Ehrenberg et al., 2002; see also p. 34). Conceptualizing advertising as publicity acknowledges advertising's inherent limitations as a sales trigger. Instead, the perspective emphasizes advertising's strength as a means of gaining publicity for the brand among very large numbers of consumers in ways that can invest the brand with carefully contrived and persuasive values and associations.

Indeed, the power of a given brand to signify particular values and impressions depends as much on the view of people who have never consumed it as upon the views of its regular consumers. The impression non-consumers have of brands contributes substantially to the brands' status and prestige. Internationally known brands have a significance in social life that reaches beyond mere product consumption: they become part of the social vernacular. Advertising is normally intrinsic to building popular awareness and creating key associations for such brands.

Advertising and the World's Top Brands

The world's top brands spring readily to mind. There are literally millions of brands in existence. Why have a small number of brands acquired such a powerful presence in the consumer culture of so many countries around the world? One important reason is that over many years and on a huge scale these brands have invested in advertising. In many cases they have benefited from the striking creative work of talented advertising agencies which has made their campaigns and their brand distinctive and memorable. It is impossible to conceive of these brands in the way that we do without advertising communication.

Communication alone does not create or sustain the brand but it does provide a space for it in consumers' lives. Brand recognition goes beyond brand usage. These brands are powerfully evocative for millions of people who have never consumed and in many cases never even seen the product. As we know brand consumers are acutely aware of the general perception of that brand. Successful brands have a cultural meaning that extends beyond purchase and usage. Awareness of what the brand means to non-consumers is part of the appeal of the brand for consumers.

The Concept of the Brand

A brand is often described in terms of four main dimensions: it is a *badge* of origin that entails a *promise* of quality and performance which *reassures* the consumer and may transform their *experience* (Feldwick, 2002: 4–9). These elements collectively differentiate the brand from others. It has been said (Aaker et al., 1992) that advertisements can lend many qualities to brands that afford a brand certain perceived attributes and confer upon it a brand personality. The notion of brand personality, well-established in professional brand management, personifies the brand and reflects the attempt to generate a sense of affinity between consumers and certain brands.

Given that the cultural status and longevity of brands are still something of a mystery to marketers, some resort to lyrical paeans when they try to describe the phenomenon of the brand. They are 'gods' with 'personalities' (Feldwick, 2002: 3). The website of the international communications organization McCann-Erickson WorldGroup describes brands as 'global icons' with 'worldwide constituencies of millions … bound by common beliefs … that transcend all traditional boundaries' by offering consumers 'experiences' that enable them to 'engage physically, mentally, emotionally, socially or spirituality in the consumption of the product or service making the interaction meaningful and real' (www.mccann.com/aboutus).

The turgid prose of brand marketing masks the substantive and important effects of brands on competitive markets. These effects are arguably unimaginable in the absence of advertising communication and can be seen to continue in spite of pockets of organized consumer resistance to brand marketing.[4]

BOX 3.3   Brand Positioning and Communication

Many major brand marketing organizations take great care to articulate the particular values of brands so that they can be reproduced through all the communications and marketing. Some (such as Unilever) undertake detailed analysis to delineate a brand's competitive environment, its target consumers, the insight that makes the brand distinctive, the consumer benefits (tangible or intangible) conferred by the brand, the values and personality of the brand, the way the brand supports those values, the feature that differentiates the brand from others and the single concept that sums up the brand essence. As an example, Unilever would need to draw out these issues for brands such as Colman's mustard, Pot Noodle snack food, Birds Eye foods, Surf detergent, Domestos bleach and numerous others. All major brand organizations use similar conceptual frameworks to emphasize the distinctive characteristics of each brand they market so that they can manage those characteristics through communication.

Brand Communication and Competitive Advantage

Communication through advertising and promotion can make consumers choose a given brand over alternatives. This confers significant market power on popular brands. In competitive markets it is difficult to make a product or service appear distinctively different from the rest. Innovations of design, process, pricing, distribution and manufacture can be quickly copied. Manufacturing technology or service operations can often be transferred to countries with lower labour costs and overheads. This means that a tangible competitive advantage is hard to achieve and even harder to sustain over long periods under competition. Intellectual property and patent rights confer some protection to innovators but rival businesses can succeed in making their offering appear to be identical to that of an innovator in important respects. In many developing economies intellectual property rights are difficult or impossible to police. Furthermore, in developed economies consumer markets are increasingly sensitive to the actual or perceived links between public events, personalities and news stories, and brands. This makes the brand vulnerable to unexpected changes in public taste.

For these reasons and others, advertising communication is an essential component of brand marketing. The competitive advantage that organizations cannot sustain by other means can be sustained by branding. A successful brand constitutes a kind of quasi-monopoly, ensuring what economists call super-normal profits. Through carefully crafted and artfully creative communications strategies organizations can accomplish the distinctiveness, differentiation and, hence, premium pricing and repeat purchasing that they cannot accomplish through other marketing or production activities alone. In a powerful sense, marketing 'is communications and communications is marketing' (Shimp, 1997: 4, citing Schultz et al., 1993). A brand lives on through consumer perceptions which are formed in engagement with advertising communication. The distinctive positioning, segmentation and targeting that is so difficult to achieve and sustain through other means can be achieved symbolically through advertising and promotional communication.

The point that communication is integral to how consumers understand and engage with marketed brands does not necessarily imply that a brand is all about superficial 'puffery' and short-term publicity. 'Puffery' is the name given to advertising copy that is so clearly hyperbolic that no reasonable person would take it literally. It is also sometimes used as a derogatory term for advertising in general. Most advertising conveys something about a brand's values and characteristics, but this is not all there is to brand marketing. Brand managers will normally argue that communications are like the tip of an iceberg, just visible above the waterline with a far more substantial structure unseen beneath. This invisible structure includes production, staffing, training, operations, logistics, supply and material sourcing, and all the other activities without which a branded product or service could not reach a marketplace. The communications dimension, the tip of the iceberg, is all that the general public can see and that is why it is so important. Most brands have a concrete existence as businesses with plant, machinery and personnel, but they also have another existence as an idea in the collective public mind. Some brands, such as Virgin, exist primarily as an abstract entity covering diverse businesses.

Brand advertising and communication, then, should not be thought of as a trivial or superficial activity in a marketing context. It is central to success in consumer, and increasingly industrial, marketing. For consumers the brand image or personality, the values and associations linked with the brand, the way the brand is talked about by friends and acquaintances, the way the brand is represented in press editorial and TV coverage, and the memory of personal experience of consuming the brand are all aspects of an holistic engagement with this entity, the brand. A consumer brand is a

BOX 3.4   BMW Brand Advertising

Crosier (1999) quotes an in-house BMW publication in his description of how a niche German motor-car brand was transformed into an iconic mass-market class leader through advertising. The London agency WCRS was appointed in 1980; since then it has produced over 300 press advertisements, 40 TV commercials and many poster campaigns. The creative themes have emphasized the aesthetic appeal and technical excellence of BMW cars and have seldom featured human beings. The brand values of 'exclusivity, advanced technology and performance' have been represented creatively through the advertising, producing the leading car brand in several classes of vehicle. The longevity of this relationship between client and agency is rare in the advertising business. The results are striking. The brand itself rests on tangible product values. BMWs are famous for the build quality of the cabin interior, the performance of the engines, and the engineering quality and aesthetic appeal of the car body. Since 1980 the brand has acquired an enduring quality of prestige and performance among many people who know nothing of car mechanics and who have never even owned a BMW. WCRS's advertising has clearly played a significant role in this brand transformation.

fine exemplar of the notion of social construction as explained by Berger and Luckman (1966). Influencing the way this abstraction is thought and spoken of is clearly a task in which communication is a primary tool (see also pp. 37–9).

When the idea of the brand is reduced to what consumers say and think about, it seems a nebulous and fragile entity. It is, then, all the more extraordinary that brands can be so enduring and powerful in eliciting the attention and enthusiasm of consumers. We take this power for granted since we are so accustomed to corporate brands such as Mercedes-Benz, Coca-Cola or McDonald's occupying a significant place in cultural and economic life. But citizens were not always so quiescent about the business wiles of big corporations. If we are to understand better the role of communications in brand marketing we have to have some sense of its evolution in a social context. Part of the reason why we have grown to take brands so much for granted can perhaps be found in the USA at the turn of the century.

The Role of Advertising in the Rise of the Brand Corporations

Even in the USA, brand marketing was not always welcomed with enthusiasm. While there are, of course, local and small-scale brands, many successful consumer brands are synonymous with large corporations: they reflect the needs and character of marketing on a large scale, what used to be termed 'mass marketing'. The activities of large corporations were met with great suspicion, even open hostility, in the USA at the turn of the century. These corporations needed some help to create the public acceptance of their activities that they required: it was to advertising agencies that they turned for that help.

The historian Roland Marchand (1985, 1998) has described how the rise of big business in the USA was facilitated by advertising and communication. At the turn of the century there were many mergers and acquisitions in US business. As a result there were fewer, bigger corporations. Many Americans regretted the demise of the local high-street store and the rise of vast soulless corporations. As corporations grew, many feared that they posed a threat to American values and institutions such as the church, the family and the local community. Serious questions were asked at presidential level about the activities of these leviathans and their influence over American cultural life. The entrepreneurs who created great corporations such as AT&T, GM, GE, Ford Motors and US Steel were acutely aware of the need to legitimize their activities and manufacture a soul for the new corporatism. Over the following decades a profound transformation took place in the public image of corporations. From being perceived as potential threats to American values, they became the very epitome.

Marchand (1998: 2) points out that this new legitimacy flew in the face of classical economic theory which held that the nature of competitive businesses is that they cannot rise above self-interest or the dictates of the market. As these companies attained extraordinary size and power it became clear that they were no mere slaves to market forces but exercised considerable monopolistic power. Not only did they have to persuade the public of their right to play a part in American life, they also had to create an identity in order to anthropomorphize and therefore soften their soulless image. The corporations addressed this pressing problem partly through welfare capitalism and patriarchal initiatives to improve the workforce through education and training. They also used grand (and grandiose) architecture to impress their status and power on the skyline, such as the gothic spectacle of the Woolworth building in New York City and the massive factories of manufacturers such as the Jell-O company and Pillsbury's.

Selling the Corporate Sizzle Through Advertising

Corporate advertising and public relations also played a significant part in creating a soul for corporate America. Their advertising agencies produced a stream of imagery and copy on postcards, posters, in magazines and press editorial and, later, on radio portraying the corporations in terms of such values as integrity, service to the community, localism, tradition and moral uprightness. This corporate advertising also served a more pragmatic purpose in helping to produce an internal sense of corporate identity (and a sense of collective purpose) for thousands of employees.

In legitimizing capitalist corporatism and selling consumption to citizens as a lifestyle, advertising was central to the development of the marketing ideal of consumer orientation. Consumers were taught through advertising that manufactured products reflected their discernment and requirements. Through responses (or non-responses) to advertising consumers could play a part in the market mechanism and cast a vote in favour of their own personal consumer vision. Consumers' collective sense of self-interest is fired by the drama of consumption played out in advertising. Clearly, in affluent economies most categories of consumer need are not fundamental and absolute but derivative and relative. Consumer goods are not created by advertising, but the social status of the attributes of goods is (Leiss et al., 1997: 299). Advertising teaches us that the social status of brand attributes is scarce and carries a premium cost.

In this important historical sense advertising has been central to the development of the idea of consumer marketing. The consumer orientation preached by marketing management textbooks can be seen as a continuation of the ideology of the early American corporations. In spite of the practical limits to consumer orientation in large manufacturing organizations, marketing texts nevertheless deploy the rhetoric of consumer orientation

BOX 3.5   The Role of Art and Dramatic Realism in Promoting Brands

With the legitimization of corporate activity in hand, advertising in turn-of-the century America was deployed to encourage the mass consumption of the stream of new products being produced. Ad agencies discovered art in this enterprise, using imagery and metaphors from classical art and literature to create aesthetically inspiring dramatic portrayals of the product along with 'an account of ... the social benefit that the consumer could be expected to derive' (Leiss et al., 1997: 79). Marchand (1985) described the advertising technique used to accomplish this effect as 'dramatic realism'. For example, an everyday situation such as dirt on clothes might be portrayed as a problem that the model housewife solves, with the help of Daz, Omo or some other branded detergent. The picture accompanying the advertising text would be carefully drawn as graphic art, perhaps with an attractive model in a striking pose, in juxtaposition with the brand logo and packaging. Advertising realized the consumer's need for aesthetic stimulation and symbolic self-expression and bridged the gap between manufacturers and creative artists. In this way the design of American advertising and the products themselves was improved (Leiss et al., 1997: 81). Consumers were treated to advertising that was aesthetically attractive and a product that could express something about consumer personality and social identity.

to promote a sense of connection between the little consumer and the big corporation. The rhetorical force and apparent popularity of marketing rhetoric (satisfying consumer needs, being customer-focused) might reflect a continuing need for capitalist corporatism to claim legitimacy (Hackley, 2003g) amid a contemporary crisis of confidence in the activities and motives of global business corporations. Advertising's success in setting the preconditions for a consumer society has been striking even while organized resistance to global capitalism is evident in the form of sporadic but numerous consumer protests and boycotts.

What Advertising Can Do for Brands

Advertising's collective cultural influence may be formidable but as a device of marketing strategy it can also be both subtle and precise. Advertising is persuasive since it draws on values that obtain in non-marketing culture and attaches these values to marketed objects. Designer clothes, prestige motorcars, executive homes, upscale holidays and so on, all impute social status to objects whose only social value is that constituted within marketing culture. In turn, brands generate an emotional response from consumers as we wonder at the aesthetic beauty of advertising images, laugh at the wit of copywriters or realize our fantasies about own attractiveness and power vicariously through owning the right brands. Advertising is an important part of the creation and maintenance of the contrived brand values that make particular brands distinctive, memorable and, above all, desirable to their target groups.

The UK IPA claims[5] that among other business aims, advertising can:

- defend brands against own-label growth
- effect change internally as well as externally to the company
- increase the efficiency of recruitment
- transform entire businesses by generating new markets for a brand
- revitalize a declining brand
- reinvigorate a market
- stop line extensions cannibalizing existing sales
- change behaviour
- influence share price
- make other communications more cost-effective
- generate rapid sales increases
- increase growth of a mature brand in a declining market
- address crises in public relations.

Through creative ingenuity and careful targeting advertising can support many differing kinds of marketing objective. It must be remembered that advertising itself is communication: ads cannot sell anything as such, neither can they in themselves create a successful brand. What they can do is to place particular ideas in the public realm to make consumers aware of brand offerings, to create a favourable predisposition towards a brand, to explain things about the brand and to tell a story of uniqueness about the brand. Advertising can also support more closely specified marketing techniques such as positioning and repositioning, market segmentation, launch and relaunch, raising brand awareness or rebranding, fulfilling corporate communication and other objectives, as discussed below.

But advertising is not all about consumer goods and services. It also plays a role in politics and social policy. Advertising can do a great many things: its uses are limited only by the ingenuity of ad agency planners and creative staff. Some examples are offered below to illustrate the flexibility of advertising in accomplishing and facilitating strategic marketing outcomes.

Segmentation and Advertising Strategy

Advertising agency research performs the essential marketing activity of sorting and categorizing consumers. The resulting campaigns reinforce those categories, making membership seem attractive to certain targeted groups of consumers. Marketing management texts have popularized the term 'segmentation' to refer to this need for categories of consumer to be broken down for easy identification, surveillance (through consumer research) and targeting. We consumers are often complicit in this categorization (Hackley, 2002), since we eagerly seek out ads and images that we feel cohere with our sense of social identity and resonate with our individual aspirations and fantasies. Most importantly, this entails creating a sense of otherness towards categories of consumer that are not us. The distinctions between categories of consumer open up the possibility for consumer discretion and choice. In a given TV or poster ad the casting, the set, the scene props and the dialogue are all powerful signifiers of the kind of human that is supposed to favour a given brand.

It is a cliché in advertising that half the budget is wasted, but no one knows which half. The value of segmentation to organizations is that it can make marketing effort appear more cost-effective by reducing the amount of the marketing budget that is misdirected at undesired consumer groups. Clearly there is a potential drawback to targeting a given segment. If the target group is wrongly identified then there is a risk that the entire marketing budget might be misdirected, instead of only half of it. As we have seen, brand planners might see sales increases as a long-term consequence of a strongly sustained brand personality. An over-emphasis on targeting might neglect to project the brand personality to non-consumers. This could be an important omission given that the brand personality depends as much on the perceptions of non-consumers as of consumers.

Advertising and Negative Segmentation

One advantage of carefully planned targeting is that it can signify to certain consumer groups that they are not wanted by this brand. By default it also signifies who the desired group is. In one example, a recruitment advertising campaign by Saatchi and Saatchi for the British Army was designed specifically to lower the quantity and improve the quality of enquiries generated from advertising. The traditional army ad had tended to glamorize army life, with action shots of soldiers skiing and racing around in speedboats. This style of ad encouraged people to apply for the wrong reasons, so many were rejected. Working to the historical ratio, this kind of campaign had to generate around 100,000 enquiries to get 15,000 new soldiers enlisted. Demographic changes meant that there was a smaller pool of potential recruits.

An integrated campaign on TV, press, posters and radio contained a range of problem-solving scenarios. In one example soldiers were carrying a wounded colleague on a stretcher. They came to a ravine. The voice-over asked the viewer if they could figure out how to cross the ravine. Viewers who felt that they could solve the problem could respond by phoning a telephone number to the recruitment line. The strapline, 'Be The Best' was used across media. The campaign used an execution that involved the audience in a dialogue and combined it with a direct response dimension. It resulted in fewer, better quality applicants. The ratio of enquiries to enlistments was almost halved from 6.7:1 to 3.4:1, which meant much more cost-efficient advertising and also more cost-efficient recruitment. In general, ads that deepen viewers involvement by engaging them in a problem-solving or other task have become more commonplace in recent years as a response to the needs of segmentation.

Another example of segmentation advertising strategy was seen in a UK integrated campaign for Frizzell motor insurance. The company enjoyed some of the longest-serving customers in the insurance business. It wanted to attract more of the low-risk type of driver it specialized in insuring – civil servants, teachers and public-sector employees. In the early 1990s cheaper rivals were winning growing market share by competing on price. Frizzell had very low market awareness (just 16%) beyond its stock of loyal customers. It wanted to attract more of the right kind of custom while actively discouraging high-risk drivers or customers motivated only by cost.

The insurer rejected the direct-response advertising strategy of its rivals because of its positioning as a slightly more expensive insurer for conservative, loyal, risk-averse drivers. Their agency (BMP DDB) designed a TV campaign based on real case histories of long-term customers. This proved tedious for non-targets but engaging for the desired target group. One ad featured a pastiche of images and songs from 1960s London. There was black-and-white film footage of Beatles concerts, flashes of newspaper headlines referring to memorable events of the time and footage (made to look like a black-and-white home movie) of slim, hirsute men enjoying happy times in their first car. The ad had a very dated but nostalgic feel and was intended to be charming to the no longer slim or hirsute drivers who were now solid citizens of 50 years of age. The ad was simply saying that Frizzell insurance was like an old friend, always reliable in an emergency. Its sub-text also clearly and effectively segmented its desired audience. The campaign was extended, with creative executions in commercial radio and national press, and a national equestrian event sponsored by Frizzell. National awareness of Frizzell increased by 200 per cent in the first year. The return on advertising investment was estimated at 24.9 per cent per year.[6]

The Frizzell campaign had used the marketing notion of segmentation to achieve a desired positioning for their brand. In the previous example the British Army wanted to signal to viewers (and prospective soldiers)

BOX 3.6   Advertising for Brand Launch

WCRS created one of the most striking campaigns of the time when they launched Orange, the mobile phone supplier, in an already booming market. Orange was trying to break into a market dominated by the major suppliers, Cellnet, Vodaphone and One 2 One. A major impact was required. It was decided to make the brand vision, 'Wirefree Communications', the creative concept for the whole campaign. An integrated campaign of posters, TV and press cost Orange £26.3 million over two years. The ads had the highest of production values with compelling cinematography and inspirational voice-overs that spoke of an ideal (wire-free) future. One of many striking images in the ads was a baby filmed in what was once called 'slow motion' as it floated happily underwater. Orange rapidly achieved greater brand awareness on some measures than the existing brands. It was estimated that the advertising generated 61,000 new connections to the Orange mobile phone network, representing a financial return of more than four times that of ad expenditure.

that it required people with problem-solving ability and personal qualities of resourcefulness and initiative. It did not want to portray itself as a sub-sidized outdoor-pursuits club for frustrated adventurers. The positioning of the British Army brand was important in attracting the desired calibre of applicant. Frizzel insurance, similarly, used a creative execution that segmented consumers by age, hence achieving the desired positioning.

Another important launch campaign which was awarded an IPA effec-tiveness award in 1996 was by the agency Duckworth Finn Grubb Waters for the South Korean car manufacturer Daewoo. With no dealer network, unexceptional cars and no brand awareness at all, Daewoo achieved its target of 1 per cent UK market share within three years with over two years to spare. According to the agency, rivals such as Hyundai had taken 12 years to achieve a market share that was not yet as high as 1 per cent. The TV campaign used a creative theme that highlighted shortcomings in other car brands' after-sales service and warranties with the sardonic strapline 'That'll be the Daewoo'. The TV ads also emphasized the direct, hassle-free Daewoo service and was supported by press advertising and other promotions. It was the most successful new car brand launch to date.

Advertising and Non-Profit Marketing

Consumer marketing is not alone in using advertising. Advertising has been extensively deployed in the case of socially important causes and non-profit organizations such as charities, care organizations and political parties. DDB London has been involved in many non-profit campaigns and also in political advertising in the UK. This has earned it the title 'Labour's ad agency'[7] in UK media circles. It has been behind many of the campaigns that persuaded British voters to elect the Labour Party to power with a large majority in two successive general elections (so far, writing in 2004). The agency is also proud of its cause-related advertising and produced a record of many of these campaigns in a hardback book[8] (replete with a quote from the British prime minister, Tony Blair, that 'The examples of work ... in this book show how advertising can contribute to social change'). Clients include the charities War on Want and Amnesty International, several unions (the National Union of Teachers and Unison, the public-sector workers' union) and local authorities, as well as the Labour Party itself.

The book examines a change in the viewpoint of the political left that has been highly significant in recent British politics. Organizations that promoted causes of social welfare, such as the Labour Party and the trade unions, were historically unsympathetic to advertising because they associated it with a sell-out to capitalism. As a result such organizations were unable to promote themselves effectively. A change of viewpoint eventually emerged which coincided with the political revival of the Labour Party.

One of the most significant campaigns to change the attitudes of left-wing organizations and campaigning charities towards advertising was the Greater London Council campaign in 1984. This campaign, sponsored by the then council of London, protested against the Conservative campaign's decision to abolish the GLC. One poster featured a close-up of the face of Ken Livingstone, the then leader of the GLC, staring directly out of the poster at the viewer. The strapline was 'If you want me out you should have the right to vote me out'. The campaign failed to change government policy and the GLC was duly abolished (although Ken Livingstone later became elected mayor of London). In spite of the outcome, the campaign was noted for its impact. The political world, public policy and also the charities and non-profit sector have now adopted the research, planning and creative techniques of brand advertising.

Positioning and Consumer Benefit

'Positioning', introduced in Chapter 1, is one of those marketing terms that can be invoked in various different senses. It normally refers to the abstract psychological attributes and associations that a brand may evoke for consumers. It may also refer to more tangible characteristics of a brand that ostensibly differentiate it from others, such as the logo, packaging colour, frequency of and reason for use and any other characteristic.

Very often positioning is linked to the benefit, tangible or intangible, the manufacturer wishes to link to consumption of the brand. For example, the chocolate 'countline'[9] Kit Kat has been positioned for many years as a reward for hard work, epitomized in the famous strapline 'Have a break – have a Kit Kat'. In contrast, rival countline brands such as Bounty bars or Cadbury's Flake are positioned as sensuous indulgences, not rewards for hard work but rewards for just being you.[10]

Positioning and the Marketing Concept

Positioning a brand in terms of some kind of abstract consumer benefit is fundamental to the marketing concept. Marketing as a business function cannot, of course, be wholly innovative as well as satisfying consumer needs. Consumer needs satisfaction must be reactive, while innovation requires leadership. Emphasizing the benefit rather than the tangible qualities of the brand itself is the way that marketing reconciles this contradiction. Advertising is often the major element in suggesting benefits to consumers. In this sense it is through advertising that marketing can symbolically realize the ideal of consumer orientation. Motor-car manufacturers started putting more cup-holders in more cars because consumers said they wanted them. The Sony Walkman, in contrast, was an innovation that initially received negative reactions from consumer research because consumers could not envisage the benefit. They had never seen anything like it and had nothing to compare it with. Once the Walkman was marketed consumers themselves learned that it solved the problem of boredom on walks or long journeys. If Akio Morita, the inventor of the Walkman and CEO of Sony, had enjoyed a large advertising budget he might have taught consumers the benefits of the Walkman though an advertising campaign. What he did have was an established retail distribution chain, so it made sense to simply put the Walkman on the shelves and let consumers discover the benefits for themselves.

Positioning and Usage Occasions

Positioning can also refer to the usage occasions appropriate for a brand. For example, advertising can be used to signal to consumers that a brand can be used in an alternative way or by different people in relation to the previous norm. The chocolate snack Mars Bar was advertised for many years with the strapline 'A Mars a Day Helps You Work, Rest and Play'. This reflected the brand's positioning as a tasty snack that gave one energy to cope with a busy life. Like many chocolate snack ads it was presented as a solitary pleasure rather than a social one. A new advertising campaign showed a group of happy-go-lucky young people pushing a broken-down car to a garage, cheerfully chomping on Mars Bars, thus repositioning the brand's somewhat dated image for a younger and more group-oriented consumer. Mars Bar consumption was now positioned as social event, symbolically signifying group membership. The breakfast cereal Kellogg's Cornflakes was the subject of an ad campaign that showed people enjoying cornflakes in non-breakfast scenarios. A couple enjoyed a romantic late-night bowl of cornflakes, and another consumer used the brand as a TV dinner. The aim was to increase sales to existing consumers by showing that you can eat cornflakes at any time.

Advertising and Repositioning Strategies

Advertising signals the consumer benefit that can be expected to result from brand consumption. Marketing folklore is replete with consumer benefit stories: Black and Decker sell holes, not drills; Revlon does not sell cosmetics, it sells hope, and so on and so forth. Positioning, linked to a consumer benefit and portrayed suggestively through advertising, is a key element of brand marketing. Advertising can be used not only to signal positioning but also to signal a new positioning that supersedes the old. In the UK an infant decongestant/cough remedy called Karvol was relaunched and repositioned through an advertising campaign combined with a packaging redesign. Qualitative consumer research showed that the benefit parents valued was their own sleep at night rather than the child's cough. They knew that while coughs are uncomfortable for the child they are temporary minor ailments. The real problem was that a child's cough could deprive the parent of sleep for night after night, resulting in chronic fatigue and stress. Karvol was relaunched as a benefit for parents' sleep.

The UK motoring organization, the Automobile Association (AA), was seen as somewhat old-fashioned in the late 1990s. Its dated image and low awareness levels among consumers were given a boost though a new campaign by the agency Howell Henry Chaldecott Lury that controversially positioned it as the 'Fourth Emergency Service'. In fact, as British people know, the coastal lifeboat service is the fourth emergency service after the police, fire and ambulance services. The AA is not an emergency service at all. The advertising strategy reflected some qualitative research in which motorists had apparently suggested that the AA was like a fourth emergency service in the sense that it was there to rescue stranded drivers. The theme played on the idea of an emergency service with all its connotations of reliability and security. It also positioned the AA as the prime motoring organization, excluding the equally long-established Royal Automobile Club, along with many newer rival organizations.

The campaign, which depicted stranded drivers on dark and sinister roads rescued by a friendly AA man, received much media attention. The creative theme played on the driver's fear of a car breakdown leaving him or her alone and vulnerable in a strange place. The AA functionary was depicted as the hero coming to the rescue.

Strategic Advertising Communication for Brands

Advertising communication can support so many marketing objectives that there are few general principles that can apply to all situations. Resorting to marketing text clichés of do-lists and models risks missing the particular value of advertising and promotional communication. It can address contextualized marketing situations with tailor-made solutions. If it is regarded as a technical discipline then its value may be lost. It can be most instructive to see case examples of how carefully conceived advertising has supported marketing objectives through a wide variety of approaches designed to fit the particular circumstances facing that brand at that time.

These few examples, then, have illustrated something of the flexibility of advertising in supporting various marketing outcomes. In each example the advertising agency took a strategic perspective and identified a key communication problem to address in order to facilitate and support the brand marketing objectives. The main problem was usually based on a fact or insight that provided a link of meaning between the consumer and the brand.

Most non-specialists say that advertising tries to sell things: those with more awareness of marketing terminology might say that it seeks to raise awareness of brands. From these examples we can already see that asking what advertising does is not a simple question. Carefully conceived and creative advertising can be a subtle and precise instrument of marketing strategy as well as an awareness-raising blunderbuss. We will return to the questions of what advertising does and of how advertising works throughout the book. For the present we suggest that advertising and pro- motion offer a range of ways of addressing complex communications problems in marketing. To ask how advertising works implies that it only operates in one way. Clearly, the objectives of campaigns for Orange, the British Labour Party, Amnesty International, Ford Ka, the British Army, Frizzell motor insurance and the rest are so different that they require differing kinds of engagement with consumers.

Brand Communication and Advertising Effect

Each of the campaigns described above were measured for awareness, recall and so on in the process of tracking their effects. But while awareness and recall were necessary to some extent for the success of the campaigns, they were not sufficient in themselves. The success of these campaigns required consumers to engage with the meaning of the ads and to respond to that meaning. The reasons for being aware of a brand or for remembering a particular ad may be quite different from the reasons for caring about an ad enough to engage with and respond to its meaning by, say, trying to solve the problem in the British Army ads or smiling at one's own lost youth in the Frizzell ads. The examples of advertising campaigns invoked here and throughout this book are intended not only to offer insights into how advertising is conceived. They are intended to also show that successful advertising can be made which reflects the complexity of human communication.

Hitherto we have examined the character of advertising and discussed how it expropriates cultural meaning in order to resonate with consumers' experiences and values. We have outlined its historical development and noted its role in marketing strategy. Chapter 4 discusses the composition of the advertising business and how advertising agencies execute their tasks. By doing so we can better understand the reasons why advertising has its powerful effect on consumers' imagination.

Review Exercises

1. Collect 10 video, radio or print advertisements and divide them between two groups. Each group should try to ascertain what each of their ads was intended to accomplish. In other words, what was the planning rationale behind the ads? Then the two groups should swop ads and perform the same exercise on the other group of ads. The two groups combined should discuss their respective analysis of each ad and decide which analysis seems the most likely to be accurate. The intention behind the ads should be considered in the light of such issues as: (a) the likely target audience for the brand; (b) other possible stakeholders; (c) the apparent brand positioning indicated by the ad's creative approach; (d) the choice of medium; (e) other marketing issues concerning this brand.
2. Discuss advertising's collective influence. What in your view is the nature of this influence and how has it arisen?
3. List as many examples as you can of marketing objectives that might be supported with advertising and promotion. Be prepared to justify your choice with examples or reasoning.
4. Is the role of communication in marketing primarily tactical or strategic? Give reasons for your answer.
5. Develop a scenario in which your group has been asked to offer outline creative ideas for the launch of a new brand of chocolate confection called 'Slick'. Focus on the segmentation, targeting (especially media) and positioning issues.

The American Advertising Association (AAF), the trade association for the US advertising industry, conceived of a campaign that advertised the benefits of advertising. It commissioned a survey among US corporations that found that, of more than 800 senior executives, a large majority agreed that advertising contributed positively to brand building, to the overall financial growth and stability of the corporation, to maintaining share values, and to sales and market share.[12] However, there were also contradictory results: only a minority of the respondents agreed that advertising would be more important in the future and that their corporation should spend more on it.

The AAF decided to develop a campaign that promoted advertising as a marketing tool to influential senior executives. The strapline that summed up their campaign (devised by agency Carmichael Lynch) was 'Advertising. The way great brands get to be great brands.' A creative approach was needed that illustrated in a succinct and powerful way that the world's most famous brands would be inconceivable without advertising. The AAF wanted to support the advertising industry by persuading sceptical executives of the value of advertising.

The creative approach chosen was one never tried before. The AAF persuaded leading brands such as Coca-Cola, Intel, Budweiser, Energiser, Sunkist and Altoids to allow their logos and creative executions to be adapted for the campaign. The press campaign was extended to TV with creative executions based on ads for Coca-Cola and Intel. The Coca-Cola company had never before allowed its unique bottle and logo to be adapted for any purpose, and other brand logos were similarly adapted for the campaign. Intel, the first microchip manufacturer to succeed in creating a powerful brand identity for their products, allowed the AAF to adapt their well-known visual identity in another striking creative execution. The wit and visual impact of the campaign drew attention to the power of advertising in creating brands. The campaign made a positive impact and attracted much media editorial coverage.

Case Exercises

1. What, in your view, was the main message in the AAF's 'Great Brands' campaign?
2. Think of ten well-known brands. Then ask individuals to list all the attributes and values they associate with each brand

in turn. Compare the results. Do many people think of the same attributes and values for particular brands? If so, why? Have many people consumed these brands? Or is their idea of the brand derived from communication? Which communications have been significant in forming your ideas of these brands?

3. Using an internet search engine, find the official websites for five well-known brands. Compare their content: do they include a history of the evolution of the brand? Do they have an archive of the brand advertising? Is there a retail interface and a chat-room area for conversations about the brand? In your opinion, do the websites enhance the brand and reflect its core values?

Further Reading

Jones, J.P. (1995) *When Ads Work: New Proof That Advertising Triggers Sales*. New York: Lexington Books.

Percy, L., Rossiter, J.R. and Elliott, R. (2001) *Strategic Advertising Management*. Oxford: Oxford University Press.

Pickton, D. and Broderick, A. (2000) *Integrated Marketing Communications*. London: Pearson Education.

Schultz, D.E., Martin D. and Brown, W.P. (1987) *Strategic Advertising Campaigns*, 2nd edn. Lincolnwood, IL: NTC Business Books.

Web Resources of Advertising Case Histories

Many ad agencies have their own case histories on their website. Some provide print copies of cases on request. All the sites below offer useful resources and links illustrating how advertising has addressed marketing and communications issues.

Account planning group: www.apg.org/uk
Advertising Association (UK): www.adassoc.org.uk
Advertising creativity: www.adcritic.com
Advertising Research Foundation (US): www.arfsite.org
American Advertising Agency Association: www.aaaa.org/
American Advertising Federation: www.aaf.org
UK Institute of Practitioners in Advertising: www.ipa.co.uk
World Advertising Research Centre (UK): www.warc.com

Notes

1 Most of the case examples cited in this chapter (and many throughout the book) are adapted from the UK IPA's (Institute of Practitioners in Advertising) collections of award-winning campaigns (see www.ipa.co.uk).

2 Source: typescript of a speech at the D&AD conference 'Creativity Sells', entitled 'Effectiveness and Creativity in Building Brands – The Agency Perspective', London, July 1995.

3 See, for example, the Global adspend trends feature on 'Adspend and national wealth', *International Journal of Advertising*, 22(3) (2003): 435–6, published by the World Advertising Research Centre (www.warc.com).

4 See Naomi Klein, *No Logo* website, or for a sociological critique of branding read George Ritzer (2000), *The McDonaldization of Society*, Thousand Oaks,CA: Pine Forge Press.

5 Examples from 'Business Questions Advertising Answers', published by the IPA in association with the *Financial Times*, taken from the IPA Effectiveness Awards, 1998.

6 The source for this and other examples in this chapter is the IPA publication, 'It pays to Advertise', Advertising Effectiveness Awards, 1996 (published 1997).

7 Source: feature article in *The Guardian* national newspaper, 'Labour's ad agency told to sell euro entry as "patriotic"', 29 June 2003.

8 *How the Left Learned to Love Advertising: Social and Political Advertising by BMP DDB 1970–2000*, published by DDB London.

9 Countline is a category of confection in the grocery trade in which chocolate is combined with another element, say, wafer, biscuit or nuts.

10 Flake and KitKat have recently (2004) been repositioned by their manufacturers (Cadbury and Rowntree Nestlé) to move away from these long-standing positioning strategies.

11 With thanks to the AAF.

12 Source: Erdos and Morgan, January 1999, AAF; see also www.aaf.org

The Business of Advertising and Promotion

Chapter Outline

This chapter offers an overview of the advertising business and describes how communications campaigns are created, from client brief to campaign launch and evaluation. The description is set in a time of rapid client-driven change in the way promotional communication is organized and conducted. The individual roles in typical agency account teams are examined. The way these roles contribute to communications planning and development is discussed. Particular issues addressed include conflict, creativity and the role of the account planning function in creative development.

BOX 4.0   Pressures for Change in the Advertising Business

The structure and priorities of marketing communications agencies are changing. Clients' pressure for integrated, **through-the-line** communications is changing the priorities of agencies that have traditionally specialized in **above-the-line** work. Ad agencies try to offer expertise in non-advertising dimensions of the communications mix such as sales promotion, web-based communication and digital television, and **below-the-line** specialists are getting into mainstream advertising. For example, the direct marketing agency Harrison Troughton Wunderman of London handle internet communications, public relations events, direct mail and also some press ads for clients such as Xerox, M & G, Jaguar cars and Microsoft. The need for integrated media solutions has increased the importance of media agencies, many of which have in recent years become separate businesses distinct from the advertising agencies of which they were once part.

> Now some media agencies are actually moving back into creative
> work by hiring dedicated creative staff or by sub-contracting
> creative work to small, independent **creative hotshops** and **boutiques**.
> Roderick White, editor of the advertising industry journal
> *Admap*, has argued that although these small independents can
> offer good creative ideas they are unlikely to have the resources to
> nurture a brand in the long term, if that is what clients want.
> It remains to be seen how the conflicts facing marketing
> communications agencies will be resolved in the longer term.

Advertising Agencies and the Professional Disciplines of Marketing Communication

This chapter will use the traditional, **full-service agency** as its point of
departure for describing the marketing communications business.
However, it should be noted that the way agencies are organized and the
range of expertise they offer are coming under increasing pressure for
change both from clients and from structural changes in the industry.
The specialist, above-the-line advertising agency may be in decline, as
clients demand **integrated solutions** and media agencies acquire greater
power and importance.

Movies and books (such as Vance Packard's *The Hidden Persuaders*,
1957) have contributed to the slightly sinister image of the advertising
profession. It is probably fair to say that advertising does not enjoy the
same kind of professional prestige as, say, medicine or architecture, or
perhaps even politics. Yet there is also a certain glamour attached to
working in advertising and marketing communication.

Competition for graduate trainee positions in agencies is intense
because careers in the area are so prized. Advertising attracts the attention
of caricaturists because it is difficult to categorize and its professional
activities are not widely understood. It occupies an industrial sector of its
own; it is a service but it is also more than that, it is almost, but not quite,
a branch of entertainment. It is a business, but then again, not exactly like
other businesses.

The integration of marketing communications has been a recurring
theme for consultants and academics in the last 10 years (Schultz et al.,
1993), but the industry of communication management remains largely
organized along specialist functional lines. As well as advertising agencies and
their traditional emphasis on above-the-line mass media there are agencies that specialize in below-the-line sales promotions, word-of-mouth and
viral marketing communications, direct and database marketing,
and also public relations, consumer and market research, industrial or
business-to-business advertising, new product development, sponsorship,

merchandising, strategic brand planning (including those dedicated solely to new brand names), corporate communications and internal marketing, internet-based promotion and interactive communications, media buying and strategy, and so on.

The remaining full-service advertising agencies may offer services to clients that include any or all of the above activities. Although their primary expertise lies in advertising, their strategic perspective covers communications as a whole and they may buy in specialist talent in other marketing communications areas for help in executing an integrated through-the-line campaign. In fact, agencies have reported increased requests from clients for communications solutions across media rather than only advertising, so they have responded by developing a more laterally integrated way of thinking about client problems. Many have developed in-house expertise in other communications disciplines alongside their core advertising expertise.

The Evolution of Advertising Agencies

The activities of advertising agencies can be better understood in the context of their historical evolution. Advertising agencies emerged as space-brokers, simply buying advertising space in the press on behalf of clients. Gradually, they extended their activities to provide more services to clients and to add value to their business. So they provided artists to draw up the ads for clients as an improvement on text alone. They acquired expertise in typography and print technology, graphic art and photography. With the development of broadcast media, some developed expertise in media planning, script writing and radio production and, later, film production. Many agencies found that because of their location they attracted certain types of business such as retail advertising in the local press or sales promotion. In these cases many regional agencies developed as specialists in these categories of work. As new communications technology has emerged many larger agencies have tried to develop in-house expertise in such areas as interactive television, internet marketing and interactive web sites, and even mobile telephony-based communications solutions such as text messaging. However, they have often found that it is difficult to maintain specialist expertise in such fast-moving areas and, in many cases, have come to rely instead on a network of independent specialists on whom the agencies can call for help when it is needed.

Advertising Agencies as Marketing Experts

The scope of activities ad agencies became involved with and the expertise their staff developed in a variety of disciplines and markets gave them yet

BOX 4.1   Thomas Holloway's Marketing Communications

Advertising is a fast-moving field but few of its techniques are entirely new. A British entrepreneur of the 1800s, Thomas Holloway, pioneered the use of marketing communications to promote his products. He was said to have employed outdoor posters as far away as China to advertise his medical remedies and tonics. Holloway was ahead of his time in other promotional techniques too. He managed to get references to his brands inserted into the script of some of the popular plays of the time. He is even said to have asked Charles Dickens to insert a reference to a Holloway brand into his classic *Dombey and Son*. Dickens declined. Holloway made a fortune and used it in philanthropic activities. Among them was the building he financed that is now a college of the University of London, called Royal Holloway.

another dimension. Agencies had to understand consumers in varied markets, and they also had to understand the businesses of their many clients. They understood marketing in a way that was free of the practical constraints that limited the thinking of manufacturing organizations. They had a special understanding of the powerful role communication could play in exciting the interest of consumers. They had, therefore, a special vantage-point from which to offer strategic advice to clients on general business strategy, product development, brand planning and brand communication, possible new markets to enter, market segmentation issues and so on. This planning function offering strategic thinking to clients on a variety of topics has grown in importance over the years. Not only does it add value to advertising agency work, it has become a consulting industry in its own right, working outside the disciplinary boundaries of advertising and marketing.

Advertising Agencies and Media

The media planning task is discussed in detail in Chapter 5. Here we need to note a few initial points. Contemporary agencies supply strategic communication ideas and sometimes production skills. They also normally possess media expertise and have a voice in deciding how ads will be targeted at given consumers through particular **media channels**. In practice, media buying is increasingly a specialist activity handled at arm's length from the agency. For media owners it is convenient to work with advertising agencies because they offer the creative expertise and advertisement production values that cohere with the values and standards of press publications,

TV programming and so on. The advertising is intimately part of the text that carries it. Advertising can even enhance and reinforce the market positioning of the medium in which it is placed. For example, glossy magazines carry ads that are like fashion photographs; ads in newspapers often fit with the typography, layout, colour and themes of the publication.

Media buying has largely become a separate activity divorced from creative services. In many countries media-buying services are provided by a limited number of companies. It can be convenient for media owners to sell advertising space to a small number of buyers rather than to thousands of individual clients. However, lateral mergers between communications groups mean that advertisers can be faced with monopoly suppliers in particular media and this places them in a poor bargaining position. For example, in the UK, licences to provide regional television or radio services are sold on a strictly limited basis so that local advertisers often have only one company to buy from. This, advertisers argue, maintains an artificially high cost for certain kinds of advertising medium.

The Character of Advertising Agency Work

Advertising and promotion agencies are slightly mysterious places. They have great (and often under-recognized) importance in capitalist economies. They produce work that is often striking and remarkable, and they attract some of the brightest and best-educated people to work in them. Yet explaining exactly how this work results from the hive of activity that is an advertising agency is not an easy task. The advertising agency remains an enigmatic place. Few academics have ventured into this area; committed and highly skilled advertising professionals themselves are not quite sure how precisely to explain their work. Like much human organization, what results can be surprising given the confusion and conflict that often surround the process of managing and producing output.

The enigmatic character of ad agencies means that a descriptive account of roles and working procedures may appear glib. A list of the components of a TV set in no way serves as an account of how it works. Nevertheless, this chapter outlines these roles and processes while acknowledging that there is much flexibility and indeterminacy in the processes. This is the nature of a creative business. The seemingly chaotic character of agency life may be seen as a reflection of the high intellects and professionalism of advertising folk. Some clients take a different view and regard communications agencies as poorly managed, unbusinesslike places that need close direction. The account that follows is organized where possible around the sequence of activities that agencies must undertake in the course of acquiring and executing business. The first step, therefore, will be to look at the nature of the agency as a business brand and how this might influence its pitches for business.

Agency Brands

Given the scope, public profile and economic importance of what advertising agencies do, it is perhaps paradoxical that the names of most agencies are virtually unknown to those outside marketing or communications fields. Ad agencies do not generally advertise themselves. A few of the world's top agency brands do have a high-profile presence in corporate life (see Table 4.1) but most are not nearly as well-known among the general public as their client brands. This is partly because client organizations prefer the consuming public to be unaware of the talented intermediaries producing the creative executions that add lustre to the brand. Agencies have had to learn to be discreet about their abilities: successful advertising must always be about the client, not about the agency. Agency success lies in bringing success to clients. Another reason for their shadowy character in commercial life is that they operate in what is essentially a business-to-business environment where work is gained through word-of-mouth, relationships and reputation among a small community of communications specialists.[2]

Even though they operate in a somewhat closed culture, agencies do have some interest in self-promotion. If they can enhance their reputation in the industry they are more likely to be invited to pitch for new business. To this end agencies try to build a reputation in the communication and marketing industry by entering case histories of their work to try to win industry awards (and publishing them in bound volumes), publicizing their history and their successes in coffee-table books and producing copies of their ads on video 'reels', CD-Roms and other media. Many agencies adopt particular creative techniques or advertising development styles and promote their expertise to differentiate their brand to clients.[3] Frequent social events for awards, campaign launches, annual reviews and so on are an essential part of the networking that is integral to the

Table 4.1 World's Top Agency Networks by Revenue, 2003.

Agency	Headquarters	Billings
1 Dentsu	Tokyo	($1.9 bn)
2 BBDO Worldwide	New York	($1.24bn)
3 McCann-Erickson Worldwide	New York	($1.22bn)
4 J Walter Thompson	New York	($1.22bn)
5 Publicis Worldwide	Paris	($1.02bn)
6 DDB Worldwide	New York	($943m)
7 Leo Burnett	Chicago	($886m)
8 TBWA Worldwide	New York	($771m)
9 EURO RSCG	New York	($756m)
10 Ogilvy and Mather Worldwide	New York	($706m)

Source: Advertising agency estimated worldwide figures for 2003, reproduced on Adbrands.net; website at www.mind-advertising.com/agencies_index_2.htm

BOX 4.2   Working in the Promotional Communications Business

Marketing communications is often seen as an elite field of work, particularly in the major international agencies. Many of these present themselves as progressive employers, reflecting their position in a creative industry that thrives on free thinking rather than the rigid control of staff behaviour. This progressiveness is often expressed in terms of loose hierarchies, informality of dress and communication, and benefits such as on-site bars, gyms and masseurs. Some agencies encourage their staff to take time to study and attend popular and cultural events at the agency's expense to maintain a close connection with the world of entertainment and mediated communication. The best agencies are meritocracies in which imagination and drive are the source of the agency's competitive advantage. The progressive employment practices and informality are genuine in many agencies but also mask an intensely competitive business which demands great discipline and motivation.

industry. Advertising is a small community and awards shows and other events create a sense of specialness and exclusivity that is important to the industry, in order to offset the lack of wider recognition for advertising expertise and accomplishment. This tendency for advertising professionals to award each other prizes seems important, sociologically, to the industry and it also reflects a self-referential insularity.

Advertising's Poor PR

In spite of the glittering prizes[4] and industry awards that are so much a feature of the advertising business, advertising and promotion agencies have largely failed to promote a greater general understanding of what they do outside their own industry. Considering the level of public and academic interest, there are remarkably few initiatives to promote better understanding of advertising in schools, universities and elsewhere.[5] Among academic researchers, the problems of getting access to agencies for information and interviews are legendary. This perceived lack of interest in the wider world creates a smog of ignorance around the industry. In some respects this may be useful: critics of advertising cannot effectively attack an enemy they cannot see and do not understand. On the other hand generally poor PR for the advertising industry means that the skills of its people are often under-recognized and the contribution of advertising to successful business is itself poorly understood – hence the need for the

AAF to produce the first ever co-ordinated advertising campaign for advertising (described on p. 75).

Agency Branding and the Pitch for Business

Many of the agency brands that appear in Table 4.1 own subsidiary agencies all over the world. In 2003 the UK trade publication *Campaign* published a table of the top UK agencies in 2002 by billings, that is, ranked by the total value of business the agencies held that year. There are over 700 advertising agencies in the UK all told; many of the major ones are subsidiaries of international advertising agency groups. Since agencies get invited to pitch for business by reputation and contacts a brand presence in the industry can be an advantage. Pickton and Broderick (2000) state that the process of pitching may be preceded by an invited credentials presentation in which selected agencies will try persuade the client that they are a credible and professional organization. Track records of successful accounts are important here, as are the reputations of the star personnel. If the agency is already a leading brand then so much the better. The client no doubt has an advertising department and public relations office of its own and needs to be reassured that the agency can add specialist expertise which it cannot provide for itself.

The client then issues a **client brief** to the agencies it deems worthy to pitch for the business, which outlines the tasks that the client wants undertaken or the objectives they want to achieve. It contains the background

BOX 4.3   Client–agency Relationships

Many industry professionals argue that effective work results from strong relationships and clear lines of communication between the client and the agency. Continuity in these relationships gives each the time to understand the other and the business. The US agency of the year in 2002, Ogilvy & Mather Worldwide, claims that their success is founded on not having a star system or 'promiscuous' clients.[6] In other words, the agency seeks to operate a meritocracy based on talent and client relationships are sustained so that trust and understanding can develop. Harrison Troughton Wunderman, a direct marketing specialist and UK agency of the year in 2002, did not lose a client between 2001 and the time of writing in February 2004.[7] Agencies that succeed in retaining client business have a much better chance of developing the kind of work that will get them noticed and earn them new clients.

BOX 4.4   The Client Brief

The client brief is an important document which sets out what the client wants the agency to do. It is vital for the mutual satisfaction of both. A written brief facilitates communication and helps each party understand the requirements of the other. The UK Advertising Association[8] publishes a guide on writing a client brief which suggests that essential items of content should include: situation analysis (expressed as 'Where are we now?'); objectives ('Where do we want to be?') and marketing and communications strategy ('How do we get there?'). Other essential topics include consumer segmentation and targeting ('Who do we need to talk to?'); effectiveness measurement ('How will we know when we've arrived?') and practical issues. The entire project should be managed with clear lines of communication and individual accountability, and not left as an informal, *ad hoc* or implicit arrangement. Following these principles reduces the risk that the client–agency relationship may become unsatisfactory or unsuccessful.

information the client feels essential to the task, such as the brand name and the nature of the product, the company, the desired market and segmentation strategy, the price, the distribution channel and, most importantly, the budget. The selected agencies take the brief, decide how they might solve the client's problem and present their ideas in a sales pitch.

Advertising is a talent-based business so the outcome of the pitch may just as well be that a new or small agency gets the business rather than the huge multinational agency group. The nature of the brief may also influence the kind of agency that is chosen. Some clients may want a full strategic communications service, in which case a larger full-service agency is more likely to be chosen. Other clients may be more interested in getting help with specific activities such as creative, production or media strategy and so may choose a smaller agency. A client who, for example, wishes to advertise a brand launch across international boundaries may have more confidence in an agency group that is already operating internationally.

Pitching for business is an everyday activity for advertising agencies. The impact of the presentation is everything; appearances are important and presentational poise and social skills are to the fore. Although it is rare for creative staff to be involved in the pitch itself the agency will be judged partly on the creative flair of its ideas, as well as on the strategic planning and professionalism of the pitch. It is the responsibility of **account managers** and **account planners** to make sure their pitch presentation is professional and competent so that the creative work and strategic thinking are seen in the best light by the client. If the client does not like

Table 4.2 Top 10 UK Advertising Agencies, 2003.

Name of agency	Address
1 Abbott Mead Vickers BBDO	151 Marylebone Road London NW1 5QE Tel: 020 7616 3500
2 McCann-Erickson Advertising	7–11 Herbrand Street London WC1N 1EX Tel: 020 7837 3737
3 J. Walter Thompson	1 Knightsbridge Green London SW1X 6AE Tel. 020 7656 7000
4 Publicis Thailand	82 Baker Street London W1U 2AE Tel: 020 7935 4426
5 Ogilvy & Mather	10 Cabot Square Canary Wharf London E14 4QB Tel: 020 7345 3000
6 Euro RSCG London	Cupola House 15 Albert Place London WC1E 7EB Tel: 020 7240 4111
7 TBWA London	76–80 Whitfield Street London W1T 4EZ Tel: 020 7573 6666
8 M & C Saatchi	36 Golden Square London W2 6JR Tel: 020 7543 4500
9 Lowe	Bowater House 64–114 Knightsbridge London SW1X 7LT Tel: 020 7584 5033
10 Saatchi & Saatchi	80 Charlotte Street London W1A 1AQ Tel: 020 7636 5060

Source: Campaign Report 'Top 300 Agencies', 27 February 2004. For other agencies' contact details try *The Advertiser's Annual*, Hollis Directories (tel: 020 8977 7711) or *The Account List File* incorporating BRAD agencies and advertisers (tel: 020 7505 8000).

the work, the account person who presented it may be accused by creative staff of not trying hard enough or of failing to do justice to the quality of the work. In some cases agencies may toil for two or three weeks on a pitch only to see the business given to another agency. The agency may charge the client for the work they put into the pitch but ultimately will do this work in hope of winning the business rather than with any realistic expectation of a profit from the pitch itself.

The pitching system is open to misuse. It is not unknown for clients to ask a number of agencies to pitch to a brief, then appoint none of those agencies and have the work conducted in-house. This obviously raises the suspicion that the client only wanted free consultancy. This results in much bitterness and/or litigation but is relatively rare. If the pitch goes well then the agency will be awarded the client's advertising business, called 'the account'.

Account Team Roles

Work is normally organized through units called account teams, which are the core of the advertising development process. The account team roles reflect different yet often overlapping areas of responsibility. The major account team roles are those of account management, planning/research and creative.

Ancillary Roles

Media planning and buying, while integral to effective advertising campaigns, is increasingly an area handled outside the agency account team. This role and function are discussed in more detail in Chapter 6. The **media planner** must ensure the campaign's effectiveness by placing the promotion before the maximum possible number of targeted consumers within the allocated budget. He or she must also try to ensure that the media chosen have the kind of impact that is appropriate to the brand and its market segment.

Another essential ancillary role is traffic, whose responsibility is to allocate work, monitor progress and ensure that tasks are co-ordinated to deadline. The **traffic controller** also ensures that there is a paper trail showing the continuous progress of all the component parts of development. If, for example, the production of a TV ad requires a script to be finished, artwork to be completed and a research brief to be fulfilled before the production company can be given the go-ahead, it will be the traffic controller's job to monitor progress and chase up the staff responsible in order to meet deadlines. Many agencies' staff are employed on production activities and are not directly engaged with the account team. Staff with expertise in graphic art and computer-aided art production, animation and animatronics, website design and other production activities can be very useful for agencies to have in-house.

The Account Manager

If an agency is appointed by a client then the account manager (sometimes called 'account executive' or 'account director', or simply 'account man' regardless of gender) will be the client's first point of contact in the agency.

BOX 4.5   What are Consumers Like? How Do We Communicate With Them?

Kover (1995) and Hackley (2003d) have each in different ways highlighted the implicit thinking that guides creative work in agencies. Kover (1995) found that creative staff hold differing implicit theories of communication while Hackley (2003d) found that account team members work to differing implicit models of the consumer. Although many agencies try to develop working practice that involves discussion and open debate about the assumptions upon which they base their communications strategy and planning, these two works illustrated how difficult it can be for agencies to draw out and articulate all the implicit assumptions that guide professional communications practice. The three main account team roles often approach marketing communications problems from intellectually incompatible perspectives. While this is a strength of the team approach it is also a source of conflict because the differing perspectives are not well understood (see also p. 27).

The account manager is essentially the business manager for the accounts held by that account team. He or she is responsible for liaison between the client and the other account team members to ensure that the campaign is planned, developed and produced on time, on brief and on budget. The account manager is often regarded as the business person or, less respectfully, as 'the suit' (Hackley, 2001). He or she has to manage the various personalities and tasks to ensure that the work generates revenue for the agency. Consequently he or she requires skills in relationship management, project management, planning and co-ordination. Account managers will normally have a good working knowledge of the whole advertising development process. On one rare occasion an account man (at DDB London, when it was called BMP DDB) actually created a TV ad. It turned out that of all the creative ideas offered in a planning meeting, his was considered the best. In most cases, though, the account person will leave the creative work to the specialists.

The account manager is normally closer to the client than any other person in the agency. In most agencies he or she will have primary responsibility for client liaison and may speak to the client daily. The account manager is consequently regarded as the voice of the client in the agency since he or she acquires a strong sense of what the client wants and will accept. This can present conflicts of interest when the creative staff want the account manager to argue strongly in favour of a creative execution that the client will not want to accept. Account managers will sometimes admit that there are occasions when they do not fight as strongly in favour of an idea as they might, simply because they know that it is not what the client wants.

The specific tasks account managers undertake during the creative development of advertising vary from agency to agency, and from account to account. In many cases they will take the lead in interpreting the initial client brief and developing and presenting the pitch for business. Once the account is won they will convene the various planning and progress meetings to discuss and agree strategy. Either alone or with the account planner they will discuss, research and write the creative brief. In many agencies account managers, rather than account planners, commission consumer and advertising research and interpret the findings at various points in the creative advertising development process. The account manager ultimately holds the responsibility of ensuring that an account is firstly won, and then retained for as long as possible. Along with the account planner (see below), the account manager will often have responsibility for measuring the effectiveness of the campaign against the objectives that were set for it.

Creative Teams

Advertising agencies produce and sell ideas and the quality of their creative output is the benchmark of their standing as an agency. The creative team is responsible for this output, and in many agencies the creative work is organized into teams of two people. There may be one creative person who specializes in words (copywriting, scriptwriting, music jingles) and another who deals in images and undertakes, for example, visualizations of story boards for TV ads, press ad layouts, poster design, typography and so on. Sometimes these roles are referred to respectively as 'art director' and 'copywriter'. In US agencies it has been traditional for the term 'copywriter' to be used to refer to the originator of any creative input, the assumption being that a copywriter without visualization (that is, drawing) skills would simply instruct a graphic artist to put his or her ideas into visual form. Quite often the two members in a creative team have interchangeable skills. In some cases, creatives prefer to work alone.

In many agencies creative teams operate at arm's length from account management. They often occupy their own sub-cultural space in the agency. Creative staff often feel disempowered by the advertising development process since the worth of their ideas is judged by other, non-creative people. However, creatives who win awards for their work can quickly acquire a star reputation that brings them (and their agency) considerable prestige. In some cases star creatives can come to dominate an agency.

Creative staff are not normally brought in to work on the account until the initial market and consumer research and strategic planning have taken place. They are then presented with a brief and asked to offer creative executions that satisfy the requirements of the brief. This brief is an important document that should inspire creative staff and excite them about the creative possibilities for an account, while also providing them with parameters to work within which are derived from the research and strategic thinking that have gone into developing the strategy for advertising. This should ensure that the creative execution will support the desired marketing objectives of the client.

When creative work has been approved internally by the agency team (usually by the internal director of creativity) it is presented to the client by the account manager. If the client likes it and agrees that it fulfils the criteria set out in the brief, then the work will be produced and offered for public consumption. Creative staff enjoy a privileged existence within agencies. They must have the discipline to produce ideas to a deadline, starting with a blank piece of paper. While younger creative staff are often very good on ideas, the task of the creative professional requires both experience and resilience, the former of which is necessary in order to know what will work as an execution in different media. Creative work requires strong craft skills aligned to a knowledge of different media and their properties, along with an intuitive sense of the excitement that consumption generates. Creative staff have to be resilient because, in the words of one experienced creative, 'of every ten ideas, only one will get made'. Creative staff must accept that the great majority of the ideas they come up with will be rejected as unsuitable for a huge variety of reasons unrelated to whether the ideas are good or not. Finally, the best creative

BOX 4.6   Creative Stars

In some agencies in which the creative staff are the stars, clients' briefs may go straight to them without any initial planning or research taking place. This can be fruitful when the creative person's intuition about the market and its consumers proves in tune with the creative execution. However, it is a high-risk approach since there is no clearly researched basis for creative work and no carefully thought-through strategy. It is likely that there are no clear criteria for assessing campaign effectiveness either. This means that in the event of the campaign failing to produce the desired results, the entire responsibility falls on the creative person. Clients may sometimes put their trust (and budget) in star creative staff. In most cases, clients would wish advertising to be based on a more transparent footing with a suitable business-like approach to planning and accountability. Generally speaking, agencies that allow the strong personality of a creative star to subvert their management systems find that there is eventually a price to pay in terms of lost business.

staff must also have a good understanding of marketing so that they can see the wider implications of their work for clients.

Account Planning

Traditionally, advertising and promotional agencies have been organized hierarchically, with the account manager leading the account team. However, in several UK agencies the account planner has equal status with the account manager and may also be directly involved with client liaison. The account planning role was initiated in the 1960s in London at JWT and BMP (now DDB London). The account planner was charged with generating consumer insights through research and with ensuring that these insights were integrated into every stage of the creative advertising development process. Originally conceived as the voice of the consumer within the agency, the account planner's role has broadened with the rise of brand marketing. He or she is now often seen as the brand custodian charged with ensuring that the brand's core values and personality are maintained through all associated marketing communications. Account planners are often assumed to have a wide range of analytical, linguistic and advocacy skills which enable them to articulate the strategic thinking for brands that contributes to the longer-term management and development of the brand vision.

Before the development of the account planning role account managers would obtain the consumer and market research they needed through the services of a researcher who normally held no management responsibility. The account manager would commission and interpret consumer and advertising research and decide whether the findings were relevant to creative advertising development. This traditional arrangement, where the account manager is the undisputed leader still persists in many advertising agencies. The account planning role and its implications for agency hierarchies have been widely though unevenly accepted in the UK and US advertising industries for some 40 years now. Nevertheless, there remains much confusion and no little controversy as to what it entails and what it can add to advertising development (Hackley, 2003a, 2003f). Those agencies that promote and espouse the account planning philosophy and function are convinced of its value; some are almost evangelical about the account planning ethos and the benefits it brings to the agency.

The account planner is the expert in marketing and consumer research. He or she is responsible for all research connected with an account and is a full member of the account team with management status and responsibility. In many agencies the creative brief will be written by the account planner. The conceptual and analytical skills associated with this role often mean that planning personnel have social science educational backgrounds, whereas account managers may often have a more formal business education such as an MBA. Planners conduct and interpret qualitative and quantitative research that feeds into the creative development of advertising. They are also responsible for market research and competitive analysis that informs the planning of the account, pretesting creative executions and, after the campaign has been launched, tracking the effectiveness of the advertising.

Difficulties of the Account Planning Role

There have been three persistent problems facing the account planning discipline, which proves unfortunate when, in the words of one account planner, they see their own role as helping creatives and making the work better. One is the hostility of many creative staff to research. When the researcher was a lowly backroom person, there was less threat, but when research is a responsibility of the account planner, it has the voice of management status. The account planner is a soft target for the angst of creative staff who feel that judging their work against research findings misses the point of what makes advertising appeal to consumers. Not only do account planners find themselves at odds with creative staff, they may also be at odds with account managers who feel that their status is undermined. Account planners do many of the tasks that were formerly the sole responsibility of the account manager, such as deciding what research to conduct, liaising with the client and writing the creative brief. In agencies implementing the account planning philosophy there often results a three-way power struggle as creatives and account management, comfortable in their mutual contempt, find common ground in their hatred of account planners.

As if these problems were not enough, account planners have a credibility problem in the industry as a whole. Just as those agencies that espouse the account planning ethos are convinced of its positive value, those that are not argue their point of view with vigour. Account planners are vulnerable to the charge that they cannot easily answer the question of what craft skills they bring to the advertising development process. Many are expert researchers with substantial educational attainments. Others are not, but have found their way into the post through a facility with words and ideas and a sense of curiosity about people. While creative staff have creative skills, and account management have business skills, account planners are sometimes unfairly seen to have no particular skills that justify their status and power on account teams.

Because of these difficulties, account planners require skills of tact and sensitivity in order simply to do their job. As researchers they require a sensitivity to consumers' attitudes, predispositions and preferences, and an ability to work these out from carefully gathered qualitative and quantitative research data.

The Client and the Agency

The client is effectively the invisible member of the account team. The client's wishes and aims are represented in the client brief (see p. 86). Surprisingly often, client briefs require a lot of work by the agency because the client may not have a very clear rationale for communication. It is often up to the agencies to research the client brief in order to understand fully the nature of the client's business, markets and brands. Even if the client is well-prepared, agencies often want to research the client brief in their own terms. Client briefs can come couched in marketing jargon that communication professionals find obscure and misleading. Marketing directors tend to compartmentalize marketing management functions. This leads to elements like pricing strategy, product design, distribution and promotion being considered separately without reference to each other. But advertising professionals have the benefit of a more dispassionate perspective on the marketing process and they recognize that the elements of marketing management and strategy are interdependent.

Brand name, price, product design, packaging, distribution and so on are all equally important strategically because each has important communications implications for the brand. Advertising that is able to portray a coherent brand strategy which makes sense to the right consumers has a far greater chance of success than advertising that is trying to use creativity to make up for an ill-conceived marketing strategy. If the account manager can act as a consulting partner to a client and gain in-depth knowledge of the marketing function, this will help the agency devise a coherent and successful campaign.

It is axiomatic that agencies regard advertising as the answer to every marketing problem. If a client is dismayed at falling sales and allocates a large advertising budget to address the problem, the agency commissioned should concede that advertising may not be the answer to the client's problem if, say, poor customer service, flawed distribution or poor product design are the cause of the client's problems. Account managers understandably feel under pressure not to turn business away but if a campaign cannot succeed because it addresses the wrong problem then it is wise to advise the client rather than risk the ignominy of a failed campaign. But clients have to be handled sensitively. Some will not accept that they have misunderstood the nature of their own business and will not be protected from their folly. The decision to allocate an advertising budget and appoint an agency is a highly political one for client organizations. And, as we saw in Chapter 3, advertising can support many different marketing, business and communication objectives. Client relations are always a sensitive area for agencies and demand astute management skills from account managers. In most cases a compromise can be reached so that the client's budget is put to good use even if the client organization has other underlying problems.

The senior board-level account director will be responsible, along with other agency heads, for deciding whether to accept a client brief. There may be reasons for declining it at the client brief stage if, for example, the agency's research reveals that communication is not the client's problem. More plausibly, the agency will need to decide if a new client will fit with existing clients. Agencies need to try to ensure that they are not open to conflicts of interest when, say, representing two clients who compete in the same market. Agencies will also have to decide if a client is suitable for ethical or political reasons. The client brief may be translated into a communications brief in some agencies. This is where the detached marketing jargon of the client brief is transformed into a more metaphorically colourful document that tries to convey the emotionality of the client's brand and its relationship with consumers. Assuming that the agency heads give the account manager the go-ahead for an account, the next stage is to devise a strategy for advertising.

The Creative Advertising Development Process

The development process differs in detail in each advertising agency. While these differences are important it is also true that each agency must do broadly similar things. What follows is a necessarily general but representative outline of the major elements of the process. In most agencies planning is conducted through lengthy meetings. From the initial meetings (sometimes called 'plans board' meetings) through to strategy development meetings views will be heard from all major parties, including the client, creative and board-level account management. These meetings are at the heart of advertising development; promotional campaigns evolve through a process of debate and argument. Although creative work can sometimes be the inspiration of one individual, in an important sense all creative development is a joint effort because of the way ideas develop and reach a certain point through intense discussion. This discussion, which sometimes can seem endless, is given direction by the use of documents.

In all agencies there are written documents that perform several functions. They provide a template for practice and thereby act as a tool of management control. Life in agencies is chaotic enough: without pro forma documents the chaos would be total. Documents provide a paper trail of accountability and a basis for contractual agreement. Client and agency have a permanent record of what, exactly, was agreed. Documents also act as stimulus tools for directing thinking along predetermined lines. They are handrails for advertising development.

The advertising development process in any major agency entails a limited number of broadly defined tasks. There is strategy development, then creative planning, pretesting and ad production, campaign exposure and finally evaluation. The evaluation should then feed back into the strategy development process for monitoring and/or reappraisal. In many agencies, particularly those which espouse the account planning philosophy, every stage of the process is informed by the consumer and market insights generated from research by the account planner (for research see Chapter 9).

The Strategy: Marketing and Communication Issues

The **advertising strategy** is all-important. There has to be a clear marketing rationale for communication. Advertising has to do something for the client's brand. The strategy expresses just what it is that advertising and promotion should do for the brand in order to support the client's marketing objectives. The strategy document, as with all the other documents in the promotional development process, normally poses a series of questions which the account team members, assisted by other interested parties such as the client, are required to address. The document states: what the client expects the campaign to achieve (for example, an increased market share, raised brand profile, changed brand identity); who the target audience is (for example, motor-car drivers between 25 and 69 years of age, **geodemographics** such as **ACORN** or other segmentation variables); what the consumer or market insight is (for example, that the brand advertised is more reliable/inexpensive/exciting than rival brands); and what reaction the campaign must produce in consumers (for example, in terms of beliefs, memory, attitudes to the brand and purchase behaviour).

The strategy is seldom expressed in marketing jargon. Agencies usually insist on jargon-free, simple and even monosyllabic expressions for strategy. The rationale for the advertising must be clearly expressed, agreed by all relevant parties, commercially coherent and easily communicable to everyone involved. As communication professionals, advertising people strive for clarity and simplicity in their own internal communications. This clarity does not preclude a certain flakiness: phrases such as 'Inject a dose of adrenalin into the brand' or make the brand 'compulsory equipment' are common. The value of such phrasing is that it resonates with advertising people who feel that they know just what is meant.

The strategy for advertising is the fundamental reason for communication and will be the measure of the campaign's success or failure. The advertising strategy will form the basis for he creative brief.

The Creative Brief

Each agency has its own pro forma documents for strategy and creative briefs. Of these, the **creative brief** is very important because it is agreed between the client's representative (often the marketing or advertising director) and the agency account management and planning team. Once it is agreed it is given to the creative team as the basis for the creative execution. It must be clear, carefully thought through and motivating. Each agency has slightly different conventions for the brief, though the aims are similar. Like strategy documents, the brief poses questions that the account team are required to answer. In many agencies the account planner will research and write the creative brief in consultation with the client and account management.

These are the kinds of question (not necessarily in this order) posed by the brief.

1. Why advertise?
2. Who is the audience?
3. What must this communication do?
4. What must the advertising say?
5. Why must the audience believe it?
6. What is the tone of the advertising to be?
7. What practical considerations are there?

Question no. 1, 'Why advertise?', invites the account planner to state the rationale for advertising, probably drawing on the strategy document. It is obvious that without a clear reason or opportunity for advertising there is little chance of a successful campaign. There must be an opportunity for communication to accomplish some outcome (behavioural or attitudinal) that will support and enhance the brand's marketing strategy. Question no. 2 asks for the target audience or market to be carefully defined. Question no. 3 again refers to the strategy to ask what the outcome of the advertising should be in terms of consumer attitude or behavioural change. It is slightly different from question no. 1 because it focuses on the outcome (for example, to make people feel more positive about the brand) as opposed to the reason for advertising (for example, sales are suffering because people feel less positive about this brand than they did five years ago). Question no. 4, refers to the bottom-line message of the ad that the client wishes the consumer to get or take away from exposure to the ad. This is sometimes called the 'proposition' or the 'take-out' (for example, this brand is the leader in its class).

Question no. 5 asks the account team to provide evidence to support the promotional claim. For example, much motor-car brand advertising tries to reassure the consumer that the brand is mechanically reliable and technologically advanced. In the case of German car brands this is not too difficult because in many countries German engineering and technology have an excellent reputation. This attitude can be symbolized economically in TV or print ads, with visual images of working engine parts or a cutaway image of an engine interior. The consumer, primed with cultural knowledge about the quality of German motor engineering, understands the inference implicitly. In the previously mentioned Levi's 501 ads of the 1980s the ads were designed to say that Levi's jeans were icons of American culture, bound up with mythical American values since Independence. The creative execution helped consumers believe this by filling the ads with period American artefacts like 1950s motor-cars, clothes and, of course, the famous launderette familiar to many baby-boomers from American movies, featuring actors like James Dean, Humphrey Bogart and Marlon Brando. The visual cue was understood by consumers who liked the glamour of American movies and literature from the 1950s. Tellingly, the American provenance ads began to fail in the 1990s because young consumers were no longer familiar with that genre of movies. They no longer understood, believed or valued the association between Levi's and the mythical 1950s America of Hollywood movies.

Question no. 6, 'What is the tone of the advertising to be?', refers to the way that brand values are reflected in the creative and production values of the ad. For example, the tone of the Levi's ad was described as 'heroic, but period' in its creative brief. Tone can also refer to other stylistic aspects of advertising production, as well as the set, music and narrative. Techniques of cinematography can give exaggerated realism. Some ads are shot in black and white (such as, for example, a later Levi's TV ad) to create an art-house feel. The aforementioned Diesel ads had a quirky, postmodern tone created by the use of vivid colour and incongruous, juxtaposed images. The tone of the ad carries implied values for the brand.

Finally, ads may have features insisted upon by the advertiser. For example, for many years BMW ads have featured no human beings. The creative staff must make the ad without actors, regardless of whatever other creative choices they make. The Levi's 501s ad featured a soundtrack but no dialogue. Levi's wanted the ad to feature in many different countries. The only linguistic sign in the ad is the word 'Levi's' and the producers were instructed to feature many shots of the jeans themselves and their distinctive rivets. Some ads have contact telephone numbers as mandatory inclusions, website addresses, particular straplines and so on. The creative brief must carry all the instructions the creative team needs to exercise their craft in ways which will fit with the advertising strategy and the brand personality.

The creative brief sets the parameters for the creative work without which advertising cannot be distinctive and memorable. The extensive work that is put into researching and writing this brief in many agencies is a measure of the importance placed on making distinctive advertising.

Tracking Campaign Effectiveness

Once ads have been produced and the campaign has been launched on selected media (discussed in more detail in Chapter 5), it is important for the campaign's effectiveness to be ascertained. This task is a perennial problem in the industry because clients need to be persuaded that campaigns are effective if they are to continue to pay high costs and keep agencies solvent. Much research is directed at this problem and Chapter 9,

BOX 4.7   Tracking the Effectiveness of BT's "It's Good to Talk" Campaign

One example of effective campaign tracking involved the use of a statistical technique called multivariate analysis to try to establish a strong correlation between a campaign and a change in customer behaviour. A famous UK campaign (called 'It's Good to Talk') conducted for British Telecom (BT) attempted to change the telephone usage habits of domestic British customers.

The advertising agency's consumer research had established that the average length of British domestic telephone conversations was significantly shorter than those in other countries such as the USA, Italy and Germany. It seemed that there was a British mentality that talking on the telephone was a cost which should be minimized. In fact the cost was and is small as a proportion of household income. In many other countries (such as Germany, Italy and the USA) domestic telephone users seemed to regard telephone conversation as a necessary expense and spoke for far longer on average on each call. This consumer research insight formed the basis for the campaign called 'Its Good to Talk'.

A series of TV ads dramatically portrayed the typically succinct British phone user as someone lacking in empathy and warmth. The message was that it was kinder to talk at greater length. The ads also suggested that telephone communication could strengthen bonds of family and friendship if people used it generously. It was claimed that the campaign resulted in a major social change: domestic telephone usage habits in the UK were substantially altered. A near 60 per cent increase in call revenues to BT was claimed. The agency (DDB London) used multivariate analysis to correlate the electronic data on telephone conversation length with the exposure of the TV ads.

looking at research, discusses some of the theoretical issues in more detail. Some of the main problems and issues are as follows.

Advertising campaigns can have various objectives. The effectiveness of a campaign should, logically, be assessed against the communication objectives, since the relationship between advertising and sales is subject to many uncontrollable intervening variables in the consumer/market environment. A rise in sales or brand awareness can always be attributed to other, non-advertising causes such as seasonality, changes in income, press coverage of consumer issues or simply inevitable random fluctuations in demand.

Agencies do try to strengthen their argument (and their pitches for business) by writing up case histories of successful campaigns. UK agencies submit case studies of advertising effectiveness to the annual IPA awards. In order to be accepted, these cases have to offer substantial, rigorous evidence supporting the case. Direct causative relationships between advertising and other variables can never be proven beyond doubt, of course, but compelling circumstantial evidence can be gathered.

Tracking campaign effectiveness is not without its difficulties. Finding a statistically significant correlation between two variables is, of course, no indication of a causal relationship. Nevertheless, correlation can contribute to circumstantial evidence about campaign effectiveness. More typically, campaigns are evaluated by using surveys to see if their communication objectives are met. In one London-based campaign for the British Diabetic Association (BDA), public awareness of the symptoms of diabetes was tested by street surveys. Some weeks after the campaign (posters placed in underground tube stations), the awareness levels were significantly higher. The BDA's desired objective was to raise awareness of the symptoms of type-1 diabetes without alarming people, stigmatizing sufferers or filling surgeries with hypochondriacs. They simply wanted more people who suspected they might be suffering from the disease to get a proper diagnosis and treatment. The campaign was a success since the awareness of symptoms increased significantly after it, according to street interviews, and doctors reported an increase in the number of people asking for a diagnosis. The fact that a high proportion of these people did in fact have the disease was, if no consolation for the sufferers, an indication that the creative executions had struck exactly the right note.

Prompted and Unprompted Awareness Surveys

Trade press publications conduct weekly or monthly consumer surveys to gauge the impact of various advertising campaigns. There are unprompted **awareness** surveys in which the participant is asked 'Which TV/press/radio/outdoor ads do you recall seeing this week?'. To simplify the explanation, if half the consumers surveyed recall seeing a particular campaign it gets a score of 50 per cent awareness. The results are tabled, with the highest percentage awareness attaining first place in the table for that week. Prompted awareness surveys involve the researcher reading through a list of ads or brands and asking whether the participant remembers seeing an ad for each in that week. Prompted awareness scores tend to be higher, of course, than those for unprompted awareness.

Awareness surveys, like most measures of advertising effectiveness, do not actually measure the effectiveness of the advertising or promotion at all. They measure the consumer's awareness of the advertising or of the brand, which is quite a different thing. Of course, awareness may be a necessary condition for effectiveness, but it is not a sufficient condition. Awareness surveys make the implicit assumption that awareness is an intermediary state in a sequence of mental states that lead to purchase. The hierarchy-of-effect model of persuasion discussed in Chapter 2 is implicitly referred to when intermediate variables such as awareness are assumed to offer some indication of the effectiveness of a campaign. This may not be the case.

Awareness is a major concern for advertising agencies. Their principal challenge is to get consumers to notice their work amid the clutter and noise of the consumer environment. It makes sense to measure it, though it can be a mistake to read too much into awareness surveys. The quality of that awareness is far more important in informing consumer behaviour and this is something that is harder to measure.

Attitude Scales and Copy-testing

Although recall or awareness is easily measured from a dichotomous question (aware/not aware), liking is usually measured with attitude scales. Scaled responses (often called Likert scales after their originator) form the answers to questions asking the respondent to rate his/her attitude to an item, on a five-point scale. For example, a statement such as 'How much do you like this ad?' is answered by ticking a box next to a range of categories, don't like at all/like a little/indifferent/like/really like. These scales are frequently used in advertising. **Copy-testing**, in particular, uses this sort of scale. Copy-testing is the term used by agencies to measure consumers' attitudes to an ad or parts of an ad before campaign launch. It is extensively used in the US advertising industry, less so in Britain. In the USA a negative copy test can result in an entire campaign being returned to the drawing board.

Split-run Testing and Regional Tests

The effectiveness of individual ads or that of components of ads such as the copy or visual can be tested by running two variants of the ad in differing regions or with differing consumer groups. As is usual with effectiveness tests, a change in sales, awareness or attitude measures cannot necessarily be attributed to the variation in advertising exposure or creative execution. Some agencies have attempted control studies in which a given ad is exposed only to a controlled TV region. Unfortunately, such studies are always subject to particular market conditions which make it difficult to draw more general conclusions. In addition it is hard to isolate communications effects demographically or regionally. The development of many regional and special interest media facilitates studies of this kind.

BOX 4.8   Direct Response Promotion and Effectiveness

There are a number of communications techniques that can be used to facilitate the measurement of advertising effectiveness. A direct response element to advertising can be useful if the objective is substantive, as it was for example when the British Army recruitment campaign wanted to increase the quality of potential recruits. The free telephone number on the TV and press ads gave the reader a direct response route (**DRTV**).

The campaign was integrated through press and direct marketing and these media deployed cut-out and post coupons and reply forms. Internet and interactive TV have powerful potential for immediate consumer response. Where an easily measured response, such as sales or enquiries, is required, the effectiveness of such advertising can be easily assessed through a direct response element.

It is just as important to know why a campaign has not been successful as it is to know why it is successful. Agencies and clients learn from their mistakes and a failed campaign may result in a new consumer insight that might form the foundation for a new and better campaign. Advertising effectiveness is continually assessed by advertising agencies and increasingly sophisticated techniques are adopted. The holy grail of advertising research is to establish cause-effect relationships between advertising and communications objectives such as awareness or even sales. The industry continues to pursue this grail with vigour.

Review Exercises

1. List the main functional roles in a typical full-service advertising agency. How do each of these roles contribute to the creation of communications strategies?

2. Form account team groups, one person each taking the role of creative, account management and account planning. Draft an outline communications plan for the launch of a new brand of long-grain rice. Then each account team should compose a pitch for the business based on their initial ideas. The pitches should cover the likely target market, the major marketing issues, the possible media plan and creative ideas.

3. List, explain and discuss some of the major problems of promotional management. How have agencies tried to resolve these problems?

4. Describe the process by which an advertising agency creates an ad. Discuss the concepts of creativity and accountability as related to this process.

5. Why is creativity such a topic of controversy in the advertising business? Does the answer have any connection with the accountability of advertising in delivering marketing value to shareholders?

CASE   The Fabric Softener Story – Velvalene VS Comfort in Australia[9]

This is the story of the introduction of account planning into a small Australian advertising agency which resulted in the planning role being adopted with notable success over the ensuing years.
David Brent, formerly of Unilever and Reckitt & Colman and an early exponent of the planning role in Australia in 1965–6 says:

'Probably the first shock for a creative writer after I took over my accounts was my urgent view to the manager of Velvalene Products that I suspected that the TVC (television commercial) for Velvasoft fabric softener produced by the agency was virtually useless! The manager had asked the agency to schedule a burst on television and after my experience in Unilever with the launch of Comfort fabric softener a few years earlier I suspected that we had a real 'dog' on our hands. The client was understandably upset, but I stuck to my guns and explained why I was worried and that a simple TVC test against the current Comfort TVC would clarify matters. This was agreed and I phoned the brand manager for Comfort at Lever & Kitchen [Unilever] and suggested that we agree on a swop of TVC dubs for testing at any time. He agreed and dispatched a dub of the Comfort TVC to us. The ad test was rapidly mounted and the results clearly showed that the Comfort TVC beat the Velvasoft TVC hands down and the qualitative reasons given by respondents clearly revealed how irrelevant the content of the Velvasoft TVC was and why it was so ineffective! The ad showed a woman running along a beach wearing a sweater, implicitly softened with Velvasoft. Consumers seemed confused about what the ad was telling them.

The client was appalled by the clear evidence from consumer interviews and questionnaires and so were the agency owners. None had ever before heard of research being used in the creative arena to check advertising performance and with such a damning indictment of the agency's work! However, the immediate problem was to replace the faulty TVC with an effective TVC and get it on air as soon as possible. A script, casting and production based on visual cues of soft bath towels were quickly devised. The TVC featured a well-known, female celebrity-entertainer and her young daughter who endorsed Velvasoft for its outstanding benefits. In addition to the celebrity's appeal and authority, the mother-daughter combination had a soft female angle which helped to further enhance the credibility of the story. This new Velvasoft TVC was then tested against the same Comfort TVC and the results showed that the new Velvasoft TVC came close to equalling the Comfort TVC on all essential scores and established a useful point of difference. The client was delighted, the agency team was relieved and we got back on track with the business. And that client was thereafter forever an advocate of the planner and his role in the agency'.

Case Exercises

1. The speaker in this case advocates the use of qualitative as well as quantitative data (for example, attitude scales) to assess the effectiveness of a given creative execution. The use of qualitative research in advertising creative development and also in campaign assessment is often associated with the account planning role. Choose a new TV ad that you can video and assess its effectiveness through a qualitative discussion group with members of the likely target audience for the brand. What do you feel are the major difficulties with conducting and interpreting qualitative research for judging the effectiveness of ads?

2. The case refers to the account planner as an industry expert whose opinion was influential in his agency. What problems do you feel might arise in the creative development process if the account planner does not have the same authority?

3. The case refers to an Australian campaign that is some 40 years old. Try to form an outline promotional plan for a contemporary brand of fabric softener to be launched in your home country. What do you feel might be the major differences in: (a) the tone of voice for the creative work; (b) the likely media mix used; and (c) the creative execution?

Further Reading

Bullmore, J. (1988) *Behind the Scenes in Advertising*, 2nd edn. Henley-on-Thames: Admap.

Hedges, A. (1974, republished 1997) *Testing to Destruction – A Critical Look at the Uses of Research in Advertising*. London: Institute of Practitioners in Advertising.

Jones, J.P. (1999) *The Advertising Business*. New York: Sage.

Packard, V. (1957) *The Hidden Persuaders*. New York: McKay.

Pollitt, S. (1979) 'How I started account planning in agencies', *Campaign* (20 April): 29–30.

Steel, J. (1998) *Truth, Lies and Advertising: The Art of Account Planning*. New York: John Wiley and Sons.

Wells, W.D. (ed.) (1997) *Measuring Advertising Effectiveness*. Hillsdale, NJ: Lawrence Erlbaum Associates.

Wilmshurst, J. and Mackay, A. (1999) *The Fundamentals of Advertising*, 2nd edn. Oxford: Butterworth Heinemann.

Notes

1 Roderick White (2003), 'Editorial', *Admap*, 444.

2 Leticia Ebb, MBA (Birmingham Business School), has kindly agreed to this insight being adapted frosm her Master's research dissertation.

3 See, for example, the explanations of proprietary brand communications tools on www.mccann.com/aboutus (September 2003). See also D. West and J. Ford (2001) 'Advertising agency philosophies and employee risk taking', *Journal of Advertising*, 30(1) (Spring): 77–91.

4 For example, in the UK, the IPA Advertising Effectiveness Awards; in the USA, the ADDY creative awards; in Thailand the TACT awards, and so on in practically every country that has advertising.

5 The UK-based initiative 'Adsmart' is one exception, funded by the industry and aiming to help children develop a more sophisticated understanding of advertising.

6 Reported in *Advertising Age*, special report, 14 January 2002.

7 Reported in Campaign, 27 February 2004.

8 The guide to client briefing is one of several joint industry guides (to finding an agency, to communication strategy, to judging creative work, agency remuneration and evaluation) produced jointly by the CAF (www.cafonline.org.uk), the IPA (www.ipa.co.uk), the ISBA (www.isba.org.uk), the PRCA (www.prca.org.uk), the MCCA (www.mcca.org.uk) and the UK Advertising Association (www.adasscoc.co.uk).

9 Case vignette kindly contributed by David Brent Pty, Brand Plan Ltd, Sydney, Australia (www.originplan.com).

Promotional Media

Chapter Outline

The media infrastructure for advertising and promotion has grown
and changed over the last 20 years. This chapter discusses the
implications of such change for media strategy and planning.
The medium on which promotional communication is conveyed
informs the consumer's interpretation of the message. In other
words, the 'medium is the message' (McLuhan, 1964), and this
chapter describes the qualities of each medium. It also indicates the
many categories of advertising and promotion that can be carried on
differing media.

BOX 5.0 The UK Media Infrastructure

In the UK in 2000 £17,000 million was spent on advertising.[1]
Most of this went on display advertising in all media, the
remainder on classified (small) ads, recruitment and business press
advertising, and company announcements. Organizations spend
significant additional sums on other forms of communication,
such as exhibitions, sponsorship, sales promotion and mail order.
In the UK there are well over 10,000 printed publications[2] serving
all types of readership. The 10 major daily national newspapers
sell in excess of 14 million copies per day in total. There are
three commercial television channels serving the UK, made up of
15 programme companies (not counting cable and satellite
channels). The UK allows up to seven and a half minutes
advertising per hour on terrestrial channels, and up to nine
minutes per hour on satellite and cable channels. Also serving the

UK are over 240 commercial radio stations, plus outdoor sites, cinema advertising and many other media.

The Media Infrastructure

The media planning task is to negotiate optimum levels of exposure for the campaign, utilizing the most cost-effective and appropriate combinations of media possible. The media planner seeks to expose the creative execution to a relevant **audience** with the greatest possible **reach** and **penetration**. The cost effectiveness of the exposure is often assessed by the **cost-per-thousand** criterion. The media infrastructure in a given country influences the character of its advertising and promotion.

Jefkins said that advertising media consist of 'any means by which sales messages can be conveyed' to audiences (2000: 74). Communication is usually said to be mediated (that is, carried on a medium) when there is some intervening vehicle between the source and the receiver, such as a newspaper or poster site. Advertising messages can be carried on radio waves, static outdoor billboards, paper and ink, ceramic mugs and ball-point pens, dynamic outdoor sites such as motor vehicles and public transport; even air balloons and loud hailers can carry promotional messages. Colloquially all promotional communication is viewed as 'advertising' although industry professionals regard advertising as those promotions carried on mass media only.

The availability of advertising media can vary greatly in different regions. In the developed north there is a complex communications infrastructure that reaches most of the population through thousands of press publications, radio and TV shows and other media. In the developing south there is a far less well-developed communications infrastructure, and also lower levels of TV ownership and adult literacy. Audiences are, in general, more difficult to reach where the communications infrastructure is less developed.

Media Planning and Strategy

Clever and thorough media strategy and planning are indispensable to the success of advertising. A promotional campaign cannot be effective if it is not seen by a sufficient number of interested consumers. The central task of the advertising media planner is to select, negotiate and buy media exposure for the campaign, to ensure that the ads will reach the largest number of desired consumers possible within the media budget. Broadly, media planning refers to the task of placing finished ads in appropriate media channels for maximum target group exposure at least cost per thousand. Media strategy usually refers to the judgements made concerning the fit between media channels, creative executions and the brand personality. The media strategy has to ensure that there is coherence between media, brand and creative execution. This distinction may often obtain without the terminology: in many professional contexts media planning is assumed to entail strategic decisions.

So, while the media planning task tends to be quantitatively driven by the cost per thousand and number of exposures, media strategy requires more qualitative judgements. Many questions need to be addressed. Which medium possesses the qualities that will provide the maximum impact for a given ad? What are the viewing/reading/listening habits of the target audience and how might they be reached? What interval frequency of advertising exposure will best support the campaign objectives? Can the campaign creative executions be integrated across differing media so that consumers' view of the brand is reinforced from a number of sources?

The tasks of media strategy and planning have never been simple, and they have become more complex because of the rapid changes in the global media infrastructure during the last 15 years. These changes need to be examined before discussing the particular qualities of each available medium.

The Changing Media Landscape

The media buying scene is today characterized by the media independents, agencies that specialize in media. In some regards the evolution of advertising agencies has turned full circle. In the UK Zenith Media[3] is the largest media independent. Many advertising agencies that formerly bought media through in-house operations now buy their media space through independent media-brokers. Some have devolved their media function into a separate business, such as OMD UK[4] (formerly called BMP Optimum), the media arm of DDB London.

In some cases the media tail is even beginning to wag the advertising dog. Media agencies are offering strategic planning services and creative work is being outsourced to specialist creative boutiques. This is a recent trend,[5] but appears logically sound when one remembers how ad agencies evolved. As media become increasingly integral to the creative development of advertising, there may well be a major challenge ahead facing advertising agencies that want to retain their current structures and working methods. In the USA media agencies are even beginning to produce TV shows, so that advertisers have maximum control over the exposure their brand receives (see Chapter 6).

The rise of the independents has partly been a response to the changing media infrastructure which has been characterized by increasing media buying costs and technological advances. The rise in the cost of advertising media, partly resulting from the monopoly position of many regional

Figure 5.1 Socio-Economic Groupings in the UK.

The socio-economic grouping system was devised by the British Civil Service in the late 1940s. It classified citizens according to the occupation of the 'head' (male) of the household because this criterion was a reliable indicator of all the household members' level of education, income, professional class and leisure habits. Today the socio-economic classification system is still used in British media, but its limitations are widely acknowledged. The categories were as follows.

A	Higher managerial, administrative and professional (3% of the UK population)
B	Intermediate managerial, administrative and professional (20.4%)
C1	Supervisory or clerical and junior managerial, admin and prof (27.2%)
C2	Skilled manual (21.8%)
D	Semi-skilled and unskilled manual (17.4%)
E	State pensioners, casual workers or unemployed (10.2%)

media owners, has not been well-received by agencies. Media buyers therefore needed more buying power to generate economies of buying scale. As a consequence there has been increased industrial concentration among media buyers parallel with that among media owners.

Circulation of Printed Media

The reduction in press production costs because of digital technology has resulted in many new newspaper and magazine titles coming on to the market, plus free newspapers, special sections in the press and a burgeoning number of specialist magazines. However, circulations, especially of the national daily newspapers and major magazines, are considerably lower than they were in the 1980s and early 1990s. For example, the national daily papers in the UK lost on average 10 per cent of their circulation between 1986 and 1993.[6] This trend is also seen in other forms of press publications. For example, between 1996 and 1998 there were 532 more magazine titles published in the USA, 1015 more in the UK, 128 more in China and the same in Japan. But circulations are shrinking; the UK's popular title *TV Times* lost 180,000 readers from its circulation during the same period, and in the USA *Women's Journal* and *TV Guide* lost 500,000 and 1 million readers respectively.[7] Many more special-interest publications allow ever more precise targeting of advertising, but to smaller groups.

Outdoor Media

There is a global trend that more public space in urban and non-urban settings is being given over to advertising. Between 1996 and 1998 there were over 100,000 more outdoor sites in Europe. In the USA there was a similar increase. It may be that changing geopolitical trends have undermined resistance to advertising in public social spaces. In a post-communist world the economic imperative of wealth generation has superseded other social values. The increase in ambient advertising assimilated into traditionally non-promotional social contexts such as bus or underground stations, pubs and bars and even schools has exploited this lowered resistance. In general, advertising and promotion inserted into otherwise non-commercialized social settings has become much more common. Walls, floors and signage in public spaces all carry advertising, and the backs of theatre programmes, bus and car-park tickets are now rarely without sponsored messages.

TV and Radio

Digital telecommunications technology has lowered start-up costs and made possible not only many new magazine and newspaper titles but also many new TV and radio stations. In the UK in 1988 there were four TV channels. Today there are over 100, with more being developed each year. As with magazines and newspapers, most TV channels carry lower viewing figures than they did when there was less consumer choice. In the UK in the 1980s it was not uncommon for the most popular TV shows to attract viewing figures of over 20 million. Today it is exceptional for a show or televised event to attract more than 12 million viewers. In contrast, in the USA the Superbowl American Football final can reach 100 million viewers, and advertising time In the many commercial breaks is the most expensive money can buy. New digital radio stations have made major inroads into the audience share of older stations. In the UK, the popular non-commercial BBC radio stations once attracted larger audiences, just like television. Today they have competition in the form of commercial, digital radio stations such as Classic FM, Heart FM and TalkSport, three stations that vie for the largest slice of advertising revenue.

These changes in the media landscape have major repercussions for advertisers. Conventional wisdom about the strategic importance of a particular medium and also about targeting, audience segmentation and cost-effectiveness has been challenged by these changes. Media strategy is increasingly relevant for the advertising strategy. Most importantly, account people and media planners can no longer easily categorize their target audience by external indicators like social class, age, income or sex. Instead they have to think in terms of the lifestyle choices of brand consumption communities and the implications of these choices for media planning.

New Media

The increased pressure for cost-effectiveness of media buying has resulted in greater attention being paid to non-traditional media, especially those arising from new technology. 'New media' is still a term used in the business although most forms of new media are no longer new at all. It is now common for brand advertisers to set up a dedicated website, to offer a web-based retail interface, to target consumers with SMS text or multi-media messaging or to produce CD-Roms, DVDs or videos for publicity purposes. Interactive television is another new medium with great marketing potential, but one that has so far proved less popular among TV viewers than the industry expected. It took TV 13 years to get 50 million users; the internet took five. The potential for marketing communications with mass coverage and targeted themes is clearly attractive to advertisers. New agencies specializing in SMS text messaging or other aspects of digital communications are emerging, chasing the popularity of mobile phones and their ability to target consumer groups using tailored messages with direct-response potential. The growth of new media opportunities is compounded by a similar rise in **ambient media** opportunities to insert promotional messages into non-advertising spaces in the consumer environment (Shankar and Horton, 1999).

Audience Fragmentation and Specialist Media Vehicles

So, while media channels have multiplied, media audiences have fragmented. This means that target groups of consumers are both easier and more difficult to reach. They are easier to reach in the sense that audiences have fragmented into narrow interest groups that are served by thousands of special-interest magazines and TV channels. If an advertiser wants to reach, say, trout fishermen, sports-car enthusiasts or TV soap opera fans, there are specialist publications and TV shows that are ideal media vehicles for targeting such narrowly defined audiences. But consumer groups are also more difficult to reach because agencies have great difficulty in categorizing audiences into target groups that are sufficiently large to be viable for general advertisers. Being able to target trout fishermen is useful if you are selling fishing tackle, but not for general fmcg (fast moving consumer goods) sales which require varied target groups. While trout fishermen probably have other consumer interests too, media vehicles that cater for one hobby are of limited use to most advertisers.

Each commercial medium that is funded by advertising has a research-based reader/listener/viewer profile which provides an idea of the typical person who consumes their medium. This information is important for selling advertising space or time to advertisers who need to know the age, sex, income and economic behaviour of the typical consumer. It is not difficult for media owners to construct this kind of profile, since there have never before existed more data on consumer habits and beliefs. Electronic communications and transactions enable organizations to construct and cross-reference massive databases of consumer behaviour, interests and activities. The difficulty brand organizations have is how best to use all these data to focus on the key characteristics of their typical consumer.

BOX 5.1   The UK National Daily Press

In the UK the *Sun* is the most popular national daily newspaper with more than 3 million sales daily. The *Sun* is an expensive publication in which to buy advertising space not only because its readership is large but also because its reader profile is relatively young and consumes many kinds of product or service. In terms of socio-economic groupings (see Figure 5.1) the *Sun* can deliver over 3.5 million B, C1 and C2 readers daily. Given that many copies of the newspaper are read in workplaces or households, the actual number of readers may be double the sales figure. These consumers are in the market for many kinds of fmcg and services. Many advertisers want to reach young consumers because they are at that stage of life in which consumption is very important and they have disposable income. If they are 18–49 they are likely to be enjoying their highest earnings and therefore have more disposable income to spare than at other times in their lives. *The Times* newspaper in the UK may be more internationally famous than the *Sun* but with daily sales of about 700,000 it cannot deliver the same volume of consumers to advertisers. Furthermore, *The Times* reader profile is somewhat different from that of the *Sun*, being slightly older, with higher average income and greater average educational attainment. *The Times*, therefore, is attractive to different advertisers. For example, the *Sunday Times* carries many pages of classified advertising for elite brands of motor-car such as Porsche and Mercedes-Benz which are priced at a level that might be out of the financial reach of a typical *Sun* reader.

The more tightly specified the audience is, the fewer the number of advertisers who will be interested in using that medium.

Demographic Segmentation and Consumer Heterogeneity

The problem for advertisers is that although they may need to reach large numbers of consumers in order for advertising expenditure to be recovered in increased sales, the behaviour of these large groups is heterogeneous. Specialist media, then, facilitate more closely specified targeting than mass media, but they tend to serve audience numbers that are much less than those formerly served by mass market media. The mass media of TV, radio and press were once regarded as easy access routes to large, relatively homogeneous, audience groups. Today, mass audiences display far more heterogeneity in their consumption patterns and behaviour than they used to. Increased income levels and social mobility mean that a person's social status no longer reliably indicates his or her consumption behaviour or lifestyle.

Demographic and social changes have rendered the old **socio-economic groups** of A, B, C1, C2, D and E increasingly redundant (see Figure 5.1). No longer can household members easily be classified and their consumer behaviour predicted on the basis of the occupation of the (male) 'head' of the household. In Western developed economies rising rates of divorce, the much higher numbers of females involved in the professions, greater social mobility and increases in the number of single-person households have changed the composition of media audiences. For example, the greater social mobility today in the West means that it is no longer so unusual for the children of a manual or unskilled worker to go to university and acquire a profession. Furthermore, the classification of manual or non-manual occupation no longer necessarily indicates income levels in Western developed economies: many non-manual workers earn less than skilled manual workers.

All these factors have changed the presuppositions that media planners bring to their task of targeting promotional messages to relevant audiences. Advertising agencies have tried to keep track of the changing currents of consumer groupings by conducting their own segmentation research. **Psychographic** profiles categorize consumers based on surveys of lifestyle behaviours and attitudes. Consumer groups are no longer segmented only by demographic criteria such as age, sex and income. Brand marketing organizations often refer to brand communities of consumers that are linked only by their consumption of a given brand. Brand consumption may be all that these people share, but advertisers assume that there is some common behavioural, psychological or social denominator underlying the motivation to consume this brand.

Brand Communities

For example, the UK soccer club Manchester United is marketed as a brand across the world and has the largest supporter base of any soccer club in the world. These supporters, united in their love for football and enthusiasm for Manchester United, are hugely diverse in terms of nationality, age, sex, income, occupation and social class. But for many of these people, Manchester United is more than a consumption opportunity – it is an obsession. They spend large amounts of money on team shirts, scarves and countless other items carrying the club crest, they invest in satellite TV to watch the matches, they pay fees to join supporter's clubs and receive regular newsletters and offers, and they engage socially with other supporters through meetings, website chatrooms and so on (see also Box 2.7).

BOX 5.2   McCann's Brand Communities

The McCann-Erickson WorldGroup is one of the largest communications corporations in the world. What they say about brand communications reflects important views in the communications industry. Their website refers to brands as 'symbols of a global community of individuals who share core values, lifestyles and beliefs'.[8] The copy explains that McCann's employs a brand 'steward' to identify brand 'citizens' in the interests of 'worldwide constituency management'. The brand steward is described as 'more akin to the leader of a nation that a manager of a product'. It is refreshing to see that even global communications conglomerates still have a sense of humour. This rhetoric is grandiose but influential since it comes from an industry-leading organization. The implication is that the characteristics that define modern brand consumers have become so subtle that only experts can figure them out in order to communicate with them. Given that someone working all the time on one topic will probably understand it better than someone who does not, this may be right.

Brand communities may cut across age, sex, geography and social class. The group may be radically heterogeneous, except for the commonality that motivates their interest in the brand, which may be very nebulous indeed, defined in terms of abstract values and intangible aspirations. The attention advertising agencies now pay to brand communities amounts to an admission that they have only the vaguest notion of what consumers are about. When age, sex, income, geographical location, educational attainment, professional and social status no longer have any relevance for brand communities such as the global group of Manchester United supporters, advertising agencies have nothing to unite the group other than by saying that this is a brand community united by a shared love of the brand. Consumers have become so eclectic in their choices and behaviour that only highly abstract notions seem able to capture the phenomenon that is occurring.

Psychographics and Segmentation

Advertising agencies and brand managers clearly have an interest in appearing to understand consumers. Since the 1970s advertising agencies have tried to formally monitor and track the changing currents of consumer groupings. One attempt has involved commissioning research to delve into consumer lifestyles and behaviour in order to form new classification systems that capture the intangibles that evade systems based on demographic data alone. Some of the lifestyle categories generated by a pseudo-science called **psychographics** became part of popular vocabulary in the UK. Consumers were classified as Yuppies (Young, Upwardly Mobile Professionals), Dinkies (Dual Income, No Kids) and many other irreverent, acronymic soubriquets. The agencies' objective was to persuade clients that in spite of the breakdown of traditional mass audience characteristics, they still understood the motivations and behaviour of discrete consumer groups. They could, therefore, claim that they had proprietary knowledge and insight that enabled them to reach exactly the kinds of consumer their clients wished to reach.

Motivation and Maslow

Proponents of psychographics drew on psychological principles to make the approach seem intellectually more robust. Abraham Maslow's[9] theories of human motivation have proved particularly useful for marketing practitioners and academics needing to lend credibility to their claim that they have special knowledge about consumer behaviour. It should be said, though, that the use of Maslow's theories by marketers, especially his 'hierarchy of needs', does not do justice to them. Maslow was a pioneer of the humanistic psychology movement which was partly a reaction against the behavioural and experimental psychology that reduced humans to entities that behaved according to rules. Maslow wanted psychology to help people find a higher and happier state through personal growth and development. Advertising agencies (and marketing academics) have used his theories to support their contention that humans can be categorized according to their consumption needs. These are said to evolve from biological essentials such as warmth and food, to the need for safety and social company, and then to progress to more egocentric needs such as esteem and self-actualization. Proponents suggested that psychographics-based segmentation systems were useful for predicting consumption from a person's position on the hierarchy of needs. While this application of the theory has some explanatory value, it does not hold any predictive capacity. In any case, the theory was not conceived with advertising in mind and is based on assumptions that do not cohere with the thinking of advertising professionals.

Reaching Elusive or Resistant Consumers

One important feature of brand communities for marketing communications professionals is that they may resist influence from conventional mediated promotion. In developed economies consumers are often sceptical of advertising claims and over-familiar with advertising techniques, and many young consumers fall outside the reach of mass media because they do not regularly watch national television or read national newspapers.

People aged 18–25 form an important group of active consumers for brand marketers and will become more important as their incomes rise and consumption needs increase. In the UK this group was notably difficult for advertisers to reach because they had opted out of mainstream media and took part only in their own exclusive sub-cultural communities. They were labelled 'Generation X' and many agencies tried to devise tailored targeting schemes to deliver this group to brand advertisers. This trend, part of a more general fragmentation of media audiences, is yet another factor in the increased complexity of media planning.

Some advertisers claimed that they could reach Generation X by placing shock advertising in cinemas. It was assumed that while Generation X would not read newspapers or watch TV they would go to the cinema and notice ads that subvert advertising conventions. Ads featuring unusually graphic violence or sex were popular for a time in the UK because agencies were trying to reach Generation-X consumers. Their success was difficult to assess. Some commentators argued that Generation X was an agency myth and that, in fact, these consumers were no more difficult to reach than other groups who shifted their viewing, listening and reading habits on a regular basis.

More important for advertisers are those consumer groups who actively resist marketing itself. There have been many news items about anti-globalization protesters at World Trade Organization meetings. Such groups tend to be against many of the manifestations of global marketing, especially the dominance of internationally marketed brands and the power brand organizations wield to influence international economic policy. Other groups (perhaps with some commonality of membership) have reacted against specific brands for a variety of reasons and called for consumer boycotts. The McDonald's restaurant brand has received considerable critical attention, especially in France where good cuisine and national culture are greatly prized; the corporatism and culinary vulgarity that McDonald's represents for such consumers makes it an obvious target. Authors such as Eric Schlosser (*Fast Food Nation*)[10], Naomi Klein (*No Logo*)[11] and George Ritzer (*The McDonaldization of Society*)[12] have written pungent critiques of brand corporatism that have been received enthusiastically by many thousands. Naturally, this groundswell of consumer resistance to brand marketing and global corporatism has created a new consumer segment that is exploited by book marketing organizations. Nevertheless, consumer boycotts and other forms of active resistance to brand marking create more problems for advertising agencies trying to categorize consumers on the basis of their receptivity to marketing activity.

The media landscape facing media planners is changing rapidly and consumers may be increasingly hard to fathom, but some aspects of media planning tasks remain unchanged. Media planners have to find suitable media with which to target relevant consumer segments with advertising campaigns that will be effective in that particular context. A prerequisite for this task is a general understanding of the kinds of media channel available and their qualities and characteristics.

The Persuasive Qualities of Particular Media Channels

Sales promotion, TV advertising, press, SMS text messaging, direct mail, radio, outdoor billboards, point-of-sale promotion and merchandising, cinema advertising, product placement and sponsorship, trade conference and exhibition stands, some types of public relations, internet and interactive-TV, CD-Roms and DVDs, even product packaging and non-mediated channels such as viral marketing, personal selling and word-of-mouth campaigns can all be understood broadly as advertising that uses differing channels to reach and influence its audience. These differing channels are increasingly used in combination in integrated and through-the-line campaigns. (Sponsorship, product placement, public relations and integrated marketing communications are described in Chapter 6.)

Choice of Media Channel

The way that major companies approach communications planning is changing to reflect the blurring of media channels and marketing disciplines. Media planning is becoming more clever and more creative. Choices of media channel continue to be made on a relatively subjective basis, often relying on conventional wisdom concerning the aura that different media channels bestow on the advertising message and, concomitantly, on the brand personality. Some media agencies have developed tools based on their research that assist planning for particular kinds of campaign. Nevertheless, rules of thumb and experience remain the most commonly used criteria. Clearly, advertising strategy is central to media channel decisions: the choices made must take account of the particular objectives that are desired for a given campaign. This is where it is important to have an informed view on the strengths and weaknesses of each medium from the brand's perspective.

The choice of media channel is often based on criteria such as the following:

- coverage of the target audience
- the type of engagement that consumers have with that medium with respect to the brand personality

- the communication context that the medium provides for the brand
- the cost in relation to the promotional budget.

These issues have to be considered in the light of specific campaign objectives. A campaign to raise awareness for a new brand launch demands a different kind of engagement with the consumer, and possibly a different medium, from a campaign requiring a direct response from consumers. Audiences engage differently with differing media. The mood of a TV viewer is likely to be relaxed, relatively passive and open to suggestion. A newspaper reader may be more critically engaged with the medium, actively reading and thinking about the content. A radio listener may be preoccupied with other tasks and may use radio as a form of minor distraction. A cinema audience may be supposed to pay greater attention to pre-show ads than, say, a TV audience. Media channels are often considered by professionals to have particular strengths and weaknesses. For example, conventional media wisdom holds that TV is good for raising brand awareness but poor for stimulating trial and purchase, and vice versa for sales promotion. The list in Table 5.1 is not exhaustive.

Television

TV advertising remains the most visible and prestigious form of advertising and the most convenient way to reach an audience of millions. It can be an expensive medium. Thirteen commercial television programme makers serve the whole UK population through the ITV network, plus Channel 4 and GMTV, the breakfast TV company. The BBC does not carry advertising on any of its stations. A single 30-second weekday exposure during the commercial break of a popular TV show on Carlton television may cost more than £30,000. In television regions with fewer viewers the price can be considerably less. For example, a similar spot on Grampian TV is a mere £870.[13] In the UK, advertising in the commercial break of a show such as Granada TV's soap drama 'Coronation Street' is usually the most expensive because of the show's regular viewing figures of over 10 million. In the USA, buying advertising time during the commercial breaks of the Superbowl American football final is possibly the most expensive television advertising in the world. In the UK all TV sets that receive BBC stations must have a television licence. The money from the 23,000,000 licences goes to the BBC for programme funding and administration. Although the BBC does not carry advertising, its existence gives UK TV a distinctive character and influences the programming of the commercial stations.

TV may be ubiquitous in developed and also in developing economies, but it is a recent social innovation. TV has such a dramatic impact that it will often dominate a room, demanding attention even if the people present are not particularly interested. Appearing on TV bestows prestige on a brand

Table 5.1 Communication Channels: Main Strengths and Weaknesses*.

Medium	Strengths	Weaknesses
TV	Audio-visual Dramatic impact/prestige Mass audience Demonstration	High absolute cost Low attention Clutter Short-lived
Newspapers	Immediacy Creative flexibility Information source credibility	Cost of national coverage Variable repro quality Not very selective
Magazines	Selectivity Colour Long life, multiple readers Reach light TV viewers	Little immediacy Long copy dates
Radio	Persistence, musical context Selective targeting Immediacy Imaginatively stimulating	'Wallpaper' Variable attention Short-lived messages Relatively low-cost
Outdoor	High visibility Frequency Wide coverage at local level New technologies (laser, 3D)	Production cost Limited message Limited coverage
Internet	Involvement Information Direct response facility	High maintenance cost Limited flexibility Clutter and resistance
Direct Mail	Personal, targeted Specified message Measurable response	Cost per prospect Database maintenance Resistance
Ambient/POS	Close to purchase Frequency, impact	Creative limitations Low attention
Sales promotion	High sales potential POS presence	Low coverage Limited message
Text messaging and email	Targeting, immediacy Low cost	Consumer resistance Low response
Conference/exhibition	High credibility Informative	Cost per unit Time-intensive

*Adapted with permission from *Admap*, November 2003, page 11.

that ripples outward to impress not only consumers but also employees, suppliers and other stakeholders. A TV ad sends a message about the aspirations of the brand and places it in juxtaposition with the most prestigious brands. TV is the media vehicle that most powerfully reflects and projects audience aspirations and fantasies. It is therefore the perfect medium for portraying brands as accessories to these aspirations.

TV has changed in the past 10 years. In the early 1990s there were four TV stations in the UK. By 2002 there were more than 80, with more being created weekly (including satellite and cable). Roughly one-third of the UK population has access to digital television and can access over 200 TV channels and other services such as the internet and interactive TV.[14] In addition to TV channels, there are over 1500 independent production companies making TV programmes. Most of the 80 new stations are commercial, funded by advertising and sponsorship revenues. Audience fragmentation into consumer communities and lifestyle groupings has made selected audiences more accessible through lifestyle and special-interest TV channels. Millions round the world now have access to satellite TV channels that cross international borders.

TV has extraordinary power to convey values and to communicate norms across cultures where the ways TV is consumed have striking similarity. TV is viewed in a relaxed mood, often in the home and in the company of other people. It can be a social occasion as well as a leisure pursuit and a source of relaxation. TV gives advertisers access to domestic settings. What is of interest to advertisers is that TV's assimilation into social settings means that people are suggestible when they are watching. TV advertising reaches those who are looking for entertainment, information and ideas about new ways of living and consuming.

TV Expenditure

TV's share of advertising expenditure has grown in most economies even while total advertising spend has grown absolutely. In the UK approximately 27 per cent of total advertising revenue goes on TV advertising, a figure of some £4.6 billion in 2001. Much of the new adspend is directed towards media which are sometimes considered more accountable and better value, such as direct mail, direct response and sales promotion. Nevertheless, TV has retained its importance because of its potential to create huge dramatic impact for the brand. The creative possibilities are vast for televisual portrayals of the brand in lifestyle settings. The global reach and prestige of TV advertising surpasses any other medium.

For many brand clients TV advertising is problematic because of its cost efficiency. Get it right and it can create a powerful sales impetus for brands. Get it wrong and a lot of money disappears very quickly. Production costs for a modest TV ad can easily reach $750,000 even before any advertising airtime has been bought. Such ads can take many months from storyboard to airtime exposure. They last only a few seconds and date very quickly. Furthermore, the individuals watching TV ads may be highly inattentive and some studies have even suggested that TV viewers do not watch the ads at all. For a brand client, TV advertising represents something of a leap of faith with potentially crippling financial losses at stake.

Newspapers and Magazines

As noted above, there are more than 10,000 press publications in the UK at the time of writing. These are of various kinds including national and local daily newspapers, local free-of-charge newspapers, local and national general-interest magazines and special-interest magazines. Daily and regional newspapers and consumer and business magazines together account for about 23 per cent of total advertising expenditure in the UK. These publications offer a huge range of possibilities for advertisers to purchase advertising space as quarter-, half- or full-page slots, multi-page inserts or 'advertorial', that is, advertising features that are inserted into the editorial content of the publication. Of more than 13 million daily national newspapers sold in the UK, the *Sun* takes the largest single share with around 3.5 million sales per day. *The Times* sells about 700,000 per day, *The Daily Telegraph* 2.4 million, the *Daily Mail* 2.5 million and the *Mirror* 2.2 million.[15] A black-and-white full-page display advertisement in the *Daily Mail* cost £31,500 in 2001 (£45,000 for full colour). *The Sunday Times* charged £54,500 for a full-page black-and-white advertisement.

Conventional media wisdom holds that newspaper and magazine readers may be more critical and more attentive than TV viewers when consuming advertising. Press advertising might, therefore, be well-advised to use more rational content and offer greater product detail, while TV advertising should rely on the simple message with a big impact. Press, especially daily newspaper advertising, has a quality of immediacy that TV does not. That is, press advertising can respond to current events in a day, whereas TV advertising requires months of production and planning. The readers of particular newspapers, while heterogeneous in their consumer behaviour, often share particular demographic characteristics of age, social status and income, which render specific newspapers useful media vehicles for particular brand advertisements.

Brand Coherence with the Advertising Medium

We have already seen how the context of interpretation is important in the meaning of an ad. The medium in which an ad appears is very significant in the reader's construct of the brand advertising itself. Press publications, TV and radio shows, even internet sites all have a sense of their own brand identity. They seek advertisers whose brands will fit with the brand personality of the medium.

Newspapers and magazines each offer opportunities for advertisers to display adds for particular brands within a coherent context set by the editorial and advertising content and tone of the publication. A press publication is a brand in its own right and seeks to convey sets of values and ideas that will resonate with the values and aspirations of its particular readership. In the USA the brand positioning of the *Washington Times* is very different from that of *USA Today*. In the UK the biggest selling Sunday newspaper is the *News of the World*, which carries highly sensationalist stories. *The Sunday Times* has a less sensationalist editorial tone. Clearly, advertisers are very keen to place their brand in a setting that complements the brand values and projects the brand personality. A given advertisement is interpreted in the broader context of the publication in which it is set. The brand can be portrayed as part of an ensemble of brands that are fitting accessories to the lifestyle aspirations of the reader of a particular publication. Placing advertising for a brand in a publication that is strongly disliked by the brand's target market is a serious marketing error. The advertiser has to act as *de facto* custodian of the brand and needs to be aware of any negative connotations that might emanate from the wrong media vehicle.

Consumption of Printed Media in Local Social Settings

Regional and free newspapers offer opportunities for advertisers to reach local consumers within the context of local news and events. This too is an opportunity to present the brand in a setting that makes it more accessible for potential consumers. In many regions of the world reading the newspaper is a symbolic social ritual, engaged in daily, often at the same time every day, perhaps in the same place, in the same company and accompanied by the same refreshments. Newspapers consumed as intimate parts of social normality are powerful vehicles for promoting other types of consumption, since the context of the advertisement implies that the products and services portrayed are also a normal everyday part of the social fabric.

Lifestyle and consumer magazines offer advertisers a route to well-specified audiences. UK magazines, such as *Cosmopolitan* with 500,000 copies sold monthly and *Marie Claire* with nearly 750,000, are bought by young women who have disposable income and a keen interest in fashion, cosmetics, holiday destinations and men, among other things. *New Scientist* sells over 100,000 copies per issue; numerous other special-interest magazines have smaller circulations but well-defined audiences. Magazine advertising costs vary: the *TV Times* listings magazine with a circulation of over 600,000 per issue in the UK charged £18,500 for a full-page colour ad in 2001, while teen magazine *Just Seventeen* charged £8,000 in the same year. The advertising cost reflects the circulation of the publication and the value of its readership to advertisers.

Radio

Digital technology has resulted in many new commercial radio stations in numerous countries. In the UK there are now over 240 commercial radio stations serving all regions. Radio has been regarded as a poor relation to TV for advertisers. But in recent years it has acquired greater credibility among advertisers for its reach and impact, and has even been used as the main medium for new brand awareness campaigns. Its increasing credibility has raised the price of radio ads, though at about £150 per 30-second slot for regional radio and £600–1000 for national commercial radio it still represents a cheaper alternative to TV (figures current at the time of publication).

Immediacy of Radio

Radio has the quality of immediacy, since many radio ads can be produced in a few hours and broadcast that very day. Unlike TV or print media, radio is seen as a medium which occupies the periphery of people's attention. It is often background music in workplaces, motor-cars or households and listeners are generally doing other things while the radio plays. However, radio ads can generate momentary listener attention if they are striking enough and with the radio on for long periods of time there is plenty of opportunity for a listener to hear and recognize a given ad. Furthermore, radio may play an intimate part in listeners' lives if they forge a relationship with a particular show or announcer that they listen to at the same time each day. Most consumers listen to the radio at some time during the week, so the medium has extensive reach to many kinds of consumer segment.

Radio's immediacy can be a major advantage. Advertising revenues at the TalkSport commercial radio in the UK increased 38 per cent in November 2003, the month England's rugby team won the rugby world cup. This increase is apparently part of a trend of increased advertising revenue for a large number of UK commercial radio stations. This may be a result of changes in the UK TV advertising scene, an upturn in general advertising revenues, or a change in the way radio audiences are measured.[16] In spite of this rise in revenue, radio accounted for less than 4 per cent of total UK adspend in 2001. It lacks the perceived glamour and profile of TV as an advertising medium, but growth in revenues and an increase in the share of listeners to commercial stations suggest that more advertisers regard it as an important medium.

Outdoor

Like radio, outdoor advertising has undergone a renaissance in recent years as advertisers have realized that it has greater impact and reach than previously thought. New approaches have developed outdoor poster sites that appear to move as the viewer goes by in a car, sites that are three-dimensional with large items (sometimes motor-cars) stuck on to the site for added effect, and laser-beam projected promotional images on the sides of large buildings. There are about 118,000 static poster sites in the UK, most

BOX 5.3   Outdoor Promotion

Outdoor promotion specialists (such as Viacom Outdoor[17]) offer packages that include (in the UK) advertising on trams, tube trains and buses: according to Target Group Index (TGI), 29 million people in the UK see an ad on a bus each week. Entire buses can be painted (wrapped) with the advertisement to maximize impact. Lenticular designs allow advertisers to use moving images, making a 3-D effect on bus sides. Bus advertising can be used regionally to coincide with TV campaigns. The London Underground is a fertile site for outdoor advertising since commuters using the underground are predominantly young (49 per cent are between 15 and 34 years old) and in the ABC1 socio-economic category. Outdoor specialists offer custom paint and design services to convert virtually any visible object in the urban environment into an advertising medium.

near or in large centres of population, especially by roads with large traffic volume. There are also numerous non-static, outdoor advertising sites. For example, many vehicles such as London taxis and public bus companies sell their advertising space. There are companies specializing in providing advertising space on air balloons or airships for exposure at large, open-air public events or simply in the sky above towns and cities.

Posters, then, can be used on either static or mobile sites. Of course car drivers are supposed to be focusing only on the road, but posters situated on other vehicles or at the roadside may be a welcome diversion from the monotonous landscape which faces the urban motorist. Agencies specializing in outdoor advertising know that static and mobile poster sites are noticed by high volumes of consumers who may see them over long periods of time. While national coverage is difficult to achieve and targeted audiences cannot be well-defined, outdoor advertising can be a powerful medium for generating localized pockets of high awareness.

Direct Mail

Direct mail (incorporating many forms of database marketing) has shown rapid growth in recent years. Direct mail accounted for about 12 per cent of total adspend in the UK in 2001, amounting to over £2 billion. Of all media, only TV attracts a higher proportion of advertising revenue. The attraction of direct-mail advertising over broadcast media is that each mailshot can be directed at a named person who may have a personal interest in the products or services being offered. As any householder knows, the belief of advertisers that direct mail is good value is highly suspect;

BOX 5.4   Charities Marketing Through Direct Mail

The Institute of Direct Marketing[18] in the UK produces case studies of direct marketing successes to promote the medium. In one such case in 2002 a charity based in Ireland called Concern achieved its marketing objectives through an integrated promotional campaign which relied heavily on direct communication. The case illustrated the flexibility of a direct and database driven-approach. The charity specialized in channelling aid to alleviate human disasters as they occurred. It began in response to the plight of people in Afghanistan whose economy and infrastructure had been devastated by years of war.

The charities sector in general has been subject to increasing competition as more charities compete for a limited well of public donations. Concern found that they were unable to pursue the aid projects they wished because of wildly fluctuating donation income. They realized, as other charities had, that a marketing-driven approach was needed and hired marketing staff with experience in the commercial fmcg sector.

Approaches included setting up and maintaining an accurate up-to-date database of donors. The administrative structure of the organization was improved so that it could set up appeals and channel donations within 48 hours of news of a disaster breaking on news media. The database was used to target donors with carefully redesigned direct-mail shots asking them if they would become long-term donors by setting up standing orders from their bank accounts. If successful this initiative would offer a long-term income stream and enable long-term planning to be undertaken. Email targeting was set up so that all past donors could be targeted within two hours of a disaster. Concern knew that speed was essential in generating donor income from disasters covered in the news media. They had to get in first before other charities. Radio and direct-response TV ads were set up in addition to email and website initiatives. The results were startling: all revenue targets were exceeded, and awareness of Concern as a charity brand increased significantly both in Ireland and mainland Britain.

much of it ends up unread in the trash, and a lot is misdirected because the customer databases driving direct mail campaigns are notoriously difficult to compile and maintain accurately. In spite of these difficulties direct and database marketing continue to grow in importance. The advent of **database mining software**, such as Viper (www.smartfocus.com), enables marketers quickly and accurately to segment their databases in many ways in order to generate new possibilities for direct mail.

Internet and New Media

As we have been, telecommunications and broadcast technology is developing so quickly that new media do not remain new for very long. The internet is still new only in relation to more traditional print and broadcast advertising media. Digital technology has reduced the cost of producing promotional print brochures, videos, CD-Roms and DVDs for circulation. New technology has produced a growth in agencies specializing in email and SMS text messaging for advertising. Some agencies have attracted a poor reputation for this sector by spamming thousands of messages indiscriminately, often for illegal or ethically dubious products or services. Used with greater discrimination, such methods can target specified consumers with messages tailored to their consumption and leisure interests. The WAP technology in mobile phones makes it possible to track the physical whereabouts of owners at any time (so long as they are carrying their mobile phone). In one experiment mobile phone users were targeted with text message promotional offers as they walked past the relevant store. All they had to do was to walk in to take advantage of the offer.

Mobile telecommunications and electronic payment and data storage have become key aspects of the integration of marketing communications with logistics and order fulfilment. New media often have the capacity for direct response. For example, the UK national newspaper *The Sunday Times* has used a CD-Rom format (called 'The Month'[19]) to carry promotional offers for many kinds of entertainment product such as music, cinema and theatre tickets, and fashion. This format, given away as a supplement to the newspaper, demonstrates products and services through audio or video clips and can interface with websites (through 'hot links to the online shop') so that users can buy instantly. The CD carries demonstrations and tryouts of movies, computer games, book extracts, TV shows and competitions. It is at once a series of advertisements, an electronic catalogue and an entertainments listings vehicle. The fact that it is given away with a Sunday newspaper means that the audience is pre-segmented: the newspaper marketing team already knows a lot about their readership and can recruit advertisers interested in a preselected audience of active consumers. At the time of writing, advertising in *The Sunday Times* can cost more than £50,000 for a single, one-page ad (more for colour). The CD-Rom format also increases the newspaper's capacity for carrying advertising and selling it at a lower cost to advertisers.

The capacity for marketing communications vehicles to provide an instant purchasing interface is one of the reasons why interactive TV was predicted to become very popular. The consumer take-up of interactive TV has not been as rapid as expected by the industry, but it nevertheless remains an enticing opportunity for brand owners to communicate with individual consumers in a format which offers a purchase capability. The internet is a powerful vehicle for this form of integrated marketing, but so far has proved a difficult medium for marketers to master. Some internet brands such as Amazon, eBay and lastminute.com have shown the massive sales leverage that an internet presence can offer a brand. The many dotcom failures have shown how difficult it can be to get this form of business right. Many brands hedge their bets in their marketing communication activities by adopting integrated strategies which link interactive websites to mass media and other advertising. A popular ad with a dedicated website can in itself provoke many 'hits' from consumers interested in the ad and/or the brand.

Sales Promotion

The category of sales promotion refers to a vast range of novelty items that can carry promotional messages or a visual representation of the brand. Often these items such as coffee mugs, pens, bags, T-shirts or other things, are given away, so the element of goodwill is bound up with the brand when they are used by a consumer. Of course in recent years brands have become so cool that it is now rare to see paid-for clothing or accessories that are not overtly branded. Brands have realized that they can have consumers pay to wear sales promotional items such as FCUK tops, Gucci bags and so on.

The category of sales promotion also refers to in-store promotions such as two-for-the-price-of-one, 10 per cent off, free gifts, redeemable coupons, competitions or money-back for returning so many bottle-tops or labels (the latter technique is called the self-liquidating premium). Conventional marketing wisdom holds that the major strength of sales promotions is that they can persuade people to try the brand. It can also be argued that some brands use perpetual sales promotions to encourage repeat purchase and brand loyalty. McDonald's hamburgers often have a promotional offer of free toys with children's meals, usually thematically tied in with a movie release. This device encourages not just trial but long-term, repeat purchase. Some sales promotional techniques converge with customer relationship management (CRM) approaches in that they seek to reward, and thereby encourage, brand loyalty.

Airlines and credit cards try to reward repeated use with air-miles for free travel and points or money-back. Mortgage providers in the UK have found that if they offer low promotional interest rates for new customers but do not offer the same for existing customers, the existing customers may take their business elsewhere. Banks rely on customer inertia: many consumers are reluctant to go to the trouble of changing their bank account or mortgage provider. But this policy can result in lost business, as more financial services consumers are prepared to consume actively and exercise their choice by switching providers. Credit-card companies often offer good rates to new customers for loan servicing (switching negative balances from another provider), but the promotional rate reverts to the existing customer rate after six months or a year. Many consumers now switch credit cards more readily to take advantage of promotional interest rates.

Some retailers have abandoned the conventional wisdom of sales promotion-inducing trial and have opted instead for continuous sales promotion to solicit bargain-conscious consumers. In Europe Aldi and Netto supermarkets are positioned as cheap, no-frills providers, in the airline market there has been a rapid growth in low-cost air travel, with firms such as Easyjet and Ryanair, and many hotel chains have developed low-cost, no-frills rooms such as the French chain Formula 1 and the Holiday Inn Express chain of budget hotels. Sales promotion, of course, implies a tactical manoeuvre which is short-term, while low-cost as a marketing strategy is rather a different approach. Nevertheless, low-cost, marketing strategies simply extend the logic of sales promotion, because many cost-conscious consumers are not brand-loyal as such but shop around for bargains all the time. Most sales promotion campaigns have a temporary effect: when UK daily newspapers compete in periodic price-cutting wars, sales rise then gradually return to a stable level once the old price is restored. Sales promotion techniques are rightly regarded as tactical rather than strategic, but some brands have taken the logic of sales promotion and applied it strategically to target cost-conscious consumers in the longer term.

Trade Conferences and Exhibitions

The UK Advertising Association has estimated that around £1 billion is spent annually in the UK on exhibitions. Many of these are trade exhibitions for business-to-business promotion but some also include consumers, such as trade exhibitions for motor vehicles, home furnishings and leisure

BOX 5.5 Email Marketing by Virgin

In 2003 Virgin Atlantic airlines created a new standard of upper-class air travel with lie-down beds and personal service in their new upper-class cabins. They sent email alerts to air travellers (targeted using their Flying Club membership database) with a hypertext link to the Virgin Atlantic website. Customers can take a virtual tour of the new cabins, check routes and buy flight tickets electronically. Perhaps more upper-class passengers will be attracted to pay the premium fare by the sense of exclusivity and comfort in the new cabins. Virgin's integrated communications make use of a membership scheme with benefits, a web presence with a retail interface, and service extras such as VIP lounges that enhance the brand and increase the happiness of the customer.

crafts. Higher education providers make extensive use of exhibitions for recruiting international students to their courses. Exhibitions can generate a massive throughput of actual and potential consumers while also acting as a presence in the market in general. Many UK universities employ teams of international officers who man stands at British Council and other educational exhibitions around the world to field enquiries and take applications for UK university courses. Universities from around the world have a presence at MBA exhibitions as they compete for the best students.

Ambient, Word-of-Mouth, Viral and Guerrilla Marketing: POS

These are important categories of marketing but not media channels as such. **Guerrilla marketing, ambient** and **POS (point of sale)** use various media while word-of-mouth (**WOM**) refers to unmediated communication (strictly speaking). **Viral marketing** originally only referred to internet-based forms of marketing communication modelled on the establishment and growth of Hotmail. These categories are often linked; for example both viral and guerrilla marketing initiatives are usually designed to create a groundswell of WOM interest in a brand. Some also seek to generate media interest and editorial coverage and hence fall into the area of publicity or PR.

Ambient media (discussed, for example, in Shankar and Horton, 1999) consist of promotional messages inserted into the consumer (usually urban) environment, frequently in novel and often unexpected ways. Ambient media come in many forms and can cross into other categories such as outdoor, packaging, sales promotion or direct mail. The key element is how the promotional message has been inserted into the consumer's environment. For example, ambient promotion has a long-standing, in-store tradition in retailing: supermarkets pipe the smell of baking bread into the shop to create a relaxed and pleasing ambience that is conducive to uncritical purchasing. They also play lift-music that relaxes shoppers so that they put more goods into their basket than they really came in for. There are countless examples of ambient advertising, such as promotional messages on the backs of bus, theatre, and car-park tickets, and messages on beer mats in bars. In the USA some telephone companies pay for 'free' local calls by making callers listen to recorded advertising that interrupts their own telephone conversation. Many land-owners in the UK receive income from mobile trailers on sites near major roads carrying advertising hoardings to catch the attention of passing drivers.

Ambient media sometimes cross into viral marketing and WOM communication strategies. Although WOM is not strictly a mediated communication channel advertisers are aware of the power of consumers talking (positively) about a brand. Many advertisers have responded to the increased difficulty of targeting particular consumer segments by creating campaigns which seek to contrive an apparently spontaneous groundswell of public interest in a brand. There are many examples of advertisers using viral, guerrilla and similar techniques to try to reach audiences that are sceptical of mainstream advertising and do not consume conventional TV and press. To some extent such techniques are similar to those of classic propaganda in that the motive and source of the message are often hidden. If people are hired to sit in bars and drink a particular brand, then engage other drinkers in conversation about the virtues of that branded drink, this is not conventional marketing communication at all but has a marketing motive. Sometimes PR stunts are deployed to try to generate popular (and perhaps) media interest in a given topic. Marketers even pose as discussants in web chatrooms to contribute positive views of a brand and thereby influence general opinion.

Guerrilla marketing, WOM and many other publicity tactics are ethically problematic because the financial motives of the information source are not necessarily revealed. The student passing around the questionnaire in class (see Box 5.7) is not deliberately hiding his or her purpose – there is no need. Fellow students assume that there is some motive behind it, but since it is not made explicit there is no resistance to be broken down. Such techniques are closer to those of totalitarian states trying to monitor and control public information and behaviour than they are to conventional advertising, which openly proclaims its bias and leaves consumer choice open. Nevertheless, such techniques are growing in influence and importance for brand marketers, as more consumers become jaded by and sceptical of mainstream advertising.

BOX 5.6   Illegal Guerrilla Marketing

In some areas of the UK spray-painted graffiti appears on the walls of derelict buildings. The graffiti depicts a website address, as if a member of the public has spontaneously committed this act of public vandalism so delighted were they with the website. Of course, the organization concerned has paid people to spray-paint public property with their web address and take the risk of being caught and prosecuted. The effect is striking: the spray-painted message is antithetical to glossy, mainstream advertising and carries connotations of an underground, people-driven movement. The messages are huge, painted on walls which thousands of cars pass every day. Illegal fly-posting has long been a common advertising technique in the music business to promote new bands or local performances. Spray-painting the message as if it is graffiti is a neat, attention-grabbing (and usually indelible) twist on this technique.

BOX 5.7   Guerrilla Tactics in Student Marketing

A Scotch whiskey brand hired a student to be a student brand representative on a UK university campus. He was asked to perform various duties such as conducting questionnaire surveys in class and recruiting participants for discussion groups which focused on tasting and talking about the branded whiskey. The manufacturers wanted to learn how to gain a foothold for their brand in the student market, given that many drinkers do not begin to drink whiskey until they are over 25. The student also promoted the brand by consuming it and setting up promotional posters in the campus bars. For his work, the student received some much needed remuneration and some experience in marketing that might help in his future career. The brand owners received far more; unrestricted access to a potentially valuable market segment at a nominal cost. To carry out market research on a student campus a brand manufacturer would normally have to ask for permission and then use designated points of access. An alcohol brand, especially, would have to go through vetting procedures before permission would (or might) be granted. Using a financially embarrassed student is not only cheap, it also means that students are accessed by one of their peers and therefore resistance is circumvented.

Point of Sale

POS advertising is a context rather than a medium, but it is nevertheless an important promotional area because of its influence over the whole merchandising context at the point of purchase. Merchandising is normally a term used in a broad sense to refer to the whole retail setting for purchase, particularly including the way the product is displayed and promoted in the retail store. POS is the point at which the sale takes place and while advertising and sales promotion might get a consumer into the store the sale still has to be made. POS promotion might entail a sales person offering free samples or cardboard models of the product to put the brand foremost in consumers' minds at the point of sale. The term can also be used more broadly to refer to any in store promotion such as liquid crystal TV screens placed in store showing continuous ads for a brand sold there, or other promotional structures such as 'tubes' – printed with promotional images of brands – which customers have to walk through.

Merchandising

Advertising and promotion at the POS are intended to create a persuasive ambience in the space where the consumer makes a decision and hands over the cash. POS should give a cutting edge to the broader merchandising activities that are common in retail marketing. In the small TCN shops (tobacco, confectionery, newspapers) that are common in much of the UK and Europe, brand marketers know that the position their branded item occupies is crucial to its sales performance. The 'golden arc' consists of an arm's length radiating from the cashier's position on each side. This is where leading brands of tobacco and confectionery will insist they are located in the shop for easy viewing and access. In larger retail stores brand marketers know that the volume of shelf space occupied is a powerful generator of sales and they will use all the bargaining power they can to get retail managers to devote as much of this volume as possible to their brand. In the frozen ice-cream business Wall's gained a near monopoly in the UK by cleverly supplying retailers with fridges for stock. Rivals were reduced to the undignified practice of going into shops and surreptitiously moving their product to the top of the fridge while burying rival brands in the depths of the freezer.

Personal Communication

Personal communication can be mediated, for instance when an entrepreneurial business person offers his or her personal endorsement for the brand in a piece of corporate advertising (perhaps more accurately described as quasi-personal communication). Indeed, advertising was once defined as salesmanship in print by an eager advertising tyro. Much early advertising did conform to the conventions of sales encounters with copy that pre-empted and answered consumers' 'objections' to purchase and emphasized the rational reasons to buy. Of course, much contemporary advertising eschews the rational appeal and develops a nebulous brand personality through vivid imagery and compelling narrative.

Personal communication is useful to organizations in many respects as a face-to-face, non-mediated form of communication. As a non-mediated communication channel, personal selling is particularly valuable for instilling confidence in consumers or potential consumers, for responding to questions and for persuading sales prospects to buy. Personal communication clearly has flexibility, the potential to attract and keep attention, and an emotional dimension and credibility that mediated communication forms lack. A skilled employee can create a lasting impression for the brand organization by appearing sincere, engaged in the consumer's life and needs, and empathetic to the consumer's experience in ways that mediated communication can never achieve. Ads, however funny or lovable, are merely impersonal communications not subject to the social rules of listening, responding and believing. Neither can they instil confidence in the listener in the way that a personal encounter might.

Personal communication at some level is unavoidable for most forms of brand marketing business. It is also very expensive in terms of possible coverage. A brand marketing organization can reach, say, a potential audience of millions with a national newspaper ad. For a similar cost, say £50,000, the organization could keep one sales person on the road for a year with a modest car and no expense account, possibly managing sales encounters with 500 potential consumers per year. The economics are quite clear: communication that is mediated is far more cost-effective and flexible.

Review Exercises

1. Devise a media plan to support the launch of a new model of motor-car. The creative executions include a 20-second TV ad, national daily press ads and direct-mail shots to current owners of cars in that class. How would you plan your targeting? Which media vehicles might you use? Explain the timings of exposure. What are the main problems and difficulties of this task?
2. Discuss the axiom 'The medium is the message'. What does it imply? Offer examples to support your suggestions.
3. Discuss ways in which media impact might be reconciled with segmentation and targeting issues. Is there an economic trade-off between impact and targeting?
4. List the main changes in the global media infrastructure over the last 15 years. What new problems and solutions have these changes generated for media planning and strategy?
5. Imagine that you are part of an account team devising a campaign for the launch of a new chocolate snack called 'Sleek'. It is to be positioned to a largely female market as a sensuous indulgence. What suggestions would you have for media planning?

CASE   Direct Marketing Specialist Innovates Through-the-line

Harrison Troughton Wunderman (HTW)[20] is a direct marketing specialist that has won clients and acclaim in recent years for its creative communications solutions. In 2001 one client, IBM Global Services, wished to target UK businesses with its

consulting solutions for information management and IT.
IBM had 40 years' experience of business consulting and wanted
to raise awareness of this among an influential target group.
HTW (part of the WPP group) felt that UK bank managers were
ideal potential clients for IBM. They needed to be targeted in a
way that was both striking and personalized. HTW knew that
UK bank executives read the *Financial Times* newspaper each day.
Their creative solution was to buy up a number of copies at 4 am
as they hit the streets, then take them back to the office to create
personalized advertising inserts. Two pages were designed as full-
page advertisements with the recipient's individual information
detailed on a business card graphic. After the newspaper had been
adapted each was couriered to the targeted individual's desk.
It looked at first sight to the reader as if IBM had bought a
full-page advertisement in the *FT* just for the named recipient.
By early 2003 the campaign had won major awards and
generated two relationships for each of the 17 targeted
companies. IBM estimate that the initiative will ultimately yield
over $50 million worth of new business.

In a campaign for the launch of the Xerox DocuColor 2240,
HTW persuaded the British artist Gavin Turk to appear outside the
Tate Britain Gallery for 45 minutes creating colour photocopies of
his work and selling them, signed, for 10p, the cost of each colour
copy produced on the machine. The event was publicized through
press and poster ads and attracted media coverage in four national
UK daily newspapers and numerous trade and regional publications.
The public queued for hours for the chance to own a piece of British
art signed by the artist for just 10p. HTW have also created TV ads
for clients such as Whyte and Mackay Scotch whiskey.

Case Exercises

1. List all the media utilized in the two examples above.
   Which categories of the promotional mix would they fall into?
   Do they challenge conventional channel categories?
2. What do the above examples mean for the organization and
   working methods of the traditional advertising agency?
   Are below-the-line specialists in a better position to offer
   integrated solutions than agencies whose primary expertise and
   experience lie in above-the-line promotion?
3. Given the 'medium is the message' axiom, what would you say
   are the messages transmitted about IBM and Xerox by the use
   of the media described above? In what ways might these media
   express the respective personality of the two brands?

Further Reading

Butterfield, L. (ed.) (1999) *Excellence in Advertising: The IPA Guide to Best Practice*. London: Butterworth-Heinemann.

Croft, R. (1999) 'Audience and environment: measurement and media', in P.J. Kitchen (ed.), *Marketing Communications, Principles and Practice*, pp. 111–34. London: Thomson Learning.

Katz, H. (2003) *The Media Handbook: A Complete Guide to Advertising Media Selection, Planning, Research and Buying*. NJ: Lawrence Erlbaum Associates.

Notes

1 The data in this section were adapted from material published on the UK Advertising Association website, www.adassoc.org.uk. Some of the figures, e.g. for newspaper circulations, were in turn adapted from BRAD (British Rate and Data), the advertising industry resource for (approximate) advertising media information and rates.

2 The Audit Bureau of Circulation (ABC) verifies press circulation figures.

3 www.zenithmedia.com

4 www.omduk.com, also linked from www.bmpddb.com

5 Reported, for example, in UK trade press publication *Admap,* November 2003: 8.

6 Source: *Marketing Week*, cited in Jefkins, 2000: 75.

7 Source: Zenith Media.

8 www.mccann.com/aboutus/citizenship/html

9 See www.maslow.com for a list of publications currently in print.

10 Eric Schlosser (2001) *Fast Food Nation: The Dark Side of the All-American Meal,* Harper Collins.

11 www.nologo.org

12 New Century edn. Thousand Oaks, CA: Pine Forge Press and Sage; website at www.pineforge.com

13 Source: www.adasocc.org.uk

14 Source: Independent TV Commission (ITC) website, www.itc.org.uk

15 BRAD, October 2001.

16 Reported in the *Media Guardian* section of *The Guardian* newspaper, 25 November 2003.

17 www.viacom-outdoor.co.uk

18 www.theidm.com

19 www.timesonline.co.uk/themonth

20 www.htw.wunderman.com

6

Sponsorship, Brand Placement and Evolving Aspects of Integrated Marketing Communication

Chapter Outline

Advertising and promotion is an evolving field. Communication strategies that challenge traditional assumptions about channel categories are now common. This chapter discusses some of these powerful influences, especially sponsorship and product and brand placement. Finally, the important roles of corporate advertising and public relations are discussed in the context of integrated marketing communications in the entertainment economy.

BOX 6.0   Cadbury's Sponsorship of a British TV Soap

In the UK the Cadbury chocolate brand engaged in a sponsorship agreement with the soap opera *Coronation Street* (a deal that was being renegotiated at the time of writing, February 2004). Cadbury's sponsorship of *Coronation Street* cost the company £10 million, according to its website. Cadbury consider this good value given that the sponsored animations showing a chocolate *Coronation Street* scene and appearing three times during each show are seen at peak viewing time (between 7 pm and 10pm) for the 52 weeks of the year. *Coronation Street* has a 35-year pedigree on UK TV and viewing figures can approach 15 million. To fully exploit the huge volume and range of audience exposure that *Coronation Street* offers, Cadbury integrates the sponsorship with sales promotions and public relations. The interactive sales promotions 'Watch and Win' competition allowed purchasers of Cadbury bars to match special symbols on the inside of a wrapper with symbols or lotto numbers that appeared in Cadbury sponsored *Coronation Street* credits.

> The sponsorship agreement allows Cadbury's family brand to appear in the context of viewers' favourite soap opera as two reliable comforts in a hostile world. As well as generating goodwill, the sponsored sections constitute significant advertising time at an hour of the day when viewers will be less likely to zap between channels because of the advertising. Sponsored scenes are inserted between the opening titles and the first scene of the show rather than in the conventional commercial break. This was an extremely successful technique and gained five awards at the Institute of Sales Promotion, including the Grand Prix Prize.[1]

Integration in Advertising Communication

As we have already seen in many examples, communications professionals are integrating media in innovative ways. Integrated marketing communication, or IMC for short (Belch and Belch, 2002; Shultz et al., 1993; Schultz and Kitchen, 1997; Yeshin, 2000), has been a topic of discussion among advertising academics for some time. Integration in this context implies planned, co-ordinated communication conceived from a strategic point of view. Strategic here means that the communication plan commands significant resources and has a carefully conceived purpose which is directly linked with the major objectives of the organization. IMC is the planning and co-ordination of marketing communications in order to portray a coherent brand personality and a consistent communications strategy across all media channels.

The idea that all communications channels might be integrated around the brand is intuitively appealing to brand organizations, which seek control over their operating environment in order to reduce risk and uncertainty. The theory of IMC suggest more control over the marketing communications environment in which consumers form their preferences and enact their consumption choices. The logic is that if a brand message is received (by a consumer) from more than one channel, the two channels might act to mutually reinforce the message, provided that the message from each channel is consistent. If all channels are operated as distinct entities with differing priorities, tactical objectives and creative executions, such consistency and control are not possible. The integration in IMC implies that all organizational communications are co-ordinated from an holistic, strategic standpoint.

A consumer may, for example, form a particular impression of a brand from a TV ad, which may be contradicted or undermined by another about the same brand received from the press or radio. As consumers we are not discerning about the source of our brand ideas. We neither know nor care whether our overriding impression of brand X was formed from a TV ad, a press story, a conversation with a friend or direct consumption experience. If, as is more likely, our impression of a brand is formed from an accumulation of encounters with it over time from every kind of communication source, then we are not aware of which, if any, particular source was dominant in framing our idea. As Percy et al. (2001) note, to consumers all promotion is 'advertising'.

If brand marketing organizations are able to co-ordinate their communications then the messages they transmit can work with each other synergistically rather than competing against each other to get and keep the consumer's attention and to promote the brand values. The theme of integration emphasizes control over the whole brand image, from corporate communication and imagery all the way through to the brand, product level and even the customer interface through service and merchandising.

Practical Difficulties of Integrated Communications

In practice, the differing disciplinary traditions and practices of the various communications agencies make true integration very difficult for organizations to achieve. It is often more feasible to create a degree of commonality that links the various channels with consistent themes and values while allowing for variation within the overall theme. In other words, organizations achieve limited yet significant control over the way that their brand is portrayed across communication channels by establishing common themes.

Even this abstract level of integration can be problematic for large organizations. In the communications industry PR, advertising, sales promotion, direct and database marketing, internal communication and so on are all regarded as distinct disciplines. Many large corporations are traditionally set up with different officers and departments handling these disciplines. Co-ordination is a difficult task when communications professionals have to liaise with so many different people, each of whom has a different perspective. Even within one organization it is common for different departments to deal with, respectively, brochures and print publicity, public relations, corporate image and customer relations, and brand advertising. These different departments do not necessarily speak to each other on a regular basis.

So integration of communication across channels can be achieved in partial ways: above- and below-the-line channels can be integrated to form 'through-the-line' campaigns. Media channels with different characteristics may be used in tandem with various creative executions in order to portray the brand personality in coherent but varied and mutually reinforcing ways. Full-scale integration of all media channels is much more problematic since it demands a degree of central control that few organizations would deem appropriate or possible. However useful in principle it may be for a consumer to get a consistent message about the brand from telephone conversations with service personnel, TV and press ads, press editorial, company brochures and written material, controlling each of these elements closely is beyond the scope of control of most organizations. Nevertheless, even partial integration is attractive to organizations because of the potential benefits in terms of control over the brand and influence over consumer perceptions.

Media Pressures on Integration

In spite of the difficulties, partial integration is an increasingly powerful influence in advertising and marketing communications because of the ways in which media channels can dovetail into each other to portray the brand identity. 'Through-the-line' approaches in which different media channels are deployed in one campaign are now common. Furthermore, conventional wisdom about the relative impact of different channels has been upturned. The rapid changes in the media infrastructure have resulted in changes in the marketing power of the differing media. TV remains highly important, but other media channels can perform similar communication functions as well as or better than TV, and often more cheaply. For example, major brands have used PR to raise awareness on brand launch. Others have led their communications strategy with below-the-line approaches such as direct response and direct mail. In fact, below-the-line promotion is now a site of creativity as fertile as that of the display ad. Creative uses and combinations of media channel have assumed more importance as technological developments and audience fragmentation drive marketing communications strategies in media-saturated, advanced economies. This general trend has blurred the disciplinary boundaries of marketing communication somewhat and has led to increased integration. The buzz-phrase **'media-neutral planning'** reflects the new order of media relations, with mass media advertising no longer necessarily the senior partner.

Sponsorship

One particularly powerful dimension of the trend for integration is the way that entertainment, marketing and advertising have merged in important respects. New forms of marketing have evolved, many of which can be traced back to sponsorship. Sponsorship takes a sizeable proportion of some companies' overall promotion budgets, although it is a new promotional tool compared with other, traditional media channels. The sum spent on sponsorship in the UK rose from £105 million

BOX 6.1   Media Agencies Developing Creative and Production Skills

In the USA some media companies are actually producing their own entertainment shows to give advertisers control over the visual and script content. MindShare North America, a media-buying arm of the communications group WPP, have agreed to jointly produce TV shows so that advertising around the shows and product placement within the shows are under the control of the advertiser.[2] The TV networks are attracted by the extra financing that media groups can provide. The trend for media interests to actually create shows for advertisers reflects the early days of TV when the original soap operas were simply sponsorship vehicles: all the script writers, actors and producers were working for the brand owner sponsoring the show. As media conglomerates increasingly hold sway over the editorial content of TV shows, and even movies, it is incumbent on brand organizations to adopt an integrated communications perspective in order to manage the brand personality through its manifestations in different media channels.

in 1982 to £781 million in 2001 and is expected to reach £940 million in 2006.

In some cases brand marketing organizations have been forced to move to sponsorship by factors beyond their control. For example, many governments have legislated against mass media tobacco and alcohol advertising, forcing brand owners in these industries to seek other advertising methods. Mass media advertising has increased in cost relative to other channels. Affluence has grown in the developed West, increasing the leisure time available to consumers, much of which is devoted to TV viewing, so TV programme makers naturally looked to new spectator events that could provide cheap TV. Many sports events now receive blanket media coverage and constitute a highly attractive media vehicle for brand marketing organizations (Amis et al., 1999; Meenaghan, 1991; Meenaghan and Shipley, 1999). In the UK entrepreneurial sports agents have introduced sponsors to sports as the popularity and media profile has grown. For example, in the 1980s snooker became for the first time a televised sport in the UK. Cigarette and alcohol companies realized that the sport needed funds for promotion and prize money. The cigarette and alcohol companies faced increasing controls on their mainstream advertising and needed to find new ways of getting their brand into mainstream media. Sports sponsorship offered the perfect alignment of need and opportunity.

BOX 6.2   Nike Takes Sponsorship to New Places

Not only cigarette and alcohol brands use sports sponsorship. Nike has taken sports sponsorship to unforeseen lengths since Phil Knight, Nike's founder, persuaded the US middle-distance athlete Steve Prefontane to wear his running shoes. Since then Nike has targeted countless sports personalities who gain international fame so that each post-performance TV or press interview is accompanied by an image of the hero of the hour wearing the ubiquitous Nike logo on his or her clothing or cap. The suggestive sub-textual power of sponsorship is telling; no explicit celebrity statement is required. The unspoken message is that Nike is cool by association. Sponsorship taps into the sub-textual element of mediated communication by juxtaposing brands with images of success and objects of desire. The message is covert and all the more powerful for its subtlety.

The Changing Face of Sponsorship

Sponsorship is essentially a mutually beneficial business arrangement with defined outcomes between two or more parties. (For definitions see Fill, 2002; Head, 1981.) Sponsorship was originally seen as a part of public relations since it offers a support medium to mainstream advertising and is not necessarily as explicit as advertising. Television sponsorship has a high profile and it has been common in the USA from the beginning of the television era in the 1950s. In 1991 the TV programme sponsorship market in western Europe was worth around $800 million (Ford, 1993). In the UK, Mintel reported that television sponsorship was worth £183 million in 2001, and it is growing annually. But other forms of sponsorship are also increasingly common.

The Economist Intelligence Unit defined sponsorship in the following way.

The essential elements of the term sponsorship as it is used in the UK today are: (i) a sponsor makes a contribution in cash or kind – which may or may not include service and expertise – to an activity which is in some measure a leisure pursuit, either sport or within the broad definition of the arts; (ii) the sponsored activity does not form part of the main commercial function of the sponsoring body (otherwise it becomes straightforward promotion, rather than sponsorship); (iii) the sponsor expects a return in terms of publicity. (quoted in Head, 1981: 4)

Such definitions, while helpful in categorizing sponsorship activities, do not necessarily capture the subtlety and intertextual character of much

---

BOX 6.3   The Persuasive Power of Televised Event Sponsorship

In the UK the Barclaycard Premiership is the major soccer league (sponsored by the Barclay's Bank Visa credit card brand), the car brand Volvo has sponsored the European Golf Championship and Toyota sponsors the snooker World Matchplay Championship.[3] Motor-racing teams raise huge revenues from the sponsorship of many brand organizations which pay to have their logo or brand name appear on the driver's racing suit and on the car itself. All these brand marketing organizations are well aware that the TV and press coverage ensure that their brand is seen in households in the context of an ostensibly non-promotional entertainment experience. Creating promotion that appears to be something else, such as entertainment, is a particularly persuasive technique since we experience the communication without any critical resistance. The brand is merely a part of the entertainment scene. Sponsorship of highly popular broadcast events achieves the dual purpose of far-reaching exposure for the brand and an implicit link between it and the event. Most importantly of all, the brand is produced as a normal everyday part of social life. It is on the way to being taken for granted by consumers and this is, in fact, a powerful position for a brand to exploit.

---

contemporary sponsorship. Very often sponsorship is used as one part of an integrated communications approach in which the sponsored element raises and reinforces brand awareness and positioning in tandem with mainstream advertising.

Arts Sponsorship

We have noted that sports events sponsorship is very popular among brand organizations because of the extensive media coverage, large audiences and positive connotations of sport. Sponsors also make use of the arts in order to appear philanthropic. A brand name seen in association with a book award or theatre production has high-brow connotations that may resonate with the target group of consumers. Such prestigious promotion can also have a positive influence on the perceptions of other interested groups such as shareholders, local government authorities or the press. Arts sponsorship provides funds for traditionally under-funded arts organizations and so there are social benefits which can generate general goodwill towards the brand organization. Gaining publicity for the sponsorship among a wider audience may depend heavily on whether the sponsored organization can gain media coverage.

BOX 6.4   Sponsorship of Non-profit Organizations

Some forms of sponsorship link the corporate brand or the product sub-brand with non-commercial organizations. For example, telecommunications' firm Cable and Wireless linked up with the charity Dr Barnardo's, in an initiative designed to prevent needy families from having their telephone disconnected because of non-payment of bills. Utility organizations face negative publicity when poor families have water, electricity, gas or the telephone cut off because of non-payment: a publicized link with a charity can in some cases deflect this negative publicity, while also providing revenue for the charity. In another example brewers Whitbread linked with local authorities in initiatives to improve the urban environment. At the product brand level Coca-Cola has sponsored a music chart show that is aired on the advertising-free, non-commercial TV station, the BBC. Sponsorship links between commercial and non-profit organizations are normally based on a mutual benefit: goodwill and publicity for the commercial organization and revenue for the non-profit organization.

Sponsorship Evaluation

Although sponsorship is an intuitively appealing communications technique because of the potentially high profile and positive connotations, it is a medium of which the effectiveness cannot be reliably measured. Certainly, the internal psychological states that might mediate between consumer exposure and sale can be measured through scaled question-naire surveys. Large sums are spent on research studies that look at brand recall, awareness, liking and purchase intention as a result of sponsorship. It is of course very difficult, perhaps impossible, to isolate recall or other effects of sponsorship from other possible causal variables. It may also miss the point by misrepresenting the way in which sponsorship exerts its influence. As discussed in Chapter 2, there is no necessary connection between the internal state and purchase behaviour. Sponsorship, like other forms of marketing communication, may exert a powerful influence on sales through a long-term publicity effect. However, like many measures of effectiveness in advertising, it is possible to gather evidence that can, with careful interpretation, provide insights into the impact of a campaign.

Measures of audience viewing habits and purchasing behaviour deriving from **panel data** provide some data-driven insights into the effects of sponsorship, which, like advertising, needs to be used in a given marketing context. Its effectiveness is invariably contingent on the objectives that were conceived for it. Measures of awareness may be irrelevant in comparison with the way that the meaning of the brand is reinforced and consumers are reassured through the sponsored link. This form of outcome can only be conclusively assessed in terms of long-term brand profitability. Sponsorship, like advertising, works to normalize a set of contrived brand values by juxtaposing the brand within a mediated context such as a soap opera (*Coronation Street* and Cadbury's chocolate, or the US TV show *Friends* and Bailey's branded alcohol beverage).

This kind of exposure can be seen to be extremely powerful, since it operates at the sub-textual level of suggestion. Brand values and the social normality of consuming the brand are implied rather than claimed or asserted.

Product and Brand Placement

It is a small step from sponsoring TV shows or movies with the sponsor's name or logo shown at the beginning and end of the show, to having the branded product placed in a scene and perhaps mentioned in the script. **Product placement** (also called brand placement) has grown in popularity as a marketing technique over the last 10 years. It has also increased in subtlety, which is one reason why it has attracted attention from some consumer groups who would like to see the practice more closely controlled by regulatory authorities. The power of brand placement to influence consumers may partly derive from its hidden character. The TV or movie viewer may not be consciously aware that the use of the brand in a scene was conceived and paid for by the brand organization. If consumers are not aware that the dramatic scene they are enjoying is a paid-for brand promotion, their critical faculties may not be as acute as if they were watching an explicit ad. In other words, product and brand placement offers brand organizations a way of circumventing consumer resistance to or cynicism towards conventional advertising. Its ambivalent status as a marketing communication in the context of dramatic entertainment makes it powerful for marketers and problematic for some consumer groups.

BOX 6.5   Brands Star in Hollywood Movies

Since exposure in *ET: The Extraterrestrial* sent sales of Rees's Pieces up by 65 per cent (according to the confectionery firm Hershey), brands have been keen for parts in major entertainment projects. Received wisdom among Hollywood marketing agents is that just 'showing the can' is no longer enough. Brand owners want to project the brand personality, so they need full creative

storyline of shows and movies. The people working in entertainment and advertising have skills and social circles in common, which helps foster this mutual accommodation. Several noted British movie directors (for example, Ridley Scott, *Gladiator*; Peter Jackson, *Lord of The Rings*; and Alan Parker, *Fame, Mississippi Burning, Evita*) learned their skills in the advertising industry. Expertise also moves in the other direction. US movie directors such as David Fincher (*Panic Room, Fight Club*) have also directed commercials. The industries may be very different, but they talk to each other and each recognizes the value of high-quality movie direction. Advertising agencies understand that good production values and striking creativity get ads noticed. Techniques of cinematography are interchangeable between the advertising and entertainment industries.

Artists and Brands

Another culture change in Hollywood that has helped embedded marketing to develop is a shift in attitude by artists towards brands. Artists are now happy to develop their own market presence through association with brands. Celebrities can reposition their personal brand and find new audiences by lending their image to an advertising campaign. Singing star Celine Dion and actor Paul Newman are two figures who have sold their services for brand endorsement in paid-for advertising recently. The actress Uma Thurman was pursued for years by the fragrance brand Lancôme before she finally agreed to feature in their ads. It is no longer uncool for serious artists to do advertising campaigns. Levi's famous launderette ad for its 501s in the 1980s was also notable for making an overnight star of the main actor, Nick Kamen. His fame lasted little more than 15 minutes but more recent beneficiaries have seen advertising roles catapult their career into mainstream entertainment. In the UK Melanie Sykes was a catalogue model until a starring role in a Boddington's beer campaign turned her into a regular hostess on TV chat shows in the UK. British comedian Paul Kay was well known only on the stand-up circuit until his cameos in John Smith's TV ads. Even the background music that brings brands to life in ads can make stars of the artists. The Dandy Warhols gained valuable exposure by licensing their music for ads. More established artists like Lenny Kravitz have used ads to pre-launch a new single, bypassing the radio playlist route to get exposure to millions for nothing. The realization that association with brands can enhance the prestige of artists, and not just the other way round, has softened Hollywood's attitude to involvement with IMC initiatives.

The Effect of Embedded Marketing Techniques

The appearance of brands in movies or other entertainment projects such as computer games is accepted by consumers because of the ubiquity of brands in everyday life. Movies reflect the social settings that we live in. Brands in movies enhance realism and communicate values. If an actor smokes Marlboro cigarettes you do not have to smoke to understand the sub-textual message. The brand is a part of our cultural vocabulary and we know we are being told that the character is a hard yet lovable maverick. Brands can act as a symbolic reference in movies to signify values, attitudes or behaviours that cohere with the narrative. The powerful cinematography and concise storytelling of advertising have been adopted by movies and TV shows. Brand references fit neatly into this style and enhance dramatic realism. Few doubt that consumers buy into brand personalities at some level. Movie audiences have always adored stars, who are marketed as if they were brands. The insight of the entertainment economy is that consumers treat each in the same way. We project personalities on to brands and we derive brand benefits from our affinity with movie stars. In embedded marketing brands are seen being actively used in an attractive lifestyle context. The brand association exists at a sub-textual level, beneath the narrative. Seeing a star actively use or refer to a brand creates a more powerful message for consumers than having that star feature in an explicit (and patently insincere) product endorsement.

Another aspect of embedded marketing is the intertextuality of our mediated experience. The tendency of differing media to draw on shared symbols and reference points can instantly convey particular values in association with a brand. The presence of a brand in an entertainment setting carries a dual marketing benefit. On the one hand, it makes that brand taken for granted because we see it in an everyday context which is important to us in our daily consumption of mediated entertainment. On the other hand, the brand has the benefit of exposure in a setting that is much more glamorous than our everyday existence, so it becomes an object of desire in our aspirational consumption field. Embedded marketing in movies and sporting event settings can achieve these two apparently contradictory objectives in one exposure.

Music and Embedded Marketing

The Levi's Launderette ad used a Marvin Gaye music track, 'I Heard it Through the Grapevine'. People in the advertising business recognize that the right music makes the targeted audience pay more attention. In some cases a campaign provides an opportunity to showcase a new artist.

The brand exposure provides leverage for the entertainment property. Car ads for Mitsubishi and Ford have been recent successes, making stars out of the artists providing the soundtrack. Music publishing companies such as BMG can license classics from artists like Iggy Pop or Frank Sinatra to current stars like Christina Aguilera and Coldplay to provide a musical hook to a broadcast ad. The track guarantees the attention of a particular audience. The advertiser who wants to use an original track to give the ad extra impact has to buy rights to both the CD master and to the published sheet music which are often owned by different music-licensing houses. They have to get the agreement of the original artists as well.

Embedded Marketing Implications

Embedded marketing reflects the merging interests and priorities of the entertainment, communication, advertising and brand marketing industries. It should be noted that, as with all marketing techniques, embedded marketing is difficult and financially risky. A brand organization might engage in a contractual agreement with an entertainment studio only for any one of many things to potentially go wrong: the movie may not be a success, the brand's scene may be cut during the editing process, the producer may have taken out side-deals with other brands that do not fit well with each other.

Brand managers and communications directors need to understand exactly what IMC developments in Hollywood can and cannot deliver. Movie audiences are self-selecting target groups for marketers. They are influential and active consumers. Furthermore, the influence of movies spreads beyond the theatre in the form of press editorial, broadcast media coverage, word of mouth, outdoor, associated websites (with retail interfaces) and franchised product links. Integrated marketing communications can become a web of influence around the brand, with numerous threads emanating from the same source.

Movies and other broadcast entertainment products such as sports coverage and TV drama provide a huge potential for powerfully synergistic marketing links. Even when sophisticated audiences are aware of such commercial arrangements, the power of the link is undiminished because embedded marketing acts at a sub-textual level. The streets are full of people wearing branded clothing and carrying branded holdalls; we have become culturally primed for the appearance of a brand symbol in almost any social context. It is inevitable, and even natural, that movie and broadcast entertainment scenes reflect this cultural reality. Embedded marketing represents the logical convergence of communications media within the cultural-entertainment-marketing complex.

Corporate Image and Public Relations

Corporate Communications

Corporate communications, corporate identity and public relations are distinct fields of study and practice. While detailed consideration of each is beyond the scope of this book, it is nonetheless important to touch on pertinent issues, since each discipline converges with advertising in significant respects and each is part of the greater convergence of marketing communications generally. As Marchand (1998) has shown (see Chapter 2), in his historical studies of corporate America, big business combined public relations, advertising and corporate communication to manufacture a sense of legitimacy for the great corporations at the beginning of the twentieth century. They used corporate advertising to give a human identity to corporations and portray them in a caring, responsible light. They also used PR techniques, including well-publicized corporate philanthropy, sponsorship of good causes and better customer relations.

Many of these corporations became strikingly successful brand names in their own right. In turn, brand advertising and marketing reflects on the 'family' brand of the manufacturer. If Cadbury promotes a new chocolate bar successfully it may be attributed partly to good product design, packaging and advertising. If the product turns out to be seriously harmful to health because of a lapse in quality control it constitutes a PR setback for the while firm. Cadbury's successful sponsorship of the UK TV drama *Coronation Street* was mentioned above (see p. 136). Cadbury also promoted a scheme in the UK offering sports equipment for schools in return for Cadbury product wrappers. This was received very poorly in the national press since many commentators felt that it was inappropriate for a chocolate company to promote itself in schools when there are serious national problems with increasing obesity among young people. Cadbury's, in fact, has one of the finest records of corporate philanthropy in UK business. The school sponsorship issue reflected people's discomfort about childhood health and the marketing power of snack food and confectionery brands.

Public Relations

The Institute of Public Relations (IPR), the main professional body in the UK, defines public relations as 'the planned and sustained effort to establish and maintain goodwill and understanding between an organisation and its publics' (Harrison, 1995: 2) The Public Relations Society of America (PRSA) emphasizes PR's task of helping an organization to interact, communicate with and win the co-operation of its public.

BOX 6.7   Unilever Reinvents Its Logo

> The global brand marketer Unilever has spent over $10 million redesigning its logo. The new logo, which will feature on the packaging of many of its brands, is 'open and friendly' and has benefited from the skills of the brand consultancy Wolf Olins. Unilever hopes that the new logo will epitomize its ethos of 'adding vitality to life by meeting everyday needs for nutrition, hygiene and personal care with brands that help people to feel good, look good and get more out of life'.[5]

PR is a function where the aim is to create goodwill towards the corporation, to deflect criticism of its activities and to foster a generally positive view of the corporate brand among stakeholders and the general public. It encompasses the dark art of 'spinning', much used and criticized in politics. 'Spinning' means putting a positive interpretation on information or news that might be interpreted negatively. It is in essence a rhetorical skill, often practised by people with media relations expertise. The aim is to put out a positive and coherent public message.

PR practitioners also try to influence the media by, for example, issuing press releases of stories they would like to be published as editorial. They also engage in informal dialogue with journalists to promote their own versions of events. Many organizations have 'good news' stories to tell. PR specialists (often former journalists) solicit stories, write them up as press releases and use their journalist contacts in order to get coverage for them. Sometimes press releases are printed in their entirety as editorial, with a house journalist taking the by-line. Sometimes they are adapted and used in part, and very often they are ignored. PR specialists need to have a journalist's nose for what will seem like a good story to practising journalists.

PR and Public Image

The PR function in an organization can have a great impact on corporate image. The discipline of corporate identity is often concerned with the visual aspects of corporate presentation (but see Melewar, 2003, for a general review). Brochures, letterheads, vehicles and all the physical manifestations of the corporation all contribute to corporate identity. In order to manage an identity programme, a corporation has to introduce a cross-functional role that co-ordinates all aspects of public presentation. Like PR, the corporate identity function seeks to manage and control the corporation's public image. All organizations have problems with the

BOX 6.8   A Free Car for Free Publicity

Sometimes PR initiatives themselves are the stories. The coach of the England rugby team Sir Clive Woodward was given a Jaguar XK8 convertible sports-car by the manufacturer as a gesture to commemorate winning the 2003 rugby world cup.[6] This gesture generated national TV coverage, most of which included an action shot of the car. Not only did Jaguar achieve as much TV exposure as they would expect from a planned advertisement, the exposure was in news programmes broadcast on prime time TV and in newspaper editorial, both media outlets with far more credibility than paid-for advertisements. The brand gained exposure in association with the England rugby team's victory, which was widely considered to be the result of astute team management by Woodward: Jaguar's exposure was brief, just a few days, but carried all the positive associations and connotations Jaguar could have wished for.

management, co-ordination and control of activities. The separation of overlapping organizational functions comes about because of the need to co-ordinate multiple activities undertaken by many people and often spread over wide geographical areas and numerous, separate businesses.

Customer Relationship-Building Through Communications

PR can take many forms, often using the advertising media listed above in attempts to influence public opinion favourably towards the brand corporation. Much communication with customers essentially fulfils a PR purpose of creating goodwill among existing consumers. For example, registered BMW car owners in the UK receive a copy of *BMW Magazine* which carries features on the latest models. The magazine contains many advertisements for prestige products and services. One of these, an ad for Fairline ocean-going motor-yachts, pictures a luxurious yacht moored off a grand riverside house. The house and garden are bathed in light as if a lavish party is under way. The strapline says 'Let there be no doubt. You've arrived'. Fairline assume that BMW drivers are attracted to quality with panache. The luxury and prestige of the yacht offer a step up in symbolic status from the BMW car. The copy plays on the literal meaning of 'arriving' and also on the colloquial use of the word to refer to someone who has 'arrived' in the big time or achieved fame for their success. *BMW Magazine* and other forms of customer relationship building through communication are attempts to develop goodwill with consumers and also leverage the interests and aspirations of those consumers.

The American Advertising Federation's
GREAT BRANDS Campaign

Intel Spot

1.

What mak

VIDEO: Black screen. Text begins to type on screen.

2.

What makes one computer more powerful than another?

VIDEO: Text on screen: "What makes one computer more powerful than another?"
SFX: Keyboard typing.

3.

VIDEO: "Advertising" logo appears.
SFX: Five-tone "Intel" signature ID.

4.

VIDEO: Light rays trace over logo.

5.

Advertising.
The way great bran

VIDEO: Fade to black. Text begins to type on screen.

6.

Advertising.
The way great brands
get to be great brands.

American Advertising Federation aaf.org

VIDEO: Text on screen: "Advertising. The way great brands get to be great brands. American Advertising Federation aaf.org."
SFX: Keyboard typing.

AMERICAN ADVERTISING FEDERATION
THE UNIFYING VOICE FOR ADVERTISING™

1101 Vermont Avenue, NW, Suite 500, Washington, DC 20005-6306 • Ph: (202) 898-0089; Fax: (202) 898-159 • www.aaf.org
Reprinted with permission of AAF.

For more on this campaign see pp. 75–6.

- Hello?
-Yo, whassup?

- Nothin'. Watchin' the game. Havin' a Bud.
- True. True.

- Yo, who's that?
- Yo, yo, pick up the phone.
- Whassupp

- Yo, Dookie
- Aaaaahhhhh
- Whassuuupp

- Aaaaaahhhhh

- Whassuuup

- So, whassup B?
- Watchin' the game, havin', a Bud.

Reprinted with permission of DDB London.

The famous 'Whassup' campaign devised by DDB for Anheuser-Busch's Budweiser beer placed the brand in the forefront of public consciousness (see also pp. 35–6). The ads showed street-credible friends drinking Bud in everyday settings, quite a difference from the 'American Hero' style of advertising that had been used previously. The major business objective was to maintain and increase value market share by the year 2000. To do this the advertising and promotion had to connect with the 18–24 year-old target group in a memorable way. The Budweiser 'Whassup' campaign's iconic status generated such interest that a website with games, downloads and a competition proved highly popular. Sponsorship and PR initiatives supporting the advertising campaign helped the brand towards the highest brand awareness scores in its category, along with increased market share and profitability.

A repositioning and repackaging initiative for the 115 year-old UK British Bakeries' bread brand Hovis was accompanied by a new website (created by Tribal DDB Interactive). The website was conceived as an information source for journalists, but also served as a useful brand presence for other internet surfers. The website helped leverage the PR generated by the radical overhaul in the brand's positioning.

DDB London created 'Dustbin' (facing page) as one of a series of television ads that accompanied the Hovis relaunch between 1999 and 2001. The agency wanted the creative work to move away from the nostalgia of Hovis's previous television advertising and instead to emphasize the healthy properties of the bread in a contemporary tone. The business objective was to revive the brand equity so that both price and sales might be increased. The campaign was extremely successful and resulted in Hovis becoming the number one brand with substantial rises in both sales volume and sales revenue.

DUSTBIN

Harry: I'm a kid. My job?

Eating junk.

I'm supposed to eat what you call good food ...like Hovis and stuff grown in earth.

OK I'll go for the Hovis - but earth!

A caterpillar could have poohed on it!

You think we have no discretion?

Reprinted with permission of DDB London.

VO: White Hovis.
Get something good inside.

A BMP DDB campaign for the UK Dairy Council had the task of branding milk. Milk drinking was in structural decline in the UK. The integrated campaign utilized product placement, packaging, outdoor advertising, TV advertising and marketing publicity to show that drinking milk is cool. The creative execution used complex wordplay to associate milk with tough and manly social practices. The 'white stuff' plays on the colloquial name for Guinness stout 'the black stuff'. It also evokes the image of highway workers surfacing roads with another kind of 'black stuff', that is tarmac. Finally, 'The White Stuff' rhymes with 'the right stuff'; a colloquial expression used to indicate that someone has a strong, tough character (has 'the right stuff').

Facing page: 'The apartment'

Marmite is a long-established UK brand of spread with a strongly traditional positioning. The creative theme for the DDB London UK TV campaign for Marmite was based on the fact that many people passionately dislike its taste. Those who like the taste are equally passionate about it. The ad showed a man's reaction after kissing a beautiful girl who had just been eating Marmite. The ads were funny and striking and ended with the strapline 'You either love it or hate it.' The campaign generated extra publicity through editorial and media comment and succeeded in broadening and sharpening Marmite's positioning with a commensurate increase in sales revenues.

- Sorry about the mess...

- Would you like to sit...coffee?
- Great

- Mmm...

- Urgh...

- Yuck

- Low Rider music begins.
Reprinted with permission of DDB London.

YOU EITHER LOVE IT OR HATE IT

MARMITE

The St Luke's campaign by Publicis Thailand (see also pp. 51–3) used visual metaphors to link the brand with its primary benefit: it cools the skin in very hot and humid weather. The images immediately identify the product's benefit and are reinforced by the metaphorical copy. One line says: 'This powder is cold (like ice cream)' but it includes a metaphor meaning 'to the heart' for emphasis. Another line says that the product cools body temperature and adds that it can be used in 'every household' – just as a fridge and fire extinguisher can (or should) be present in every household.

This award-winning campaign helped to consolidate St Luke's as a number one brand. (Translation by Amy (Rungpaka) Tiwsakul.)

Reprinted with permission of Publicis Thailand.

Advertising and Marketing Communications in the Entertainment Economy

The expression 'the entertainment economy' draws attention to some notable features of post-industrial economies. Of course, marketing activity is not all about entertainment; it is also about innovation, materials sourcing, design, organization, manufacture, logistics and more. But important features of marketing are converging in the entertainment and communications areas. In post-industrial economies increased affluence and leisure opportunities have created a huge demand for entertainment. Furthermore, the emergence of the internet and digital communication technologies have created opportunities for consumption itself to become an arm of the entertainment industry. Technology has driven a boom in this area, as demand has grown for the individual consumption of movies, magazines, music and anything that can be covered on TV such as sports and popular shows. Electronic audiovisual goods are a derived demand since they are required because of the initial demand for MP3 music, DVD and video-format home movies and so on. The entertainment industry is driving the technological development of new entertainment media.

Symbolic Consumption and Entertainment

Many consumers now use the internet to research and buy all kinds of consumer products from houses to holidays. Indeed, the availability of information and purchase opportunities on communications media has shifted consumption itself into the entertainment arena. Many people shop for pleasure, whatever the goods or services on offer. Cable TV stations like The Shopping Channel, QVC and The Auction Channel are entirely devoted to consumption as entertainment. People watch and shop purely for pleasure. Most consumption categories have special-interest websites and magazines through which people can research and communicate their interests, whether it is cosmetic surgery, haute cuisine or body-building.

The boom in demand for entertainment and the movement of consumption into the entertainment arena have many implications for marketing. Entertainment and consumption have become so closely associated that they are at times inseparable. Watching a movie exposes the viewer to product placement and advertising. Consuming mobile phones, DVD players and other electronic goods is functional, but also fun. As consumer affluence in developed economies has shifted the emphasis of promotion away from utilitarian values towards symbolic values, even purchases such as shoes, cars and detergent are portrayed through brand advertising as lifestyle choices that enhance the user's sense of status and social identity. Many researchers have alluded to this symbolic aspect of consumption (Elliott and Wattanasuwan, 1998; Holbrook and Hirschman, 1982).

Consumption of virtually anything, then, can tap into symbolic values of social status and identity. A great deal of consumption is linked with entertainment. We view ads or product placements while we are being entertained by movies, TV shows and radio shows, or while we are reading magazines and newspapers. Frequently, direct-response ads, interactive TV or websites mean that we can engage with a retail interface almost instantly. The insertion of images of consumption in entertainment and news media powerfully signifies the central importance of consumption to economies and lifestyles. The symbiotic relationship of entertainment, communication and marketing represents an ideologically powerful mix that promotes the consumption of brands as it promotes the consumption of communicated entertainment itself. The culture industry written of by Horkheimer and Adorno (1944) has come to pass in the sense that entertainment, marketing and news media are now intimately linked in the promotion of corporate interests. The absence of an explicit sales message in much embedded marketing communication does not impair the promotional effect: humans are interpreting creatures, we seek to impose meaning and coherence by making sense of our experience. We actively make the connections between brands and values that are left implicit in embedded marketing initiatives.

Review Exercises

1. Video an evening's TV viewing on commercial channels. Play back the video and list the number of sponsorship and product placement events. Categorize these using the categories explained in this chapter. What do the results tell you about the changing practices of sponsorship and brand placement on broadcast entertainment? What impact do you feel such events have in comparison with conventional TV advertising? Has the character of TV advertising changed to reflect the growth in sponsorship and its variants?

2. How can sponsorship of TV shows generate tangible benefits for brand organizations?

3. Discuss the possibilities and limitations of IMC as an approach to promotion and marketing communication. Can you think of examples of IMC practice?

4. Imagine that you are the public relations officer of a soccer club, a university or a retail organization. Think of six ways in which you could draw on other communications disciplines to promote a positive public perception of your organization.

5. What is meant by the phrase 'the entertainment economy'? What are the major features of the entertainment economy? Form two groups to debate the social implications of the entertainment economy and the economic benefits.

The London agency WCRS's work on their First Direct financial services account[7] illustrates the axiom that how advertising works cannot easily be separated from the influence of other non-advertising media. The relaunch of the First Direct brand entailed a multimedia campaign that enlisted 1 million customers, a figure reached three years ahead of target. First Direct pioneered the telephone-access banking service in the UK. When WCRS won the account in 1995, the initial success of First Direct had been copied by the major banks. Less than two in five consumers realized that First Direct offered a full banking service rather than just loans, limiting its growth potential. WCRS designed a relaunch using TV as a communications magnifier, leveraging the effect of other media in an integrated campaign. The research agency Millward Brown[8] conducted a tracking study that demonstrated that in two years the number of people who knew that First Direct offered a full banking service had doubled. The effectiveness of the campaign was judged against the overall use of media rather than relying on channel-specific measures alone. In other words, in an integrated campaign, there were cross-effects from TV to other direct-response media. The TV campaign was effective partly because it primed consumers for a more positive response from below-the-line media.

Case Exercises

1. How does the First Direct case demonstrate the principle of IMC? In what tangible ways did the brand benefit from the integration of media channels?
2. Is the financial-services sector a special case in communications planning or could any brand category benefit from integrated communications? List four brand categories that might so benefit and discuss possible integrated communications strategies for each brand category.
3. Do you feel that some media channels and vehicles work better together than others? Explain your answer using examples of current or recent communications campaigns.

Further Reading

Chaffey, D., Mayer, R., Johnstone, K. and Ellis-Chadwick, F. (2000) *Internet Marketing: Strategy, Implementation and Practice.* London: Prentice-Hall.

Tiwsakul, R., Hackley, C. and Szmigin, I. (2004) 'Explicit, non-integrated product placement in British television programmes: an empirical study', *International Journal of Advertising* (in press).

Van Raaij, F.W. (1998) 'Interactive communication: consumer power and initiative', *Journal of Marketing Communications* 4(1): 1–8.

Van Riel, C. (1995) *Principles of Corporate Communication*. London: Prentice Hall.

Varey, R.J. (2000) *Corporate Communication Management: A Relationship Perspective*. London: Routledge.

Webley, P., Burgoyne, C.B., Lea, S.E.G. and Young, B.M. (2001) *The Economic Psychology of Everyday Life*. Hove: Psychology Press.

Notes

1 Source: Cadbury website, www.cadbury.com

2 Reported in *The Guardian, Media Guardian* section, 2 December 2003: 22, 'US advertisers gain more say over shows'.

3 Quoted in Fill, 2002.

4 This section on embedded marketing draws on a previously published article, by Chris Hackley, 'IMC and Hollywood-What Brand Managers Need to Know', *Admap* (November 2003c): 44–7.

5 Source: WARC Newsletter 14 May 2004; original story in *Financial Times*.

6 Announced on national TV news in the UK, 5 December 2003.

7 Case adapted from IPA Advertising Effectiveness Awards 1998.

8 www.millwardbrown.co.uk

Advertising Brands Internationally

Chapter Outline

Brand marketing is now conducted in an international space which crosses national and cultural boundaries. Standardizing brand marketing communication across the globe is attractive to organizations because of the potential savings and control over the brand image. However, communicating to different cultures raises many difficulties. This chapter discusses some of the major managerial opportunities and problems of promoting brands internationally and explores some of the wider implications of the globalization of the marketing environment.

BOX 7.0   US Brands Under Pressure

The research organization NOP World has reported[1] that there is 'diminishing respect for American culture' with a subsequent 'domino effect on US brands'. The research, conducted among 30,000 respondents in 30 countries, highlights a change in reports of general perceptions of the USA among non-US consumers. Country-of-origin effects are well-known in marketing, meaning that certain countries confer prestige on brand perceptions. This research appears to show that the prestige of the USA as a source of brands may be suffering a general decline, although whether this translates as downturns in specific sales or market share remains to be seen.

The World Advertising Research Centre (WARC) reported[2] that the DDB Worldwide chairman, Keith Reinhard, conceived a 'Business for Diplomatic Action (BDA)' plan in 2004 to promote US brands internationally. BDA planned to raise $1 million to fund work countering the declining global prestige of America and American brands. The initiative gained urgency because of a NOP World survey finding that trust in American brands had fallen to 35 per cent.

Advertising Promotion and Cultural Interpretation

We have already seen that even within one country a given advertisement will be exposed to heterogeneous consumers whose interpretive **frame of reference** is informed by highly specific cultural norms which reflect ethnic, religious, family, **sub-culture, peer-group** and other values and presuppositions. Clearly, this is a problem for those who wish to communicate across cultures. It may seem glib to draw attention to the self-evident differences in cultural and meaning systems, and, as we shall see later, these differences may not always be particularly significant for globally recognized brands. Nevertheless, it is important to see that all of us can fall into conventional, culturally-bound ways of seeing the world. We interpret visual and linguistic signs where the meanings, as we easily forget, are highly specific to our own culture.

Differing Cultural Practices of Communication

In many countries similar gestures carry quite different meanings, which illustrates the varied communicative practices of cultures and carries profound implications for international marketing communication. Non-verbal communication is an integral feature of many visual promotions. In Britain, raising the first and second fingers to another person in a V-shape is normally considered an insult, unless the palm is facing outward in which case the V is taken to stand for 'victory'. Other cultures have their own insulting gestures, such as the fingers scraped outwards under the chin in an Italian gesture of contempt, or the hand thrust outward, fingers separated and palm outermost, in Greece. Soccer players in continental Europe seem quite accustomed to spitting at each other in moments of anger, but if the object of the bile is a British player the British media become very excited, regarding spitting at someone else as an especially contemptible insult.

Crossing one's legs while sitting is commonplace in many countries. But in Thailand, if the sole of the foot is exposed in the direction of another person, it is considered a serious breach of social etiquette, although allowance is made for foreigners. The giving of gifts to business associates is relatively rare in the West but common practice, and sometimes compulsory, in the East where gift-giving is an important part of the complex practices signifying relative social status. In the UK a recent series of HSBC (formerly known as the Honk Kong Shanghai Bank) advertisements

BOX 7.1   National Stereotypes in Promotion

In Europe there are stereotypical beliefs that the best policemen are British, the best chefs French, the best mechanics German, the best lovers Italian and the best organizers the Swiss. As the old joke goes, 'Hell is where the police are German, the chefs are British, the mechanics French, the lovers Swiss and it is all organized by the Italians'. Such stereotypes can be exploited in promotions that humorously draw attention to them while also using them to illustrate a serious point. Advertisements for HSBC and VW Passat have been successful in drawing attention to cultural differences. Clearly, there is also potential to offend or disparage audiences if the communication is not handled sensitively.

entertainingly depicted many of these cultural differences of gesture and behaviour. The message was that an international organization such as HSBC was well placed to understand the cultural differences that can hinder attempts to do business in foreign cultures.

Of course national stereotypes can work both for and against advertisers. If they are invoked to represent a positive and enduring stereotype then they can support the brand. A creative execution for the DDB London Volkswagen Passat campaign in the UK used the stereotypical British belief that Germans are good at motor engineering to present the Passat at the best of German engineering. The scenarios gently mocked Germans while also admiring the personal dedication of VW engineers ('A car born of obsession' went one strapline).

Signification in Cultural Context

Signification must occur in context and it is the context of the behaviour or gesture that confers the precise meaning. Viewing ads in the company of people from countries and cultures other than one's own can be a salutary reminder of this truism. Advertisers therefore need to be especially sensitive to the uses of such gestures in a TV commercial script or press ad, in case meanings are construed that do not reflect well on the brand. The international marketing world is awash with stories of brand names, packaging designs or ads that failed because they were interpreted to mean something inappropriate or outrageous in some regions because the planners did not think outside their own cultural frame of reference. This, however, is a communications lesson that even domestic advertisers and marketers must learn. It is a fundamental precept of brand planning that the cultural beliefs and practices of target consumers have to be thoroughly understood if communications are to be designed that resonate with meaning for them and project the brand personality effectively.

Before we look at some examples of how international advertising was developed to address the difficulty of communicating across cultures we need to understand better why marketing on an international scale has become so important.

Internationalization of Marketing

Notwithstanding the commercial risks that global marketing entails, there remain sound and pressing reasons why brand marketing organizations want to operate on a global scale. Perhaps the most powerful aspect of globalization is communication itself. Information and advertising cross cultural boundaries and raise consumers' lifestyle expectations. The scenes

BOX 7.2   The International Appeal of the BMW Mini[3]

BMC (British Motor Corporation), formed from the merger of the UK car brands Austin and Morris, launched the Mini in 1959. The car, owned by Rover, ceased production in the UK in October 2000 after over 5 million had been manufactured[4]. The revolutionary front-wheel design of Sir Alec Issigonis created a car with great appeal, but sales were falling sharply by the late 1950s. BMW bought the brand in 2001 and Frank Stephenson redesigned the car, keeping the sense of fun and style but producing a vehicle that is contemporary in substance and performance. The promotions for the new Mini have positioned it as a pan-global small car. Brand communications have utilized conventional (though quirky) mass media advertising (with the tag-line 'It's a Mini adventure'), web-based communications, sponsorship of TV shows, brand placement in movies, numerous publicity stunts, outdoor promotions and extensive PR coverage (both solicited and unsolicited). The new BMW Mini has been a resounding commercial and critical success across the world, even selling heavily in the large-car-dominated US market. Its international success reflects a conscious effort on the part of BMW to position the car internationally rather than over-exploiting its British heritage. Many new consumers of the Mini are unaware that it is an icon of 1960s' Britain. But this connotation of the car, while arguably an important part of its appeal, was not a feature of the marketing communications for the new BMW Mini.

of affluence portrayed in brand advertising or in movies viewed round the world on satellite TV have a powerful effect. This helps to stimulate latent demand for brands and in so doing helps to wear away cultural and political resistance to controls on the movement of labour, goods, services and capital. Organizations and entire economies thrive through growth: when domestic demand reaches a point of slow growth because of increased competition or saturated demand, foreign markets offer a means of continued organic growth. Of course, domestic competition drives up labour costs and foreign countries seeking inward investment can offer global brand corporations cheap labour and production costs, continuing the cycle.

The impetus for global marketing may often derive from competitive activity. If brand X is active in a particular foreign market, then brand Y will want to be there too in case it loses ground against the competition by not having a presence in that market. Another factor in the globalization of markets is the relative ease of technology transfer. National boundaries no longer hinder the transfer of production capability to low-wage economies. The competitive need for international expansion, the ease of access to new consumer markets and low-wage labour markets and the cross-cultural communication driving an ideology of brand consumption are, taken together, important drivers of the globalization of corporate activity.

Managerial Problems of Marketing Internationally

Marketing in non-domestic markets presents a number of managerial problems that are less acute when dealing with domestic markets alone. For example, the marketing and communications infrastructure may differ widely between regions. In advanced economies well-developed road, rail and air transport links, the presence of wholesale distribution facilities and easy access to local retail or other sales outlets facilitate marketing by domestic or non-domestic firms. In less developed economies the absence of a well-established communications and marketing infrastructure may present real difficulties. Logistics can be a problem: while densely populated cities may have good communication links, vast numbers of people may live in areas with poor communications and few retail outlets. Rates of literacy and access to TV and telephones may differ widely from region to region. This clearly has major implications for the design of marketing initiatives.

Business Behaviour and Cultural Difference

There are often differences in the cultural practices of international business. For example, the difficulty of getting distribution agreements for Western brands in Japanese markets is legendary. This is at least partly because the Asian tradition of building mutually advantageous business relationships carefully over long periods of time is difficult for the Western business mentality, based on instant rapport, agreements of convenience and instrumental relationships. The language and dialect used in neighbouring regions may have nuances that can only be understood by local people.

Communicating and doing business may be very difficult for foreigners who do not have a deep knowledge of local culture, language and business practices. Systems of business regulation and attitudes to communication may differ widely from culture to culture. For example, what is acceptable in advertising in one country may not be allowed in another. In Muslim countries the portrayal of females in advertising must adhere to the public standards of dress and conduct expected. Portraying sex and nudity in advertising is often more liberal in Europe than in the USA and the UK. Specific rules about advertising of particular goods can differ. For example, in Sweden no TV advertising directed at children under 12 is permitted. Marketing internationally encounters numerous differences in regulation, infrastructure and consumer culture.

BOX 7.3   Germany and New Zealand United in a Co-branding Promotion

The German sports wear manufacturer Adidas[5] won a contract to supply kit to the famous New Zealand All Blacks rugby team. This was more than a promotional agreement, it was a cross-national, co-branding initiative. The association of a German sportswear brand and the New Zealand rugby team might seem incongruous on the face of it. Thus initially it met with resistance from the New Zealand media. New Zealand people are passionate about the All Blacks and the team represents the national identity in a far-reaching way. Many people felt that a local sponsorship deal was more appropriate. Saatchi and Saatchi developed creative executions for advertising that played on the reverence New Zealanders feel for All Black players and reflected the proud winning tradition of the team. In one TV commercial execution a film of the famous Haka Maori war dance that All Black players perform before matches ended with a simple 'Adidas'. In another, a plaintive song about heroes accompanied a gathering of All Black players pulling on their jerseys. Again, the Adidas name was an under-stated presence at the end of the ad, tapping into the passion for sport felt by New Zealanders and seeking to legitimize the Adidas brand in this highly charged emotional context. The incongruence of the respective national cultures (rugby has few followers and little tradition in Germany) seemed overridden in this case by the linked connotations of the respective brands.

Standardization and Localization of Marketing Communication

One important question facing brand organizations is to what degree they ought to try to standardize their marketing communications throughout the world. We have already seen that the meaning of advertising narratives is often unstable and open to a variety of interpretations, even within relatively homogeneous consumer communities. How much more difficult must it be to control the interpretation of brand communications across different cultural and language communities?

In spite of the self-evident difficulty of standardizing meaning across cultures, advertising and marketing communications have been at the forefront of the globalization of corporate activity in recent years. Many markets have grown beyond national boundaries and media and telecommunications developments have created opportunities for brand marketers to reach global audiences. Indeed, while globalization itself can be seen as a nebulous, even a mythical, notion the global manifestations of advertising are clearly apparent. Consumers the world over are often aware of global brands because they have encountered branded goods, brand ads, logos, sponsored sports events on satellite TV, branded computer games and movies. Marketing communication is a significant thread in the globalization debate. Certain brands have global recognition because advertising has been created that resonates with consumers of every origin. As brand organizations compete to internationalize their brands they face the decision of how best to do this in a way that minimizes costs.

The Converging Cultures Debate

The standardize-or-localize question arose partly because the communications infrastructure evolved to make standardized global advertising possible. Hollywood movies have been popular the world over for many years. The emergence of video technology, satellite TV, the internet and international travel allowed this popularity to gain full expression through the global consumption of entertainment products. Another factor in the debate was the tendency of academic and consulting business writers to cast it in the rhetoric of dichotomy: an either- or choice, to standardize globally or to adapt locally. In an article in the *Harvard Business Review* Professor Ted Levitt[6] raised the question of whether heterogeneous cultures around the globe are converging in attitudes, aspirations, tastes and beliefs. The main site of this apparent convergence was consumption.

The logic of the argument was simple. If you can see Nike trainers and McDonald's hamburger joints in practically every capital city in the world then is this not evidence that consumers the world over are essentially the same in their needs and wants?

In a post-9/11 world the suggestion that the aspirations and values of differing cultures have united under the ethos of consumerism seems far-fetched. In fact the free-wheeling ways of capitalism and marketing are at the centre of the cultural fissure between the secular and the religious mentality. For example, Muslim beliefs hold that advertising of loans is inappropriate because the charging of interest on loaned money is forbidden. Many Christian religious influences are concerned about the way advertising seems to promote materialism and emphasizes social status and physical beauty, while concerns are raised from both Muslim and Christian quarters about advertising's portrayal of gender relations and female sexuality.

It is important to specify just what might converge in differing cultures and what clearly cannot. Indeed, the notion of converging cultures makes little sense since cultures are defined by enduring and powerful differences. In important regards what is of a particular culture can only be understood in terms of its difference from other cultures. But in the smaller world of advertising it is still worth posing the question because of the evident commonalities between cultures that make global consumer brands possible. One of the reasons why the question gained credence among the academic and consulting circles of management was the appeal of the idea of global standardization for brand marketing organizations. Not only does having a global reach appeal to the adventurism of brand marketing organizations, it also makes business sense.

Economies of Scope and Control of Brand Image

The appeal of standardized marketing practices lies in two main areas: economy and control. In communications, if a brand organization appoints a local advertising agency in each country the expense may be considerable. The cost of commissioning creative work, producing many creative executions and buying local media exposure is multiplied. Economies result from using one production team, one ad agency and one media-buying agency to produce one standardized ad campaign for the whole region. Costs are kept low in relation to the scale of the advertising operation.

Control results from keeping creative executions under central command rather than having to co-ordinate the work of local agencies, so that brand values and the brand personality are portrayed in exactly the desired way in every region. International brand organizations take a great deal of time and trouble to develop the ideas of their brand's values and personality, and to plan how these values might be portrayed in communications such as advertising. Giving control of advertising away to an agency in another country is not feasible for major brand organizations because they know how costly mistakes in communication can be. Local agencies will invariably employ a culturally-specific interpretation of the brand values, which may not always be the interpretation that the brand organization conceived of in its strategic planning.

In practice the question of whether to standardize or localize marketing communications is not merely dichotomous. Most international organizations reach an accommodation between the need for localized communications strategies driven by culture-specific knowledge, and a need for control over costs and creative executions.

'Glocalization' as a Response to Difficulties of International Marketing Communication

Most international brand marketing organizations have found that neither localization nor global standardization serves their purpose. What they require instead is a policy that reconciles the need for consistency of presentation of the brand in all communications across the world on the one hand, and the need for advertising to resonate with culturally-specific consumer groups on the other. To achieve the specificity required, the brand values and personality have to be portrayed in terms of local language, priorities and practices. The broader marketing mix activities, in addition to the advertising, have to reflect local realities and practices.

The term **'glocalization'** was coined to refer to the local adaptation of globally oriented marketing themes and products. Global brand marketing organizations often seek to impose control over the presentation of their brand at a certain level, allowing local marketing agencies some licence to portray the brand in ways that will cohere with local cultural meaning systems.

One can argue that many globally recognized brands represent something that does not cross cultures at all but transcends cultures. The fact that many global brands are American in origin cannot be a coincidence: US-based brands have global exposure through Hollywood movies. Of the most widely recognized global brands, most are still US in origin. Only two of the top 10 brands listed in Kochan (1996) are not US in origin: Mercedes-Benz and Sony. After the Second World War US products gained a reputation for representing luxury, affluence and high-quality production standards, a perception which is often enduring. Goods of US origin have long lost their technological advantage over Asian-produced goods, but nevertheless a fragment of the glamour of postwar America – chewing gum, silk stockings and Coca-Cola – is retained. Other aspects of US culture are also important as marketing symbols. Subaru cars used a movie star, Kevin Costner, to feature in their Japanese press ads for the Legacy range: pictures of the range (including the Subaru Legacy 'Lancaster') are seen below a picture of him portraying his rugged screen image.

As the world's major economic, political and military power, the USA is a brand in its own right. Perhaps branded consumer items that are known to originate from the US have the advantage of this cross-over effect. Certainly, in many economically disadvantaged countries, products known to be of US origin are powerful symbols of an affluent consumer culture that can only be dreamt about elsewhere (but note the changing image of US provenance, see p. 157). Perhaps this is something to do with the simultaneous fascination and resentment that specific symbols of the USA hold and in some quarters the high global visibility of the symbols of US popular consumer culture has turned into a liability.

Country-of-Origin Effects and Brand Boycotts

In France there have been popular movements against the establishment of Walt Disney attractions and McDonald's restaurants. Of course, France has a powerful and well-developed economy in its own right. These movements are a reflection not merely of resentment against the symbolic power of richer nation-states, but also of concerns that these US brand icons represent a kind of capitalist imperialism in which the massive financial power of huge US corporations allows them to establish brands that obliterate local culture. But there have also been more specific concerns about the way that global brands represent corporate interests against the interests and needs of local consumer communities. The McDonald's ethos of fast and simple food is anathema to French cuisine, but the restaurants remain popular in France as elsewhere. McDonald's has also attracted criticism for its effect on agriculture. In the USA, the brand has created a supply chain establishment that has apparently changed the structure and culture of the farming and cattle processing industries.[7] French farmers have been worried that the same thing might happen in France. The protests against the Walt Disney theme parks may have an element of cultural prejudice however they were not built to serve the expressed leisure needs of local people, but rather to attract international tourists.

Nike was the subject of considerable adverse press coverage because of media stories that they manufactured products in low-wage economies where labour laws were either inadequate to protect children or were not applied. The suggestion that your $100 Nike trainers were stitched together by a 10 year-old Asian making a few cents for a 12-hour day of factory work does not make great copy. Even mainly US-produced brands such as Levi's attracted bad press coverage because of the way they tried to save production costs by shutting down a factory. Global brands make excellent copy for media editors, and hostile stories make better copy than favourable versions. It is right that global brand corporations should be subject to close scrutiny regarding their social and environmental responsibility. It is all too easy for global corporations to use free trade as a cover

BOX 7.4   International Brand Boycotts

Global brands that are closely identified with the values of their country of origin run the risk of being attacked or boycotted for reasons that are only indirectly connected with the brand itself. In other cases, the high profile of a global brand attracts close critical scrutiny of its sourcing and manufacturing practices.
In 2003 UK university students organized a boycott of Coca-Cola products because of stories that trade union organizers had been killed by paramilitaries at Coca-Cola plants in Colombia.[8]
The stories were not verified and there was no allegation that the Coca-Cola corporation itself had anything to do with the killings. Coca-Cola GB tried to enter into dialogue with the students' union representatives in order to defend their position. Nevertheless, the matter illustrates the perception that big brand corporations have a duty to be highly solicitous in their operations all over the world.

for sourcing ever-cheaper labour and materials in regions where labour laws and health and safety regulations are often flouted, if they exist at all. But there can be little doubt that global brands have become convenient weapons in media circulation and political contests.

The activities and consequences of global brand corporations operating in local cultures is an important area of debate and investigation for many reasons. It is the global profile itself that makes the corporation both more powerful and more vulnerable to criticism. Our concern here is not with the wider issue of the corporate social responsibility of big corporations. Nevertheless, the general values of the organization will influence the perceived values of their brands. Global brand corporations have certain resources and media, especially advertising, under their direct control. They have influence rather than control over others, such as public image. News stories, from whatever source, that are connected to global brands wield important influence over them. Global corporations are well aware of the importance of public perception. Consumer movements that turn attention away from consumption of the brand and towards the activities of the producer can be powerful influences on corporate behaviour.

Consumer Enchantment with Things Foreign

Foreignness can be a marketing virtue. Country-of-origin effects can bestow a halo of prestige on brands emanating from particular countries. For example, in the UK, German motor-car design and engineering,

Japanese technology, Swiss watches, French food and wine, Italian fashion, Colombian coffee, Indian tea, Belgian beer and holidays in Thailand are all thought to have special qualities. In many Asian consumer markets brands with a European connotation are often thought to have special glamour or prestige. UK press ads for an executive Volvo model featured an elegant woman of east Asian origin, whereas the Japanese ads for the same car showed a blond Caucasian woman. Each ad had a symbol of desire that might appeal to the domestic business executive who might be a typical sales prospect for that particular model of car.

The French Renault Clio car ad for the UK featured an attractive woman with an amused look in her eyes and the strapline 'The New 16 Valve Clio. Size matters'. Japanese press ads for a very similar Renault model showed a new French-sounding name (the 'Lutécia') and a circus trapeze scenario, suggesting fun and excitement but safety too. The differential advertising signifies different positioning and targeting strategies in each country, as well as adaptation to various cultural norms of advertising. Japanese advertising would be most unlikely to use an image of a woman with a humorous double-entendre, although such themes are common in the British tradition.[9] Later the Publicis agency created the famous 'Papa, Nicole' TV campaign for the Clio that became a huge popular success in the UK. The campaign traded on French elegance and sexual sophistication to position the Clio as a car for independent young females not afraid to shock older people in the cause of having fun.

Other country-of-origin effects may be based on cost. Taiwan and China have become associated with mass-produced, low-cost, low-quality goods. It has been estimated that 70 per cent of the toys and games British children play with are produced in China and Asia. In general, consumer acceptance of foreign culture has proved remarkably flexible

BOX 7.5   Western Celebs Reap Dividends in Japanese Advertising Roles

Japan has been a particularly lucrative source of extra income for Western celebrities prepared to appear in brand advertising. Movie and TV stars such as Leonardo DiCaprio (Orico credit card), Matt Le Blanc (cosmetics), Arnold Schwarzenegger (energy drinks) and Brad Pitt (Edwin jeans) have all appeared in advertising in Japan, as have pop singers Maria Carey (Nescafé) and Jennifer Lopez (Subaru). The British soccer player David Beckham and his ex-Spice Girl wife Victoria promoted Tokyo Beauty Centre salons. In spite of well-developed Asian movie and sports industries, Western stars remain potent symbols of glamour and affluence for many Asian consumers.

BOX 7.6   International Influences in Thai TV Advertising

Many ads on Thai TV reflect an interest in non-Thai culture and global brands, for example, those that mix Japanese with Thai language and culture. An ad for Japanese snack food Bun Bun carries Thai-language subtitles; other brands such as Lays seaweed-flavour crisps, Pote snack food and Giffarine facial cream (a local brand) combine Japanese and Thai influences in their advertising. Thais are also very interested in international brands such as L'Oréal, McDonald's (the 'I'm lovin' it' jingle is sung in Thai) and Scott's toilet tissue (showing the same ad as in the UK). Sony, Samsung and Orange all create Thai advertising executions. Chinese culture influences Thai TV ads for Choice soup mix, Mistine powder for oily skin and Pond's facial foam.

and well-produced or inexpensive goods have become acceptable even when the consuming country has had a long-standing historical antipathy to the producing country. Since the Second World War Japan has acquired the largest international trade surplus of any country, reflecting the popularity of its goods worldwide. China is rapidly developing its export markets. But Britain, once the cradle of the Industrial Revolution, has become a post-industrial economy and has ceded most of its domestic manufactured goods markets to manufacturers from countries with which it was at war just 50 years ago. National cultures, it seems, are quick to put historical animosities aside if someone can market a better or cheaper product or service. Perhaps the global advertising agencies are right and brands really do now transcend national and cultural divides.

It is very human to feel desire for the unattainable or the unfamiliar. No doubt there is something of human nature in the country-of-origin effect. National or regional reputations, myths and symbols that resonate with consumer aspirations are clearly powerful drivers of consumption. It can be a strong lever for advertising and marketing internationally. And, as we have seen, there can be an adverse effect for brand marketing corporations if they happen to be closely associated with a country that acquires negative press coverage and receives international disapproval for whatever reason.

Standardized Global Advertising Campaigns[10]

The UK's IPA has documented some striking examples of standardization in international advertising. In some cases standardization was possible because the commodity0 being promoted had the same meaning to consumers in different cultures. This common meaning was not immediately apparent but emerged through consumer research. This commonality offered a fact-based platform for creative work. One such example concerned a campaign for De Beers gem diamonds.

De Beers Gem Diamonds

De Beers is a South African diamond producing and cutting organization. It mines diamonds in many places, including Botswana, South America and Russia, as well as South Africa. Gem diamonds have no functional use (say, in cutting tools) but are in demand as jewellery. In 1996 De Beers commissioned JWT to design a campaign to strengthen positive attitudes to diamond giving in order to protect sales against small but growing pockets of competition from West-African produced diamonds. De Beers wished to encourage diamond consumers in high consumption countries (for example the UK, USA and Italy) to trade up to more extravagant jewellery while also stimulating demand in places like Thailand, Mexico and the Gulf. The cultural practices of gem diamond consumption for special occasions (especially marriage and engagement) were central to De Beers' marketing problem, but in the West marriage rates have fallen significantly and divorce rates have increased. In addition, marriage often happens at a later age. Thus cultural change may influence the consumption opportunities for commodities like diamonds.

JWT had to identify a powerful motivation that unified consumers of different cultures. Take a moment to think about diamonds and what they mean in different cultures. Do you feel that diamonds have some universal meaning that transcends cultural differences? Diamonds might mean wealth, and perhaps social status, if worn in public, especially at a glamorous or prestigious social event. They may be a symbol of commitment if given by one lover to another. Diamonds were 'a girl's best friend' according to Marilyn Monroe, and can signify eternity when they are given in a spirit of enduring love.

The social practices of diamond consumption vary in different cultures. In the UK a diamond ring might be given on the occasion of a wedding engagement, a marriage, or a 50th wedding anniversary. In Islamic cultures diamonds often form a large part of a bridal 'set' given by both sets of parents as a nest egg. The quality (and quantity) of the bridal set reflects the wealth and social status of the families involved. In some cultures gold or pearls replace diamonds as important symbolic gifts on significant occasions.

JWT designed a campaign for De Beers that used the differences in regional social practices of diamond consumption to portray a universal meaning for diamonds. The 'Shadows' campaign, shown in 23 countries, was a winner in the 1996 IPA awards for advertising effectiveness. The worldwide marketing budget ran to many millions of US dollars. TV was used in a new, more aggressive style, in contrast to historical reliance on press and magazine advertising. The production cost for the first three TV executions was $700,000, but the production techniques enabled diamonds to be shown in far more striking detail than was possible in static poster photography.

Diamonds are universal symbols of love, especially in the context of being given as gifts to mark a loving commitment. Three main ads were designed in the same cinematic style with the same themes, but using differing regional contexts and language voice-overs. One ad was UK-based and showed a couple in silhouette with classical English music playing over a pictorial narrative of a man giving a diamond ring to his intended bride. Another used Arabic music and showed images not of one diamond ring but of a diamond necklace, earrings, bracelet and ring in a bridal 'set'. Although such displays of wealth may not be typical of ordinary Arab people, the images made a striking visual display of diamonds in a regionalized context. A third ad depicted a mature couple with a child, again in the cinematic style of silhouette figures. The voice-over and music were Spanish and the ring was, in the Spanish tradition, being given to a woman by her man after they had been together for some years.

The ads, created in the same cinematic style, were presumably the work of one production company. Each ad was culturally relevant to a geographically wide region, with some commonalities in language, the social practices of diamond giving and ethnicity. They all portrayed De Beers as the choice for those who truly love the person to whom they wish to give diamond jewellery. By implication, to present diamonds that were not De Beers devalued the sentiment and made the giver look cheap. The tracking studies indicated positive results from the campaign. In the USA an 8 per cent increase in retail sales was reported (worth almost $3 million).

Advertising's Symbiotic Relationship with Culture

Both within and beyond cultural boundaries advertising and promotion have the curious property of both exploiting existing cultural norms, meanings and practices, and changing them. Sometimes they do the latter by expressing a cultural meaning that in retrospect appears to have been powerful but latent, like the global demand for denim jeans as symbols of American provenance. Sometimes, perhaps, advertising consumer research can discover these latent meanings and acute creative executions can express them so that consumers instantly recognize an aspect of their own identity and experience in an ad. For consumers, perhaps advertising sometimes expresses something that they already feel either individually or collectively, yet have no means to express. Maybe advertising is fascinating to us partly because it teaches us about ourselves.

BOX 7.7 Global Brand Advertising and Cultural Change

The De Beers campaign is reputed to have changed the consciousness of some cultures towards diamonds. In Japan, for example, pearls and not diamonds were the gift of choice for major occasions. The De Beers campaign introduced a word for diamonds (*diamondo*) into the Japanese vocabulary. Before the 1960s there had been no word for diamond in Japanese.

Of course, there are countless examples of advertising changing established cultural practice. The UK Cadbury's Smash ads of the 1960s and 1970s got millions of UK households eating dried instant mashed potato for the first time. Häagen-Dazs ads in the 1980s repositioned ice cream as a luxury indulgence for adults rather than a children's treat. The famous (or infamous) Hofmeister Beer ads in the 1980s changed the UK beer market for ever by promoting a sweeping change in the consumption of light lager beers in the UK.

Sometimes cultural changes in meaning are neither caused by nor reflected in advertising. Cultural change occurs and leaves advertising looking out of date. The cultural (or in this case, cross-cultural) meaning of signs and practices is not stable indefinitely.

As the ideological sharp end of capitalism, advertising has a crucial role in promoting consumption itself by teaching new approaches. Consumption becomes much more fun if we attach abstract ideas to material goods. Advertising and promotion show us an array of states of mind, ways of being and relating, and forms of enjoyment, all of which are orientated to consumption. We are more than happy to be offered these choices, which we take according to the preferences that we are taught through our exposure to marketing. Globally successful ad campaigns, then, might be seen not as triumphs of cross-cultural communication but simply as examples of creative brand advertising that transcend cultural borders.

Advertising in Asian Economies

Some examples of advertising in South Asia might serve here to illustrate issues of advertising in developing countries. Some Asian economies, notably Japan, are among the most advanced and wealthiest in the world. Many other national economies in South Asia can be categorized as developing because economic growth is uneven and GDP per head is significantly lower than that in countries of equivalent population with advanced economies. Nevertheless, because an economy is developing does not mean that there are not large and sophisticated consumer markets in the urban centres. In developing countries the cultural juxtaposition of Western-influenced consumer advertising and local cultural and economic norms can seem particularly discordant.

The economic and cultural influence of advertising in Asian economies is difficult for a Westerner to appraise. There is a well-established link between advertising activity and economic growth. Advertising is a powerful driver of consumption. In countries in which poverty is the greatest enemy of social progress, advertising does not always attract the critical scrutiny that it does in more affluent countries. Nevertheless, developing countries should not have to turn themselves into servants of the global corporations, providing both cheap manufacturing and large consumer markets for global brands. They need to develop wealth on a model that fits with their culture, traditions and particular needs. Consumption itself might be said to be a practice that unites differing cultures, but the particular context for consumption differs from culture to culture.

Advertising and Promotion in Malaysia

In Malaysia, for example, many magazine ads[11] seem to promote Western values in an Islamic cultural context. Malaysia is a culturally complex country, with three main ethnic groups, Indian, Chinese and Malay. Each has a separate language and many differing traditions, but there is also a great deal of commonality. There are also groups of Thais, Filipinos, Taiwanese and Indonesians. Advertising in such a context has to be distinctively Asian and must conform to local sensitivities. Approval for

BOX 7.8   Muslim Values in Western-style Advertising

A Bahasa fashion magazine has many examples of 'glocal' advertising portraying Western products with Western values but in a creative execution that is adapted to be acceptable to Muslim readers. One product, Johnson's pH5.5 cooling body wash, is intended to be used in the shower. However, it would not be allowed to show a photograph of a female in the shower, so the ad shows a woman with naked shoulders in a sensuous pose while a graphic, water-like abstract design fills the background. The model's hair is fixed in place so that she might even be wearing a headscarf. The ad's suggestion of a female in the shower is clear, but the advertisers can claim that it does not show a naked female.

ads is often given directly by government officials. There are detailed codes of practice for the advertising of different products and services.

The art of adhering to advertising codes and regulations literally while going beyond them is symbolically a mark of advertising under advanced capitalism. Ads such as the one described above illustrate the ideological force of advertising, which promotes the values of consumption while subtly circumventing other cultural values. Clearly, capitalism and the ideology of consumption have had to chip away at religious and other values in Western countries as well as Eastern ones. Advertising does this precisely because it is seen as trivial and benign. It is also the case that the imperative for wealth creation means that advertising is usually seen as a lesser evil than poverty.

Other Malaysian ads portray females in a way that offers a compromise between the traditional values of home-making and husband-nurturing and the less traditional values of female independence. One ad for a 'Pewani' savings account offered by Bank Islam (in a daily newspaper) promotes a savings account for women with the strapline 'Nurturing success for today's women'. The visual shows a woman in a traditional headscarf with her husband and children and promotes the idea of the account as a gift to her family. Presumably, the ad has become necessary because more Muslim women in Malaysia are going out to earn money independent from their husbands.

Many aspects of tradition impinge on advertising in Malaysia. One (possibly apocryphal) story about an ad for the US Barbie doll illustrates this. A government minister was asked at a dinner party why advertisements for pork were being permitted on Malyasian TV. This was a cultural misunderstanding: in the Bahasa language 'babi' means 'pig' and some Malaysians who did not speak English thought the doll was made of pink pork meat. The agency was allowed to continue running the ad provided it placed a halal sign in the commercial to signify that the product advertised did not contravene Muslim rules on food consumption. Many non-food products such as shampoo and luxury goods advertised in Malaysia carry the halal sign to reassure Malays.

Japanese Ads and Consumer Individualism

Japan is a very different economic, religious and ethnic proposition for brand advertising from Malaysia. Even so, advertisers have to use symbolism to suggest meanings that they hope will prove persuasive to consumers. Indeed, symbolism, particularly erotic symbolism in advertising, seems to be a mark of the state of development of the consumer markets it serves and reflects. Tanaka (1994) (see also Chapter 2) employed a distinction between covert and ostensive meaning in advertisements. The use of covert meaning, in which meanings are suggested but in such a way that the intention or identity of the speaker is not made clear, allows ads to suggest associations which would be considered outrageous or forbidden were they made in an ostensive, explicit way.

In one pair of examples (in Tanaka, 1994: 46–51) two ads for a miniature TV set were shown, each of which appeared in the risqué publication *Fookasu* in 1985. In one, the TV set was pictured in a scene with two girls embracing intimately, and a man embracing one of the girls from behind. The sexual innuendo is supported by the advertising copy which claims that the satisfaction of curiosity is the key to mankind's development. It goes on 'Can't do this, can't do that … there are many things forbidden in this world. What's the point of living unless we can at least watch what we want to when we want to …'.[12]

The other ad shows the TV in a scene with two girls embracing intimately over a piano. Neither sex orgies nor lesbianism are commonly the subjects of public discourse in Japan. The magazine or ad agency could easily deflect accusations that they were promoting either in a literal sense. But, as we saw in Chapter 2, much of the power of advertising lies in its ability to suggest meanings which are not accessible unless read by the audience, thus imputing the meaning to audience interpretation rather than to the artifice of the advertiser. The ads were in tune with the risqué editorial tone of the publication in which they appeared. They allowed a mundane item to be portrayed in a way that made it seem, perhaps, far more interesting to some readers.

While these ads are not typical of Japanese advertising as a whole, they do illustrate how advertising can be devised which undermines, or at least evades, local cultural taboos and norms. Consumption can therefore be made to appear an act of symbolic self-realization that reinforces individual identity because it (symbolically) transgresses social conventions. This individualistic dimension of consumption is often taken for granted in the West, but in the more collective social culture of the East such implicit individualism may promote and also reflect far-reaching cultural change.

Advertising in Thailand

Thailand is one Asian country that shows intriguing examples of sophisticated advertising in a developing economy that has sharply contrasting centres of urban development and rural poverty. The Thai advertising industry is a mixture of locally owned agencies and branches of global communications conglomerates such as Saatchi and Saatchi, JWT, Publicis, Dentsu and many others. It leads other southeast Asian countries in advertising expenditures (Punyapiroje et al., 2002). From 1987 to 1996, its advertising expenditure increased by almost 800 per cent from 4.9 billion baht to 42 billion baht.[13] Thailand was also ranked sixth among the world's 20 fastest growing countries for advertising expenditures between

1987 and 1996.[14] The annual TACT awards (now in their 29th year) celebrate creativity in the Thai advertising industry. Production standards are as high as in any developed country, as are standards of creativity. In this respect Thai advertising is more like Western rather than Malaysian advertising, possible partly because the ethnic mix in Thailand is less complex. Also, since it is a predominantly Buddhist country, Thailand is less subject to specific broadcasting rules concerning behaviour, dress, eating and other practices than predominantly Muslim countries.

According to Punyapiroje et al. (2002), the Thai advertising industry draws heavily on Western influences modified to suit Thai culture. However, there is at least one major difference between Thai and Western ways of doing advertising business. Advertising consumer research using questionnaire surveys and experiments in which respondents are asked to answer questions are common in Western advertising, but according to Hoy et al. (2000) Thai social etiquette demands acquiescence and people do not like to offer views that might offend by contradicting their interlocutor (Mulder, 1996). Thai advertising professional strategy is to combine research results with their intuition, emotion and creativity (Punyapiroje

BOX 7.9   Sexual Symbolism in Thai Advertising

Thai brand advertising tends to be soft-sell and replete with scenes of humour, fun and love, reflecting the easy-going and creative character of Thai consumers (Supharp 1993). Advertising is very visual, reflecting low literacy rates among the rural population and indicating the subtleties of tone, image and gesture in communication to which Asian consumers are attuned. Thai consumers love freedom and novelty and this is reflected in brand-switching behaviour (Sherer, 1995). Symbolism, particularly referring to sex, gender roles and social status, is powerful in Thai advertising. A TV ad for a Samsung washing machine employs a strikingly stylized scene of a man whose shirt is being flayed from his body by females with whips as he whirls in a vortex. The agency decided that it was difficult to portray a clothes washing machine in a visually interesting way without allowing the creative staff a great deal of licence. The sensuous and risqué suggestiveness of the ad is amusing and attention-getting. It is hard to imagine a washing machine being advertised in a similar way in the West. Perhaps in developing economies there is sometimes a more pressing need to dispense with functional appeals in favour of the richly symbolic. Thailand is, in fact, a socially conservative country in which good manners and proper behaviour are regarded as especially important. In this ad

> consumption itself is being portrayed as mysterious, taboo-breaking
> and fun for its own sake.

et al., 2002). Incidentally, as we shall see in Chapter 9, some in Western advertising hold the view that the Thai approach is best because of doubts about the integrity of questionnaire-based and quasi-experimental consumer research data.

Thailand is one of the Asian economies that has demonstrated enormous potential for further economic development. Ownership of Western goods once signified membership of a social elite (Tirakhunkovit, 1980). Today Thailand is a developing country with very uneven distributions of wealth and educational attainment. In this hierarchical society ownership of branded goods has become important in signifying the social status of the owner, as it is in the West. As long as the Thai economy can survive the periodic economic depressions that hinder development in Asia it will continue to be a fertile source of creative advertising and new brand markets. The role of advertising in this context is particularly powerful in promoting a brand-conscious mentality and in encouraging consumption as a lifestyle. The extent to which this influence may be seen to be complementary to local traditions and values or merely exploitative of them will offer valuable insights into the cultural influence of advertising in other regions too.

Promotional Management in a Global Context

Advertising agency management is subject to much the same kinds of cultural variation as advertising itself. A great many international agencies are organized along similar operational lines with account management, account planning or research, creative and media roles in account teams. There are, nevertheless, differences in approach that reflect broader cultural differences. West (1993) refers to apparent differences in approaches to creativity in advertising in different regions, and Hackley (2003a) has indicated some differences in approaches to consumer research in major UK and US agencies. While the Thai advertising industry has evolved under Western influence (Punyapiroje, et al. 2002), it has also developed a distinctive style reflecting the particular cultural mores and traditions of Thailand.

From the examples above we have seen that a glocalization policy in international advertising is often pragmatically the best course. The attractions of international markets and the appeal of brands that cross national boundaries have to be understood in terms of local cultural meaning systems. Local agencies can place the brand in an appropriate localized context while preserving some aspects of a generic brand personality. If a brand is known to have a global presence this in itself adds appeal to the brand personality. A relatively small number of brands have been able to standardize advertising cross-culturally if their ad agency can find a common denominator of meaning that transcends cultures. They also have to exploit this common meaning by devising ingenious creative executions. Finally, even brands with a global presence are subject to the forces of change. No communications solution is effective indefinitely and brands must remain connected to the ebb and flow of consumer cultures if they are to retain vitality and relevance in the marketplace.

Review Exercises

1. In groups, decide upon a local brand that you feel has potential to be marketed internationally. Decide on the core brand values that may be communicated. Devise an outline communications plan with creative themes and executions using integrated media channels. How will you ensure that the brand values are interpreted appropriately? What are the major difficulties of promoting this brand internationally?
2. Choose six print or TV advertisements that promote internationally marketed brands. Discuss the need for advertising globally marketed brands to accommodate cultural differences. Use specific examples of cultural differences of behaviour, attitude or social practice to inform your discussion.
3. Try to find examples of advertisements for the same brand in different countries. Compare and contrast the respective ads and try to work out the possible differences in local segmentation and positioning and communication issues.
4. What is glocalization? In what ways is the concept relevant to advertising internationally? Offer examples to illustrate your points.
5. Try to think of potential international co-branding opportunities. To explore the coherence of the respective brands, you will need to list all the possible associations and connotations of each brand and discuss their various merits both singly and in conjunction with the co-brand. What opportunities do you think might arise from such co-branding initiatives?

CASE Levi's 501s and the Changing Cultural Meaning of Denim Jeans

Bartle Bogle Hegarty's legendary 1980s TV campaign for Levi's 501s caught the imagination of denim jean wearers the world over. The original ad (called 'Laundrette' because it was set in one) was produced to show all over the world. There was no copy or voice-over, so there were no language problems to overcome. There were lots of shots of the jeans, along with many images suggesting their American provenance, many of them evocative of the style that actors such as Marlon Brando and James Dean brought to 1950s Hollywood movies. The ad was played to a classic music track ('I Heard It Through the Grapevine' by Marvin Gaye). The campaign targeted male jeans wearers aged 15–19 as an influential style leading group, but the ad also appealed to other age groups of both sexes because of the wit of the narrative and sex appeal of the actor. A young man enters a laundrette, takes his clothes off down to his boxer shorts and washes them in a machine, then puts them back on. The astonished reactions of the other customers are nicely contrasted by his laconic style. The male jeans wearer is cast in the same light as Brando or Dean, rebellious, sexy and heroic, a universal symbol of teenage rebellion and timeless cool. The denim market had been in recession and the Laundrette ad began a revival that saw denim jean sales leap by a reputed 800 per cent across all brands.

The stunning success of the 'American hero' style of Levi's ads lasted for a decade until the allure of American provenance faded. The jeans market as a whole lost sales and fragmented into niches, each with a somewhat younger profile and different style values. The Levi's 501s campaign was right for its time and struck a chord in many cultures. Its values seemed to transcend the cultural particularities of the countries in which it was shown; it shamelessly played on Hollywood iconography to confer a powerful sense of style to clothing that was merely everyday workwear in the USA. But by the early 1990s the cultural meaning of denim jeans had changed. For young people who had never heard of Brando and Dean and never saw movies like *Rebel Without a Cause* the American hero ad style meant nothing. Jeans simply meant comfort and informality. They no longer represented rebellion or any distinctively adolescent virtue: how could they when your dad was wearing them?

Later Levi's Campaigns

Levi's changed its approach to cater for niche markets and ended its long successful series of hero ads. One later campaign was, however, international and made a huge impact. A campaign for Levis Sta-Prest range by the UK agency BBH achieved highly successful results by featuring a hand puppet called Flat Eric from an art student's short

▶ film. The character generated huge popular interest and media coverage. The levi.com website received more than 1.1 million hits around the time of the campaign. The research company Millward Brown found it was one of the most popular ads they had tracked in the UK for Levi's. Sta-prest volume sales increased by a factor of 21 in the UK in four months, and the sound track to the ad achieved 2.5 million sales across Europe.[15] The contemporary and youthful feel was continued with a campaign for 'Twisted' Levi's. In 2003 a UK TV campaign produced for Levi's by TBWA/Chiat Day/San Francisco used a similar creative theme to 'Twisted'. The 'Flyweight Jeans' ad showed a Hispanic youth walking through a teeming urban scene with a quirky post-production twist to his gait.[16]

Case Exercises

1. Ask four of your colleagues under 25 years old to list all the associations they can when they think of denim jeans. Now ask four people over 40 years of age to do the same thing. Are the responses different? If so, why do you think this is? Could it be that the two groups are interpreting denim jeans from differing cultural frames of reference?
2. Levi's developed integrated campaigns for some of their products by creating websites that featured the characters in the ad. How can websites add value to marketing communications campaigns? Why does it matter for the brand that the website achieved a million hits in a few weeks? What other ways can you think of which might add value through the use of additional media?
3. What problems of cross-cultural promotional communication did the 1980s Levi's campaign solve and how did it do this? In a group, draw up an outline global campaign plan for a well-known brand of your choice. What particular difficulties arise when conceiving of cross-cultural communication for this particular brand?

Further Reading

Banister, L. (1997) 'Global brands, local contexts', *Admap* (October): 28–30.
De Pelsmacker, P., Geuens, M. and Van den Bergh, J. (2004) *Marketing Communications: A European Perspective*, 2nd edn. London: Financial Times/Prentice-Hall.

Forceville, C. (1996) *Pictorial Metaphor in Advertising*. London: Routledge.

Tanaka, K. (1994) *Advertising Language: A Pragmatic Approach to Advertisements in Britain and Japan*. London: Routledge.

Usunier, J.-C. (1993) *International Marketing – A Cultural Approach*. New York: Prentice-Hall.

Notes

1 Source: WARC email newsletter, 10 May 2004, citing www.adage.com as its source for figures.

2 WARC email newsletter, 14 May 2004: original story in Brand Republic, www.brandrepublic.com

3 With thanks to Kate Laidlar, BCom (University of Birmingham, UK), for conducting the research into the new Mini.

4 Source: www.mini35.co.uk/history

5 Case described in J. Motion, S. Leitch and R. Brodie (2003) 'Equity in Co-branded Identity – The Case of Adidas and the All Blacks', *European Journal of Marketing*, 37(7/8): 1080–94.

6 T.Levitt (1983) 'The Globalisation of Markets', *Harvard Business Review*, (April/May): 92–107.

7 See Schlosser's, *Fast Food Nation*.

8 'Students gear up for Coca-Cola boycott', *Times Higher Education Supplement* (5 December 2003): 52.

9 With thanks to Miyuki Otomo, MBA, who sourced some of these examples of Japanese advertising in 1999/2000 while researching her MBA dissertation at Oxford Brookes University, UK.

10 The examples are adapted with permission from the published IPA awards, 1996, and featured on an IPA video, 'Advertising Works'.

11 I am grateful for these examples, taken from 1999/2000, to Monikha Bohra, BA, who researched her dissertation into Malaysian advertising at Oxford Brookes University.

12 The copy is written in Japanese and translated by Tanaka, 1994: 50.

13 *The Advertising Book: Thailand 1999 Advertising, Marketing and Media Guide* (1999), p. A-10. Bangkok, Thailand: Bangkok Publisher.

14 'Global adspend trends: Asian adspend, a review of its development and future prospects', *International Journal of Advertising*, 17(2)(1998): 255–63.

15 Source: a presentation by Martin Smith, Deputy Chairman of BBH, to the Advertising and Academia marketing educator's forum, IPA, Belgrave Square, London, September 1999.

16 Source: http://ad-rag.com/749.php

Advertising and Ethics

Chapter Outline

Advertising and promotion, as we have seen, occupy a particular cultural space and elicit strongly contrasting judgements from consumers and policy-making bodies. This chapter explores some of the many ethical problems raised. The notion of ethics is briefly addressed and some potentially useful concepts are introduced for analysing the ethical status of advertisements. Advertising policy and regulation are also discussed.

BOX 8.0   Interpreting the Meaning of Offensive Ads

Advertising regulation tends to hinge on debates about the meaning of ads, which often assumes that they carry distinct meanings as with legal or scientific material. As we have seen, much advertising carries both ostensive and covert communication which, in combination, leave the precise intended meaning of the ad open to interpretation. Cook (2001) uses the example of a British TV ad for Cadbury's Flake chocolate bar to illustrate that ads, like any discourse, have connotations that are subtle and personal. Some UK viewers find the Cadbury's Flake ad an amusing and sexually risqué visual metaphor. However, drawing attention to this feature of the ad risks the response that such an interpretation says more about the viewer than it does about the ad. As Cook (2001: 51) states: 'This kind of dispute, with its assumption that meaning resides in the text quite independently of group or individual perceptions, is depressingly common in discussions of advertising'. Of course, the fact that certain individuals, perhaps even large numbers of individuals, might read such a connotation into the ad might well be a stratagem of the advertiser. Such indeterminacy makes ads a more intriguing and more compelling communication. Ads are frequently accused of using sexual suggestiveness and symbolism; they are able to do this without risk of official censure by locating risqué communication within the covert dimension of the ad, where its presence cannot be proven nor agreed upon.

Advertising and Ethical Controversy

Ethics refers to what is right, good or consistent with virtue. The study of ethics is often concerned with abstract principles, and the study of morals is seen as an applied field that focuses on personal behaviour in specific situations. However, the terms are also linked and sometimes used interchangeably, as in 'applied ethics'. Advertising offers complex ethical questions for our consideration. Is it right to advertise to children using the same techniques that are used when advertising to adults? Should advertising be permitted to use imagery and words that shock, offend or insult particular groups? Should advertising intrude on such a large number of social spaces? Indeed, is advertising intrinsically a medium of exaggeration, mendaciousness and illusion? Should it be permitted at all?

Advertising communications commit many acts of dubious ethics in their attempts to seduce us into buying. Some are listed here.

- Overselling
- Exploitation of vulnerable groups
- Deception
- Misuse of lists
- Intruding on privacy
- Promoting racial or sexual stereotypes
- Promoting prejudice against certain vulnerable groups
- Promoting socially or personally harmful values or behaviours
- Offending public taste
- Vulgarity
- Exploiting base motives of greed and envy

The problem with advertising, as we can see straight away, is that ethical judgements in general are predicated on certain values and interests that are not universally agreed upon. People cannot concur on matters of civil governance that are, on the face of it, quite concrete and substantial. How much more difficult is it to agree on the ethical status of an ad when we cannot even agree on what the ad means?

Controversial Advertising

The subjectivity of ethical judgements means that questions of ethics in advertising are clouded in a fog of contrasting opinions, which are often held very strongly indeed. Particular ads or campaigns occasionally become topics of controversy, that is, they attract widely diverging opinions that are expressed in public forums such as newspapers' letter pages, editorials, TV documentaries and even in parliamentary debates in the House of Commons. Of course, not all controversy over advertising is based on questions of ethics. But many disagreements emerge from differing ethical standpoints. Promotional campaigns for brands such as Benetton, Calvin Klein, French Connection UK, 'Opium' fragrance and even for charities such as Dr Barnardo's in the UK have generated much editorial coverage in the media. Often the media stories are given their narrative hook by strongly held opinions about whether an ad or campaign should or should not be permitted.

BOX 8.1   'Opium' Fragrance

Many complaints are received from the public or from special interest groups on the grounds that specific ads are more sexualized than (some people feel is) appropriate and therefore give offence.

In 2001 an ad for Yves Saint Laurent 'Opium' fragrance that featured the model Sophie Dahl (see also p. 42) apparently naked attracted around 1000 complaints to the UK print advertising regulatory authority the Advertising Standards Authority (ASA), considerably more complaints than any other ad that year.[1] In comparison, the most contentious print ad of 2002 attracted some 315 representations to the ASA. Many of the complaints about the 'Opium' ad were from young women. The ad had attracted little attention when it was displayed in the pages of fashion magazines where portrayals of sexuality are the norm. The complaints poured in when the ad was made into a poster and displayed on street billboards. As we have seen in other examples, one important factor in interpreting the meaning of ads is the context in which they appear. The 'Opium' ad was regarded as normal in the context of a fashion magazine but inappropriately sexual on a billboard. Billboards are viewed by a far wider social group. The complaints were upheld and the ad returned to its magazine setting. The public reaction to the 'Opium' ad seems curious given that advertising has become far more sexualized in the last decade. It is now commonplace to see forthright sexual encounters posed

> by beautifully photographed models on TV, billboards and of course in magazines. Often these are for brands of fragrance or clothing (and even ice-cream, as in the case of Häagen-Dazs).

In some cases controversy over advertising is nothing more than a marketing technique: brand owners know that if they can succeed in antagonizing groups other than their own target market there are likely to be useful side-effects, such as free editorial publicity and a stronger brand identity. Sales of Calvin Klein clothing ranges reportedly rose considerably even as child protection groups in the USA and elsewhere were campaigning against the use of apparently very young models in (arguably) sexualized poses in CK ads. The success of the Benetton brand of clothing is legendary, and some Benetton advertising has generated huge amounts of public and official protest. Here the ethical sensibilities of citizens seem to be being exploited for commercial advantage. If the brand personality has a rebellious and anti-establishment aspect, then creating promotions that irritate social authorities is an astute way of endearing the brand to its young target audience.

To some extent media coverage reflects advertising's mature status (in advanced economies) as a part of the media complex. It is only natural that advertising is often used in the editorial content of the popular press and TV shows, given the symbiotic relationship between advertising and other media such as the press, movies and TV entertainment. Substantial sections of the media are funded entirely by advertising revenue. The interests of media vehicles such as TV shows, newspapers or magazines are economically locked into those of brand marketing corporations and other sponsors of advertising. In developing countries advertising is part of the effort to generate increased economic growth. It is therefore bound up with the interests of state officials and governing political parties.

Advertising has only become a topic of public discourse in very recent times. The growth in advertising volume may be part of the reason for this, which has changed the general tone. With so many ads competing for our attention advertisers push the boundaries of content and try more striking kinds of appeal in an effort to get consumers' attention. As noted in Chapter 1, public interest in advertising has also grown in a positive sense. It fascinates people, it has become more sophisticated. It often seems as if TV ads are more entertaining than the actual TV shows. But advertising's high profile makes it an easy target of blame for all manner of social evils. Advertising has evolved into this high-profile hybrid of the entertainment, media and publicity industries because of its economic importance.

Advertising's Economic Function

A consideration of advertising and ethics must take into account the context which gives rise to advertising. Advertising performs the indispensable economic function for capitalist economies of communicating offers to consumers. Through advertising producers are able to expand their markets and thereby take advantage of economies of scale to reduce unit production costs. Through advertising producers can sell the large stocks they produce and stimulate demand for new offers. Through advertising consumers are aware of far more choices than they would be without it. Arguably, consumers enjoy lower prices and better quality because, even after the cost of advertising is taken into account, the competition that advertising facilitates acts in the consumers' interest.

Advertising in the past is valuable historically since it can be used to discover the social norms and conventional values. The implication is that advertising reflects current standards of public taste and decency and modes of public discourse. In other words, we get the advertising we want and deserve. Of course, the 'we' in question is a heterogeneous group with the sharply differing views and values of the communities in which we live. Controversies about advertising, then, can serve a social function as a public forum for revealing fundamental differences between social groups.

The UK Codes of Advertising Practice

It is rare for advertising in the UK to fall foul of the law since it is well-known and most agencies and advertising media have legal advisers to check ads

BOX 8.2   Advertising Law and Industry Regulation

Each country has its own regulatory codes for ads. We saw in Chapter 7 that rulings from government ministers can influence advertising in Malaysia. In the UK advertising must conform to Acts of Parliament such as the Trades Descriptions and Sales of Goods Acts. It must not describe the goods that are for sale incorrectly and those goods must perform the functions claimed for them. Specific categories of advertising must conform to the relevant laws. For example, recruitment advertising in the UK must not contravene the Equal Opportunities Acts and must not discriminate on grounds of sex, race or disability. Other laws have an indirect effect on advertising because they rule on matters such as product safety. Advertising must be careful about claims regarding the efficacy of products or services, offers of prizes or guarantees.

before publication. There is, though, another level of regulation that governs advertising. Voluntary regulatory agencies, funded by the advertising industry, devize detailed codes of practice for advertising and police the industry to ensure compliance. In such a voluntary system, advertising agencies and the sellers of advertising space agree to be bound by the rulings of these agencies, though there is no legal requirement for them to do so. The ASA is the UK body that rules on press and print advertising (it also rules on email and SMS text message advertising), and the Independent Television Commission (ITC) rules on broadcast advertising. From 2004 the ITC became part of an industry-wide regulatory authority, Ofcom. While the rulings of these bodies do not have the force of law they do offer a quicker, more flexible and more efficient regulatory system than the law could provide.

Advertising regulatory bodies have general rules that they try to apply in specific cases through codes of practice for particular circumstances. The UK ASA publicizes its ruling maxim as being to ensure that all (printed) ads are 'Legal, Decent, Honest and Truthful'. The Hungarian code of advertising ethics uses the principles 'Lawful, fair and true'.[2] The ways in which such principles are applied differ in various regulatory systems. In the UK, for example, TV ads are viewed by the Broadcast Advertising Clearance Centre (BACC) before campaign launch to ensure that they conform to the ITC guidelines. The BACC can tell an agency to make substantial (and costly) changes to the ad if it deems these necessary, to ensure that the ITC code of practice is satisfied. There is no pre-vetting procedure for poster or print ads and in the opinion of some commentators this is the reason why some occasionally seem to be more cavalier about offending the public than TV ads.[3] The ASA sometimes require advertisers who have complaints upheld to have future ads vetted before exposure. FCUK poster ads were required to do so after some serious transgressions of ASA rulings.

BOX 8.3   The ASA Rules on 'Secretary'

One ad in *Time Out*, the London listings magazine, and also shown on a poster, promoted a film called 'Secretary' about the sado-masochistic relationship between a secretary and her boss. The ad attracted seven complaints on the grounds that it might 'cause serious or widespread offence, particularly because children would see it' and also because it might appear to 'condone sexual harassment'.[4] The visual showed a woman dressed in mini-skirt and stiletto heels bending over with the strapline 'Assume the position'. The complaints were not upheld; the ASA panel rejected the view that the ad might cause serious or widespread offence.

> It also rejected the charge that the ad could be seen to promote
> sexual harassment because, the adjudication said, the female lead in
> the film 'played a strong and wilful character'. Of course this would
> be quite beside the point for the many people who would see the ad
> but not the film. The adjudication does show that a high level of
> tolerance is afforded in some cases to sexualized advertising.
> But interpreting the ad's imagery and words in a sexualized way
> presupposes some understanding of sado-masochistic sexual practices.

Many countries require advertisers to conform to certain rulings about
content or the mode of exposure.

- In France TV advertising for movies, alcohol, tobacco and
  medicines is not permitted. The ban on advertising books and newspapers
  has recently been changed to allow limited advertising.[5]
- In eastern Europe alcohol advertising is heavily restricted.
- In Sweden TV advertising for toys cannot be directed at children under 12.
- In the UK tobacco advertising is banned.
- In Argentina all advertising was banned on subscription cable-TV
  channels in January 2004.[6]
- In Austria and Finland the use of children in ads is heavily restricted.
  Italy also banned the use of children in advertising in 2003.
- In many predominantly Muslim nations advertising cannot portray
  practices that are not permitted under Muslim law, for example females
  must be fully clothed and wearing headscarves, and advertising of non-halal
  food products is not allowed.
- In Hungary, it is prohibited 'to use erotic and sexual elements in advertising
  for purposes not justified by the object and substance of advertising'
  and no advertisement 'may be such as to reduce the reputation of the
  advertising profession or undermine public confidence in the advertising
  activity'.
- In the UK alcohol advertisements cannot use actors who appear to be
  under the age of 18 and they cannot show people drinking quickly; they
  must sip their drinks.
- In Greece TV advertising of toys to children is banned between 7 pm
  and 10 pm.

Public Complaints about Advertising

The UK regulatory bodies are useful to the advertising industry since they
act as a mechanism for gauging the limits of public tolerance towards
advertising content. If members of the public object to an ad for any

reason they can make a complaint to the ASA or the ITC. Their complaint will then be investigated by a panel who judge it according to their interpretation of the codes of practice. If the complaint is upheld, the regulatory body may tell the agency concerned to take the ad out of circulation and in some cases may censure the agency or the brand commissioning the advertising. The system is reactive because regulatory agencies merely respond to public complaints (and, as noted above, posters are not normally even reviewed before public exposure). All the judgements of the regulatory bodies are published on their respective websites.[7]

FCUK Advertising Regulation

The notorious FCUK acronym used by French Connection UK to brand their clothes has featured in a copious number of ads. It is obviously a risqué English-language joke and has attracted much criticism from social commentators. Clearly, in earlier periods, slang terms or those that sounded like words generally regarded as obscene would not have been permitted in public discourse. After one campaign ten public complaints were received about posters on the grounds that they were offensive. The posters featured the FCUK logo and added lines such as 'my place now' and 'all night long', allowing the viewer to add the missing word. The complaints were not upheld. The advertisers mounted a defence that included video interviews with other consumers who did not find the ads offensive.

BOX 8.4   Cultural Attitudes to Vulgar Language

FCUK campaigns have often been severely criticized by the ASA, but they persist apparently without fear of censure. The reception FCUK has received in other countries with more conservative standards of public discourse has not been so favourable. FCUK posters on public buses were greeted with outrage in Singapore. The strength of public opinion forced the bus company to demand changes.[8] In the UK the increase in the use of swear-words in public life, and especially on TV, has probably softened attitudes and made this kind of campaign possible. FCUK saw its profits rise by 84 per cent in the first half of 2000, the year it launched its campaign in the UK. French Connection's advertisers are acutely aware of the power of the acronym to get attention. A High Court judge in the UK commented that the campaign was 'obnoxious and offensive' because it was a 'euphemism for the obscene expletive 'fuck", according to a report on the BBC News website homepage dated Friday, 3 December)

1999. The French Connection legal representative is quoted as replying that while she and His Lordship might find it offensive, young people who buy French Connection clothing 'find it amusing'.[9] The key point from a brand marketing point of view is that the use of the logo enables the brand to appear cool and anti-establishment in the eyes of some of the young people who are the targeted market segment for FCUK clothes. The more the logo irritates authorities such as High Court judges, the cooler it appears to its own consumers.

A complaint to the ASA about an email advertisement for FCUK condoms was upheld on the grounds that it might 'cause serious or widespread offence'. The ads contained slogans such as 'Practice safe sex, go FCUK yourself' and 'FCUK safely'. The ASA referred to previous adjudications in which it had ruled that 'Fcuk' should not be used in an advertisement if it could be interpreted as 'fuck'. To some it might seem odd that the word 'fuck' is replaced by asterisks in most daily newspapers to avoid offending the readers, but the word 'Fcuk' is displayed on roadside billboards in letters 3 ft high, featured in TV ads and worn on countless T-shirts. It is a clever piece of wit for the advertisers, a striking marketing device for the manufacturers and, for others, an example of the way advertising erodes public standards of speech and behaviour and mocks its own attempts at self-regulation. On one poster FCUK used the slogan 'FCUK the Advertising Standards Authority'.[10] The ASA upheld a complaint about this poster.

It is curious that the advertising industry was once concerned to promote and legitimize mass consumption by representing brand marketing corporations in a paternalistic and socially responsible light. Today, corporate social responsibility (CSR) is a major field of consulting, academic and policy research, but some advertisers seem keen to represent brand corporations in a way that suggests they are openly on the make and do not even pretend that they are making any positive social contribution other than making people snigger.

Reading these judgements offers a useful insight into how the voluntary regulatory system works. The complaints also reflect current public tastes and trends. What was acceptable in advertising in 1950 or 1960 may not be considered acceptable today, and of course, the reverse would also be said to be true – much advertising today would seem excessively vulgar or sexualized to a 1960s audience. Alcohol advertising is a particularly powerful indicator of changing social roles, especially with regard to gender relations. Ads that are taken for granted today might well have provoked heated complaints 10 or 20 years ago, and many ads from earlier times now provoke amusement or astonishment in modern viewers.

Changing Cultural Norms in Alcohol Advertising

The representation of gender in UK alcohol TV advertising has turned full circle over the last 30 years. The ads for Hofmeister lager (mentioned above) featured a man in a bear suit who was the centre of an admiring crowd of young men and women. The ads featuring the lager drinker as a cool, streetwise and charismatic male character allowed females only to be the grateful objects of male lust. These ads replaced those that portrayed females only as domestic drudges. In recent campaigns for Archer's and other alcoholic drinks targeted at females it is female alcohol drinkers who are portrayed as independent, quick-witted and rebellious. The men portrayed are mere accessories. Such advertising would be unthinkable in 1960s Britain.

BOX 8.5   Alcohol Advertising in the UK

The agency DDB London held the Courage beers account for some 25 years. A compilation video was produced which is a revealing document of social history. The tape runs from the 1970s ads with elderly Northern English men enacting scenes of conspiratorial male congeniality in ads for John Smith's Yorkshire Bitter, takes in the change to light beers drunk by younger 'Jack the lad' heroes in watershed advertising moments such as the Hofmeister bear ads, Foster's and Castlemaine XXXX, and ends with ads replete with surreal scenes of 'Mad Max' post-nuclear destruction, self-deprecation and ironic humour. The 1970s UK TV ads for John Smith's and other beer brands were dominated by narratives of males ingeniously escaping nagging wives for the masculine companionship of the pub. Women were portrayed as men's jailers and the pub represented an exclusively male habitat. Such ads were typically not taken to be serious and did not attract widespread complaints, but they would jar with today's heightened sense of political sensitivity over gender relations and sexual politics.

Advertising and Children

In recent years there has been rising concern about the influence of advertising over children worldwide. Entering the words 'advertising to children' on the google internet search engine produced 4,760,000 results. The debate is intense. Arguably, many children under 10 are often unaware that when they are watching TV advertising but what they are watching is in fact an offer to buy. They have not yet grasped the nuances of commerce-tinged communication. They are, therefore, defenceless against the sophisticated techniques of persuasion used by advertisers. Some advertising industry lobbyists claim that in fact children are very commercially aware and are capable of critically evaluating advertising.[11] But the concern about certain topics, (for example the rise in child-onset obesity in the UK, has caused the government to be involved) Ads for Coca-Cola, placed on drinks dispensing machines in Scottish schools have been removed at the insistence of the Scottish Regional Assembly.[12] This reflected a general tide of opinion turning against food and beverage advertising that promoted high-sugar, high-fat, high-calorie and low-protein products.

One general area of ethical concern is the tendency of ads to promote acquisition as a virtue. Adults are in a position to understand that other values are more important to health, happiness and relationships, but children view advertising from a much less well-developed frame of moral reference. In the absence of moderating influences on their development, advertising shows children a world in which you are what you own, and if what you own is not a desirable brand, you are not worth very much at all. At least, that is one possible construction that can be placed on much children's advertising.

There is a total ban on TV advertising directed at children under 12 years old in Sweden, and there are strict limits on TV advertising of toys in Greece. Young children make demands on parents if they want a product that they see advertised. These demands are not necessarily well informed by an understanding either of the nature of commercial messages or of the economic implications for parents.

An opposing point of view to the Swedish one is that early exposure to advertising enables children to develop a critical commercial awareness. However, this view presupposes that the social context children occupy when engaging with commerce is supported by adult attention and counsel. Where this context is lacking, for example when children engage in consumer activities such as watching TV unsupervised, there is no guarantee that they will develop a sophisticated understanding of commerce. Children may not become more critical consumers by watching ads if their domestic circumstances are not conducive to their moral and intellectual development in other ways.

Infantilism in Brand Advertising

The UK Hofmeister beer ads were a turing-point in alcohol advertising not only because they contributed to a major shift in UK beer drinking habits from dark to light beer. They also used imagery attractive to children to advertise adult products. The bear in the ads was developed into a character that children enjoyed and understood. Previously, a man dressed in a hairy bear suit would only have been seen at a children's entertainment. The ads took a cultural sign that denoted kids' entertainment and placed it in an adult context in connection with an adult pastime, beer consumption.

The ITC code of practice today forbids alcohol ads that use imagery attractive to children, but much alcohol advertising seems to be consciously designed to do exactly that. Campaigns for Budweiser have featured animated talking reptiles and recent UK TV ads for Foster's lager show obviously faked but amusing scenes of people being beheaded by animals. The use of imagery in adult advertising that a short time ago one would only associate with children's shows has become commonplace. Many ads on UK TV use animated cartoon characters but are ostensibly directed at adults to sell, for example, branded chocolate, tea and gas central heating.

This trend towards infantilism in advertising reflects the relentless pursuit of novelty in advertising but also springs from the increasing awareness of brand marketers that children are very important to advertisers of adult products. Children enjoy advertising, they remember it and they discuss it. The attention of a child brings a brand into the household and it then becomes a brand that is considered in household buying decisions. Not only do children influence the household budget: they learn about and become conscious of brands at a very early age. Innocent viewing of children's TV shows, such as 'Recess' on the Cartoon Network cable station, are frequently interrupted by ads for personal loans even though one has to be over 18 and in employment to qualify for a personal loan in the UK. Not only do children influence the household budget, they learn about and become conscious of brands at a very early age. Market researchers showing logos for adult brands to kindergarten children find very high rates of recognition for these as well as children's brands.

The Social Role of Brand Recognition

The act of recognition seems to carry emotional significance for both children and adults. It is psychologically reassuring to recognize a feature of one's environment. Brands play on this psychological need. An adult recognizing a brand in a shop will often feel enough reassurance about the quality of the product to buy it, even though similar, non-branded products may be just as good. Of course, many brands really do get their quality control right and the reassurance consumers feel is well-founded. But children do not have the opportunity or experience to critically appraise brands. They simply enjoy recognizing them because it gives them a sense of power over their environment and can signify their knowledge of the world of adults to other children. They keenly shout out the names of brands such as Pepsi, Coca-Cola and children's products when the logos are held up for them to look at. In fact most children, when asked their favourite ad, will cite an adult brand.

Children's recognition of adult brands takes place in the absence of actual brand usage or purchase. The marketing industry in the UK is aware of the tendency for children (and also adolescents, see Ritson and Elliott, 1999) to use advertised brands as symbols of social and group identity. This gives brands a powerful social presence that is quite independent of the product or service associated with it. For brands on sale to children this awareness gives sales an extra leverage because children may pester their parents to buy. The influence goes beyond advertising when sponsorship, product placement or other communications channels are used to insert brands into the daily mediated experience of audiences. When a chocolate brand sponsors a TV soap opera or where condom and cigarette brands sponsor televised sports events, the brand gains exposure to children of all ages.

Children as Objects of Advertising

Ads for children's causes can also generate controversy. Ads for the children's charity Barnardo's have featured a striking image of a baby apparently injecting itself with heroin. Another campaign showed a baby with a cockroach forced into its mouth. The images are unpleasant but are shown ostensibly in the interests of children: charities know that shocking ads generate increased donations and gentle ads are ignored. The ASA allows ads for charities and government public service campaigns such as AIDS awareness or public safety more licence to shock than brand advertising, on the grounds that the cause is good. The Barnardo's ads generated complaints both from the public and from other charities[13], who felt that the ads misrepresented the lives and attitudes of the poor and the socially disadvantaged.

Advertising industry groups lobby to maintain the freedom of advertisers to target children with responsible advertising (for example, in the USA, the Children's Advertising Review Unit). Other groups try to raise awareness of the potentially damaging effects to children of unrestricted advertising. For example, one website for teachers carries an 'Adsmart' resource that points out that a million children start smoking cigarettes each year and that many children aged 3–6 are able to recognize the Joe Camel cartoon character and link it to the cigarette brand.[14] Other sites address internet advertising to children and the special issues of influence and control that this topic raises.[15]

| BOX 8.6   Children in Advertising |

The use of children in advertising can also be controversial.
In Italy it has been common practice to use children as actors in ads because cuteness sells. The use of child actors and models in Italian advertising became subject to strict regulation from 2003.

Ethics and Alcohol Advertising in the UK

Alcohol advertising has become an area of considerable controversy because of possible links with increases in alcohol-related diseases such as cirrhosis of the liver, especially in young British females. TV campaigns such as those for Bacardi rum have attracted complaints that their scenes of wild partying so glamorize alcohol consumption that they may implicitly promote high-risk sexual behaviour in both sexes.

Alcohol Advertising and Social Identity

The World Health Organization made alcohol advertising control a key priority in its anti-alcohol campaigns (WHO, 1988, in Nelson and Young, 2001). The sexualization of alcohol advertising and its role in constructions of gender have been linked with increased alcohol consumption[17] among young women and the promotion of a binge drinking mentality.[18] The website of the ASA (www.asa.org.uk) carries many case reports of complaints made against advertisements of this type.

As cigarette advertising since the 1950s has changed the historical view of femininity and promoted cigarette smoking as a normal social practice of the liberated and independent woman (Williamson, 1978), alcohol advertising is seen to be playing a similar role in locating alcohol brands as discursive resources for the construction of female (and male) social identity (Lemle and Mishkind, 1989; Young, 1995). The changing behaviour of women in relation to alcohol consumption is a particular

---

BOX 8.7   Promotion and Patterns of Alcohol Consumption in the UK

Although very high levels of alcohol consumption per head are not characteristic of the UK, according to recent measures, patterns of alcohol consumption in the UK are unusual. There is, apparently, a culture of drinking alcohol at a young age as a rite of passage and of drinking very large quantities in each session, both dangerous to health. Alcohol brand marketing techniques, especially advertising, that target segmented consumer groups differentiated by age, ethnicity, affluence and attitude to risk-taking have raised particular disquiet. Alcohol-related groups (for example Alcohol Concern[16]) have expressed concern over the role of advertising in these trends. Advertising researchers (Ambler, 1996) have tried to ascertain the influence of advertising over excess alcohol consumption.

concern (Day et al., 2003). Young people are often thought to be particularly vulnerable to this form of marketing (Calfee and Scherage, 1994; Ritson and Elliott, 1999)

Advertising and Obesity

There are now new concerns about the effects of advertising for fast food on growing rates of obesity in the UK and USA. Clearly, the existence of codes of practice and voluntary regulatory regimes does not reassure these groups that the brand marketing and advertising industries are exercising proper social responsibility. Debates about advertising's influence on social issues are invariably clouded in supposition, since there is no proven causal link between advertising and behaviour. Yet while textbooks have regarded this lack of a causal theory of advertising as a problem, the industry itself has managed very well regardless.

In this book we have seen many examples of advertising campaigns for which compelling circumstantial evidence has been gathered showing that they did indeed influence consumer thought and behaviour. Even if this point is accepted, the idea of stricter advertising regulation jars with the freedom of choice that advertising represents. Certain individuals and groups have always been quite favourably disposed towards lifestyles which might be regarded by some as unwise or unhealthy. Advertising presents a smorgasbord of options and consumers have the right to exercise their choices as they see fit. Then again, in some regards advertisers have far more power than individual consumers, especially young or poor ones. The ability of consumers to exercise truly individual choice may be sharply circumscribed where there is an acutely asymmetrical power share between consumers and brand marketing corporations. For all the marketing textbook rhetoric about consumer sovereignty, consumers clearly do not have multimillion dollar budgets to spread their point of view all over the media.

Applied Ethics and Advertising Regulation

Advertising regulation has a connection to ethics since it is concerned with values. Advertising regulation is inspired by an idea of what is good in the applied context of social policy. But there is also a significant difference: by its very nature public policy regulation is political and pragmatic, while ethics in its pure sense is the study of value in itself. Advertising regulation is a political process in that it acts under the influence of complex interests. The values that influence advertising regulation policy are not always those of what is good but those of what is possible in the circumstances. They may also act according to the values of commerce irrespective of what is good, but there is an assumption that the values of commerce are themselves good in that they promote wealth creation and freedom of expression and therefore benefit individuals. While ethical study is concerned with principles of value, it also embraces the study of morals: it asks how ethical principles might be applied by individuals in practical situations.

Advertising regulation presupposes that advertising itself is legitimate because it reflects the interests not only of the public but also of advertisers and brand marketing organizations. Politically, bodies such as Ofcom exist as much to protect advertisers from the wrath of the public as to protect the public from the excesses of advertisers. A mechanism exists through which regulation is seen to act in response to public concerns. Simply having this mechanism serves the important political purpose of superficially democratizing advertising policy, almost regardless of the adjudications that are actually taken. The presence of regulatory systems reassures the public even though they know very well that regulators represent interests that are, in the end, far more powerful than those of any consumers. Nevertheless, there is an implicit ethical dimension to advertising codes of practice. However obscured advertising regulation may be beneath complex webs of interest, its rationale at some level is to make life better or finer than it would otherwise be without regulation.

Advertisers know that many individuals will complain about ads which are not offensive or inappropriate for the majority. The regulators have to try to represent the majority view. In many cases this may leave many individuals feeling disempowered and unhappy. Voluntary regulation does have the virtue of being efficient and, within its limits, responsive. In many cases the UK regulators take ads out of circulation after complaints by as few as a dozen individuals. As a reactive system it depends on public feedback. In a typical year the ASA receives only about 12,000 complaints from individuals or groups about print advertising. If vast numbers of the public do not complain about ads the industry can only assume that people are, in general, happy with the state of advertising.

BOX 8.8   Guerrilla Marketing Tactics Outlawed

In 2004 a North London council authority tired of seeing illegal music business posters plastered over walls by organizations such as BMG and Sony sought recourse through the law.[19] Under anti-social behaviour legislation the chief executives of each company may be held personally responsible for the illegal bill-posting, which saves BMG and Sony an estimated $5 million per year compared with buying advertising space on paid-for media. The executives could ultimately face custodial sentences if they were to be prosecuted under this law.

Ethics and the Good Life

Ethics is broadly concerned with asking questions about the best or most correct way to live, but using terms such as 'better' carries implicit value judgements that complicate ethical debates. The study of **ethics** has its roots in ancient religious and philosophical systems. It entails thinking about which particular acts, thoughts or practices are consistent with living the good life. The good life is one of virtue according to given standards. For many followers of formal religious systems, living the good life means living in accordance with particular moral precepts and codes of behaviour that have been set down by religious authorities. The Jewish, Muslim and Christian religions place great importance on these codes and compliance is compulsory. Observation of the codes is therefore a matter invested with both individual as well as collective significance. But secular ethical systems such as humanism deny the need for prescribed codes of behaviour or belief and aver that reason and experience, not religious authority, are an appropriate basis for all moral decisions. Humanism denies the need for either the fixed codes of morality or the eschatology[20] of formal religions.

Although it is difficult to generalize, it might be fair to draw a distinction between the emphasis on specific behaviours found in the Jewish, Muslim and Christian group of religious traditions and the emphasis on living according to abstract principles found in eastern religions such as Hinduism and the many versions of Buddhism. The former group of religious traditions have abstract principles also such as honesty, compassion, piety, non-violence and so on. The former groups' belief systems are supplemented by rules about wearing head coverings (for females), not eating meat on Fridays, not consuming alcohol or pork, as abstaining from sexual relations outside marriage (compare Chapter 7, where examples were given of religious traditions providing norms of social behaviour in given cultures). Advertising has to negotiate sensibilities in regions where religion is the chief authority. In the West, where secular values predominal, the religious point of view, while still important, becomes one among many.

The Historical Status of Advertising

Discussions on everyday or applied ethics often concern areas not covered by pure ethics. The conduct of business in the twenty-first century creates many situations which were impossible to predict and are difficult to assess according to ancient ethical codes. The great moral and religious thinkers of the past two millennia did not offer thoughts on the ethical status of fragrance advertisements. But many people would not take this omission to indicate that advertising is too trivial to enter ethical discussion. Indeed, religious groups are often among the most active lobbyists about advertising standards. Western philosophy since Socrates has been highly influential in framing the ethical principles of Western religions.

In many periods the social elite regarded commerce as a necessary evil and its exponents as trivial, sinister or both. Traders and shopkeepers were seldom lionized like poets, kings and soldiers in ancient literature. Commerce was not normally considered an occupation worthy of the educated upper classes until late in the nineteenth century. And while advertising may be a part of commerce, it is also a part of literature because it entails the creation of public texts. Advertising might be regarded in the same light as the street-corner storyteller in that it recounts the myths and legends of its time. Of course on another level it is also analogous to the street hawker, and perhaps sometimes to the bar-room comedian.

The Ideas of Plato, Aristotle and Mill and Advertising

Advertising is a uniquely modern form of communication and it is difficult to find enlightening parallels from the past. It might be fair to say, though, that it would come under the area of literature for some ancient thinkers, because it panders to popular sensibility, is seen on a wide scale, and excites and alters the emotional states and values of those to whom it is directed. The poetry of Homer and the plays of Aeschylus were written to produce a similar effect. Plato specifically mentioned Homer's poetry in *The Republic* as a candidate for censorship because of its morally degrading influence on young people. There are those today who would take a similarly stringent view of the influence of advertising.[21]

One might infer that Plato would not appreciate advertising, though as a member of the elite social class he had no need to respect the imperatives of commerce. But Aristotle eschewed social engineering in his *Nicomachean Ethics*, written for his son Nicomachus. He seemed to have little paternalistic interest in the improvement of the plebs but rather adopted the view that individuals should take a balanced approach to personal ethics based on their own predispositions and needs.

Aristotle's view of advertising might be liberal, in the sense that advertising would be seen as but one of the challenges individuals must face in the world.

BOX 8.9   The French Object to Sloggi Underwear Ads

Triumph, the manufacturer of Sloggi underwear, has been asked by the French advertising association to remove its billboard ads featuring semi-naked women posing around poles in a setting that appears like a striptease-show stage. Triumph, which has shown the ads in many European countries, declined to remove them. The *Observer* newspaper noted that placing the billboards near schools taps into a national debate over whether schoolgirls should be allowed to wear the thong style of underwear to school.[22]

By coming to a moderate accommodation with advertising one reaches an ethical standard that is personal to oneself. Aristotle saw the world as a place full of potential deceit, indulgence and temptation that one must learn to live with ethically. He took no account of the need for vulnerable groups to have some degree of protection from the wiles of the powerful.

Another, more contemporary liberal view came from John Stuart Mill, whose book *On Freedom* famously argued that free and unfettered expression and behaviour were necessary prerequisites for a progressive society in which individuals were free to develop according to their needs and imagination. Advertising, it is often claimed, is one form of free expression that should not be regulated. But Mill was aware that some popular voices can drown out those of others and he warned against a 'tyranny of the majority'. In other words, free expression that allowed the loudest and most populist voice to dominate public discourse was not consistent with genuine freedom. Perhaps Mill would have regarded advertising as a tyranny of the majority, because it takes the ordinary person's experience of daily life and reflects it back bathed in the warm glow of consumption. The voice of commerce dominates public discourse and makes alternative (not consumption-oriented) ways of thinking, being and behaving difficult.

Ethical Concepts for Judging Advertisements: Deontology

The ethical status of an act may be judged according to whether it is regarded as intrinsically good or bad. Such judgements can be said to apply a **deontological** principle because they assume that acts in themselves may have an ethical status. For example, if an ad promotes condoms, some people judge this to be ethically inappropriate because their religious beliefs forbid the use of birth control. If an ad uses vulgarity or swear-words it may be judged unethical on those grounds alone if the person making the judgement regards either of these as not to be uttered in public.

Deontological judgments, then, rely on preconceived moral values. In some cases there would be wide agreement on the ethical status of an ad if, say, it promoted something that was illegal. In matters which do not in themselves have legal status, like eating, everyday social interaction or drinking, deontological judgement would depend on a person's individual sense of right and wrong. Clearly, deontological judgements regarding the ethical status of advertisements have limited use where there is a wide divergence of views on what is intrinsically good or bad.

Consequentialist Approaches

Where people cannot agree whether an ad is intrinsically good or bad in itself, they may be able to agree on its ethical status by evaluating whether the consequences of showing the ad are likely to be good or bad. Good or bad in this case may be concerned with positive or negative social effects. For example, an ad promoting the use of condoms in safe sexual behaviour might be shocking to some who feels that the public depiction of sexual relations in any context is indecent and therefore wrong. However, if the consequences of the ad were that fewer members of the general public became infected with sexually transmitted diseases then the consequences of the ad might be good, at least from the public health point of view.

Utilitarianism, the doctrine that acts should be judged on the criterion of the greatest good for the greatest number, is a **consequentialist** doctrine. Advertising that has socially good or benign consequences would be permissible when judged according to a consequentialist ethical approach. Of course, we still have the problem that deontological and consequentialist approaches entail implicit value judgements about what is a bad act in itself or what is a good consequence. But it is perhaps useful to refer to ethical concepts such as these in an effort to clarify the intractable questions of advertising and ethics. It may be useful to refer to one final case of controversial advertising in order to reflect on what kinds of ethical approach might prove most useful.

How Might We Apply Ethical Analysis to Advertising and Promotion?

Benetton campaigns are perhaps the most fruitful source of material for examining the cultural status of advertising with particular reference to the ethical dilemmas of advertising communications. The case at the end of this chapter (p. 205–6) outlines the circumstances by which Benetton advertising earned such notoriety. Benetton ads have probably generated more high-profile public controversy across the world than any other campaign in brand advertising. But they are very different from, say, the Calvin Klein, Yves St Laurent 'Opium' or French Connection FCUK ads discussed above. Unlike these, the Benetton ads did not display sexually provocative scenes or use vulgar words.

The Benetton ads which generated most complaints (for example, the kissing nun and priest, the images of men condemned to death under the American penal system, the dying AIDs victim and his family, the black woman breast-feeding a white baby, the black and white hands handcuffed together) did so on a wide variety of grounds. Some generated outrage and offence, though in most cases the outrage was expressed by relatively small groups who interpreted the advertising in terms of their own particular political beliefs. For many complainants the use of certain imagery in the ads was wrong *per se:* in a deontological sense it offended their code of moral decency, although the use of similar images in other contexts such as news programmes would probably not have been seen in the same light.

Few had complaints on explicitly consequentialist grounds, although some might say that were such images allowed it could lead to adverse social consequences. For example, the theme of racial integration was seen as a bad social consequence by racist consumers. And it should be remembered that the great majority of people who viewed the ads saw no reason to complain at all, although reading a default position into non-complaints is problematic. Inertia may prevent offended people actively registering their disapproval, so advertising regulation has to assume that complaints received reflect a larger body of opinion.

Some people felt that the Benetton ads were exploiting vulnerable groups rather than raising awareness of their plight, although permission had been given for the more intrusive ads such as the scene of a man dying of AIDS with his grief-stricken family. Other ads were misinterpreted, for example the black-skinned hand photographed handcuffed to a white hand. The ad does not necessarily imply that the white hand belonged to a police officer. That implication was, revealingly, read into the ad by some British viewers. Other ads revealed the prejudices of consumers, such as where posters of a newborn baby and of a breast-feeding woman were greeted with complaints. The fact that the breasts were black-skinned and the baby white exacerbated the effect for the racially sensitive. Nevertheless, as Oliviero Toscani pointed out, there seems no intrinsic reason why such images of life should be regarded as objectionable. Of course, as we have seen in this book, the interpretation of the meaning of a cultural sign as in the case of an ad is highly influenced by the context. It may not have been these images in themselves that generated the complaints; it may have been seeing the images as advertising that was the difficult thing for people to understand.

What is Appropriate Material for Advertising Communication?

Toscani's final campaign, the death row series of ads, was commercially ill-advised and insensitive to those whose lives were damaged by crime. It did, however, have an ethical position at its core, the case against capital punishment. Capital punishment is a legitimate topic for public debate. What Toscani did that was new was to frame the issue in a commercially loaded context. However strong the views people hold on the topic, they can accept debate about it in the context of late-night TV talk shows or Sunday-morning radio shows. Many people could not reconcile the topic with its context when it was seen as an advertisement. The fact that the matter was directly personalized in a way that it rarely is in current affairs debates clearly made a difference, in addition to the context. The (alleged) perpetrator was photographed and the family of the victim knew his identity.

But the negative reaction to this campaign, seen most strongly in the USA, raises another paradox. People often complain about advertising's triviality, but when Toscani raised non-trivial matters in advertising the reaction was very mixed. His ads were sometimes accused of using serious topics such as crime, racism and AIDS to sell sweaters. It was almost as if people felt that advertising had stepped beyond its cultural remit. Ads that address serious or unpleasant matters for good causes sometimes generate uneasy reactions, such as the Barnardo's or National Children's Homes (NCH) charity campaigns described above (p. 194). But such ads are generally accepted because they are in a good cause. Toscani claimed that his Benetton campaigns were not about selling knitwear but about raising the profile of social issues. He enjoyed the power of having every high street and magazine in the world display his photographs of the social world he saw around himself. His claims about the awareness-raising motives for Benetton advertising were greeted with cynicism. It is clear, though, that the campaigns met both objectives to some extent. They generated a powerful brand image for Benetton in association with social values, and they simultaneously placed the social issues they raised high on the public agenda.

Whether they did so in a way that was constructive is another question. Toscani argued that images of war, starvation and AIDS had become banal and clichéd when seen in the conventional news media. As advertisements they had a fresh impact. Toscani's justification for the advertising could be seen as somewhat disingenuous given his expert knowledge of the cultural role of mediated communications. Images of human suffering have arguably become news media clichés but is not their use in advertising simply drawing attention to the cliché and not to the suffering involved?

The Ethical Status of Benetton Campaigns

What, then, of the ethical status of Benneton ads? Many of the most controversial print and poster ads did not seem to contravene formal advertising codes of practice. The creative themes evaded regulatory codes by being so novel. It had simply not occurred to the people who devise advertising regulations that anyone would want to publish photographs of copulating horses, newborn babies or breast-feeding mothers in the name of brand advertising. The regulations did, of course, cover consumers' feelings of offence or disgust in response to ads, but reactions to the Benetton ads were very mixed. Some newspapers refused to publish certain ads because of the sensitivities of their readers. In fact, in some cases it seemed as if the ads raised more objections from corporate interests, ostensibly fearful of a consumer backlash, than they did from consumers themselves. It cannot be denied, though, that the negative reaction to the death row ads was serious and sincere. The Benetton ads were contrived to be difficult to categorize in terms of codes of practice or ethics. They crossed boundaries by using images of social reality in a brand advertising context. In some cases they seemed to reveal the prejudices of the people who complained about them with regard to racial stereotypes or public (and cross-racial) breast-feeding. They do illustrate the deeply provisional nature of social agreement on advertising as it is expressed through codes of practice and tacit agreements between advertisers, media owners and the public. The Benetton campaigns seemed to open up some of these tacit agreements to scrutiny and this made for uncomfortable viewing. They mocked the notion of ethics in advertising by questioning and challenging advertising's cultural role and status.

Advertising is normally a purely commercial text that links images of health, happiness and success with consumption of marketed brands. Images of social reality are normally confined to news media or government-sponsored campaigns. Toscani's advertising created a new form of cultural communication but one that generated unease. Advertising as a whole is a powerfully ideological medium, perhaps the 'super-ideology' of the age (Elliott and Ritson, 1997). It expropriates values and signs from non-commercial human culture and assimilates them into a text that promotes consumption above all else. Toscani's work simultaneously revealed and undermined advertising's ideological character and this created a frisson of unease that, perhaps, revealed the profound cultural significance of advertising. The tacit agreements and interpretive consensus that surround the public face of advertising were fractured. Ethical judgements applied to advertising were seen in themselves to be based on highly provisional and culturally sensitive notions of value.

Review Exercises

1. How is advertising regulated in the UK? Describe the voluntary system of regulation that is present in such countries as the UK and France. Illustrate how it is applied with examples from the ASA website.
2. Discuss the ethical status, as you see it, of three specific print or TV ads. What ethical concepts might you employ to bring some intellectual clarity to the debate? In your view, do these concepts bring clarity to the debate?
3. Using the ASA website, print off five recent adjudications on ads for which you can obtain printed copies. Ask a group of your peers for their views on the ethical status of each of these ads. Discuss the views expressed and compare them with the ASA adjudications. What do the various opinions reveal about the people who hold them?
4. Is advertising ethical? How can ethical principles be applied fairly with integrity in a diverse, market-driven society? Use practical examples and theoretical concepts to discuss your response to this question.

5. Examine the arguments for and against advertising regulation.
What might be the result if advertising were not subject to any
regulation at all?

CASE Benetton[23]

Perhaps the most well-known examples of ethically controversial
advertising come from Toscani's Benetton campaigns. Oliviero
Toscani, one of Italy's top advertising photographers, was given
sole control over Benetton's advertising by Luciano Benetton in
the early 1980s. He decided to change the focus of Benetton
advertising from product to lifestyle. Toscani's work turned
Benetton from a quality, local clothing company into one of the
world's most recognized brands. From 1984 the creative
executions increasingly carried Toscani's personal agenda of social
injustice into the commercial world. The 1984 campaign featured
teenagers of different races together with the slogan 'All the
Colours of the World'. The print and billboard campaign was
distributed by JWT in 14 countries and generated complaints
from racists in South Africa and also the USA and the UK.
Toscani, suitably encouraged, continued with the United Colours
of Benetton theme for subsequent campaigns. From 1989
Benetton took all its advertising production in-house to give it
complete independence and control. The ads were consciously
provocative to racial sensibilities. They outraged many consumers
while continuing to give a massive profile to the Benetton brand.
One poster featuring a black woman holding a white baby to her
naked breast generated such protest in the USA that it was
withdrawn. For some consumers it evinced an era of slavery. For
others, public breast-feeding itself was offensive. The ad also
received more praise than any other Benetton visual and won
awards in five European countries. Other ads continued the theme
of racial juxtaposition. One featured a black hand handcuffed to a
white hand. It generated complaints in Britain where it was
assumed that the white hand belonged to a police officer. London
Transport refused to display the poster.

Other themes of social injustice attracted Toscani's attention.
Ads featured brightly coloured condoms and a dying HIV-positive
man surrounded by his grieving family. They also featured a wide
variety of striking images, including a snogging priest and nun,
copulating horses, a newborn baby with its umbilical cord still
attached and HIV-positive people with an HIV stamp on their naked
body. Some newspapers refused to publish particular ads, afraid of

the backlash from irate customers or other advertisers. Reaction to the ads was mixed. The French advertising regulation body, the Bureau de Vérification de la Publicité (BVP) recommended the withdrawal of the poster showing the kissing priest and nun. The same poster won an award in the UK. In the UK the newborn baby ad (titled Giusy) generated 800 complaints to the ASA and was withdrawn. It was also banned in most other European countries, but it won an award in Switzerland.

The Turning Point for Toscani

The controversial themes continued and were often greeted with (by now predictable) outrage from various parties. Toscani's last campaign for Benetton preceded his leaving the company in 2000. As Benetton had gained a bigger reputation for provocative advertising, sales had begun to suffer in some markets. Occasionally, Benetton retailers themselves had suffered; some shops were even vandalized. Several hundred Benetton shops were closed down in the USA. In an attempt to recover lost ground there, Benetton entered an agreement with Sears to put Benetton outlets in their stores across the country.

Toscani, meanwhile, decided to raise awareness of the plight of the thousands of young black men on death row in America's jails. He gained entry to a prison, took photographs of some of the prisoners and used them in a poster campaign. Although the permission of the prisoners and their families had been obtained, Toscani had neglected to tell the prison authorities what he was planning. This oversight added to the furore when the campaign was launched. Families of the victims of the murderers pictured in the campaign waged a passionate protest against Benetton and picketed the Sears stores. The campaign against Benetton gained pace in the USA and Sears cancelled their agreement. Toscani left Benetton three months later, after 18 years in charge of their advertising.

Case Exercises

1. The Benetton campaigns illustrated that advertising discourse, while loose and flexible as a category, also has limits to which audiences were sensitive. In other words, some people felt that certain Benetton ads had violated the rules of advertising discourse by raising issues and using images that were not suitable in the contexts used but were appropriate only for news and documentary media. Discuss the limits that seemed evident from the reactions to three different Benetton ads.

▶

2. The Benetton ads created controversial reactions because they did not obviously contravene existing regulatory codes. Discuss the question of whether this reveals weakness in the current codes of advertising practice in various countries. Are codes of practice ultimately impotent against creativity? If so, how can societies defend themselves against advertising?

3. Arguably, Benetton dispensed with its controversial advertising themes when the commercial consequences became clearly adverse. What do you feel this reveals, if anything, about advertising discourse and its relationship with ethics?

Further Reading

Hackley, C. (1999b) 'The meanings of ethics in and of advertising', *Business Ethics: A European Review* 8(1): 37–42.

Kitchen, P.J. and Hackley, C. (1999) 'Ethical perspectives on the post-modern communications leviathan', *Journal of Business Ethics* 20(1): 15–26.

Macklin, M.C. and Carlson, L. (eds) (1999) *Advertising to Children: Concepts and Controversies.* Thousand Oaks, CA: Sage.

Manchanda, R.V., Dahl, D.W. and Frankenberger, K.D. (2003) 'Does it pay to shock? Reactions to shocking and nonshocking advertising content among university students', *Journal of Advertising Research* 43(3): 268–279.

Pollay, R.W. (1986) 'The distorted mirror – reflections on the unintended consequences of advertising', *Journal of Marketing* 50 (April): 18–36.

Notes

1 Reported on Guardian Unlimited website, 'Naked Sophie is most offensive advert of 2000', http://media.guardian.co.uk/advertising/story/0,7492,477315,00.html

2 The Hungarian code of advertising ethics http://www.mrsz.hu/eng_ethics.html

3 Source: Conor Dignam, editor of *Media Week*, quoted on 18 December 2003 on a BBC news website, http://news.bbc.co.uk/1/low/uk/140490.stm

4 ASA adjudication, published on www.asa.org.uk/adjudications

5 After a 35-year ban, books and newspapers were allowed to advertise on cable and satellite TV in France from 1 January 2004. Source: *The Times*, 26 December 2003: 15, 'Burrell's book in historic TV advert'.

6 Source: WARC email newsletter, 3 January 2004. With a penetration of 50% of Argentinian households the cable-TV advertising market was the biggest in South America. The COMFER (Comité Fédéral de Radiodefusion) the Argentinian regulatory body, argued that too much time was being given over to advertising during movies which subscribers had paid to see.

7 www.asa.org.uk

8 BBC news website for Asia-Pacific region at http://news.bbc.co.uk/1/hi/world/asia-pacific

9 http://news.bbc.co.uk/1/hi/uk/548249.stm

10 Source: BBC News online web pages.

11 http://www.toy-tma.com/industry/publications/fbcurrent/advertising.htm

12 Source: story on World Advertising Research Centre newsletter 30 December 2003: 'Coke to pull ads from Scottish schools'. www.warc.com

13 'Barnardo's ad provokes storm of protest', feature by social affairs editor, John Carvel, 13 November 2003, on Guardian Unlimited website at http://society.guardian.co.uk

14 http://scienceu.fsu.edu/content/adsmart/docs/tobaccolist.html

15 http://www.mediafamily.org/facts/facts_internetads.shtml

16 www.alcoholconcern.org.uk

17 See Cristol, H. (2002) 'Teen drinking on the rise', *The Futurist*, Washington 36(4):14.

18 UK *Sunday Times*, 17 August 2003: 'Alcohol lads' ads to be sexed down'.

19 Source: WARC email newsletter 4 June 2004, original story in *Financial Times*.

20 Eschatology, the doctrine of last things, e.g. concerning death, judgement and resurrection.

21 This section draws on ideas in a paper by Hackley and Kitchen (1999).

22 Reported on http://ad-rag.com/106244.php

23 Further information on 'Benetton Campaign Causes Controversy', *Daily Mirror*, www.dedham.k12.ma.us/dhs/mirror/February2000/Benetton.htm, and for a detailed case study on Benetton see the INSEAD-CEDEP 'United Colours of Benetton' case, 1996, available through the European Case Clearing House, Cranfield, Surrey.

Advertising Research

Agencies act as intermediaries between consumers and brand
marketing organizations. In order to fulfil this role they need to have
research knowledge and craft skills that can generate actionable
consumer and marketing insights. The aims, methods, purpose and
relevance of research are all matters for intense debate both within
agencies and between agencies and clients. This chapter outlines the
main research techniques used in the field and sets this within
a discussion of the major debates.

BOX 9.0 The Limits of Pre-launch Testing*

Valentine Appel, a revered figure in advertising research, once
claimed that research of finished commercials could do two things
well. One was to eliminate 'dogs', advertising that is really bad.
The other was to select advertising that is really good. Often,
however, really innovative advertising does not test well because it
cannot be captured by the rational measures of much advertising
research.

   Given the limitations of advertising research to pre-test
commercials, one wonders why it is required. The answer is partly
political: advertisers need to gain budget approval from many
individuals. They therefore need statistical evidence, even if it merely
supports the obvious. The other, related reason is that advertisers are
highly risk-averse. Advertising research can provide reassurance. It is
close to a truism that much advertising is neither good nor bad, just
mediocre. Research can test three executions, for example, and show

if one is preferred to the others. The advertising manager has the basis for a decision based on concrete numbers, on science, even though the chosen commercial is not really different from the rejected ones. It makes little difference what he or she selects. Cynical? Yes. Reality? Yes. Advertising testing may not be important for decisions but it is necessary for careers.

*This vignette was kindly contributed by Professor Arthur J. Kover, former editor of the *Journal of Advertising Research*.

The Contested Role of Research in Advertising

Guiding Assumptions About How Advertising Works

The British mathematician and economist John Maynard Keynes was once reported to have commented that most politicians were 'the slaves of some defunct economist'. In advertising, conventional ideas on how advertising works, like ideas on economic policy, bear the faded signature of past theorists. What this means is that much research in advertising is based on taken-for-granted assumptions. It is true that science (and social science) cannot be judged on assumptions alone. Very often these are provisional and have less importance than the predictions that a theory yields. Nevertheless, it is important to understand what they are.

Development of Professional Advertising Research

Advertising research has a long history. Agencies have typically been highly sensitive to the need to know as much as possible about the client's business, the market sector and the relevant consumers before devising an advertising strategy. The advertising legend David Ogilvy (1983) points this out emphatically. He refers to the need for advertisers to do their homework, in other words, to find out as much about the client's problems as they can before trying to devise solutions. According to Richards et al. (2000: 20), JWT began to commission research in 1916 to acquire greater understanding of the social and demographic trends and structures that formed consumer groups. Universities were called upon to add methodological sophistication. For example, the behavioural psychologist John B. Watson was diverted from his university career to become an advertising man for JWT. Behavioural psychology aspired to provide a unified theory of human learning and behaviour. If the behaviourists were right, then ads could be conceived as teaching devices, changing human behaviour through **operant conditioning** and behavioural reinforcement.

BOX 9.1   Advertising Research and Organizational Politics

It was reported that a new campaign for a carbonated drink brand departed from the usual sip, smile 'n' sing format and took a less obvious narrative route, with the dramatic resolution ('the brand as hero') at the end of the ad. In a copy-test the ad was shown to a group of franchise-holders who were all surprised when the usual image of the brand being consumed by an ecstatic (and attractive) actor did not appear within the first five seconds. The franchisers were not impressed by the agency's creative execution and demanded that the ad be scrapped and replaced by another one in the old format. The client advertising director, who had agreed to the new style, was removed from his post as a result of the bad test results. Many creative professionals deplore this kind of pre-launch testing.

Agencies followed the trend for research and established their own research departments. The distinct fields of audience, attitude and mass communications research later developed. Eventually, many research departments that had begun in advertising agencies became separate market research agencies.

Hedges (1997: ii), writing on the uses of research in advertising, maintained that 'What we need urgently in this field is a better and clearer understanding of what we are about – a longer and broader perspective – will lead to a reordering of priorities'. There is a view among some practitioners that research in advertising is often used in the same way that a drunk uses a lamp-post, for support rather than illumination. Clarity about the aims, limits and purpose of research can help to focus the illumination it can offer.

An Academic/Practitioner Divide?

Academic researchers have drawn on models and techniques developed by advertising people and tested or adapted them to different situations. For example, some of the academic research into creativity and idea-generating techniques has drawn on models originally developed in advertising (Osborn, 1963). In turn, the advertising profession has arguably been more receptive to academic ideas than any other marketing or management field. Most professional advertising research techniques began life in psychological, sociological or anthropological studies. But in spite of sharing some common concepts, research can mean very different things in the two fields.

Some advertising practitioners feel that the contribution to the field from academic empirical social science has been negligible (Hedges, 1997: 86). Entire volumes on advertising research have drawn attention to the difference in mentality that divides academics and practitioners on the topic (see Wells, 1997). Cook and Kover (1998) feel that this divide is based on language. They draw on work by Wittgenstein to suggest that the two professional fields of academic and practitioner research in advertising are separated by differing language games. Hackley (2003g) maintained that the divide could also be understood in terms of differing **representational practices** in the two fields. In other words, each field applies quite different criteria to judge the value and contribution of research and consequently research in each field is often described in quite different terms.

Most obviously, professional advertising research has to be justified in terms of outcomes or practical implications in a way that academic research does not. It has to pass the 'so what' test. But academic research has to be justified in theoretical terms. Indeed, much academic advertising research is entirely self-referential, because it makes sense only in terms of its connection to other academic theories. Of the 250 or more advertising research studies reviewed by Vakratsas and Ambler (1999), a small number derived from, or were used in, practical advertising management.

BOX 9.2   Viral and Buzz Marketing Seeks Legitimacy

In 2004 BrandRepublic (UK) reported that agencies including GD & SM Advertising (USA), VM-People (Germany), Go Viral (Denmark), KetaKeta (Israel), Spheeris (France) and Maverick Media, The Viral Factory and Digital Marketing Communications (all UK) were among the founding agencies of a new trade body, the Viral & Buzz Marketing Association. The WARC email Newsletter[1] reported that the new body would establish a code of best practice and establish international collaborations and a case study resource. From a research perspective, this reflects rapid developments in marketing communication practice and offers a useful source of data for research. But research in itself can offer no insight into general principles or even rules of thumb for practice. Research is merely a name for a broad collection of theoretical assumptions that govern what may logically be inferred from empirical data. Research requires that the particular theoretical assumptions in a given case are clearly specified. Buzz and viral marketing initiatives face the same centuries-old problems of accountability and effectiveness as mainstream advertising.

Nevertheless, there is common ground. Professional advertising research uses many concepts and techniques that have their origin in academic work, even if the theoretical aspect of academic research is largely ignored by practitioners. As Kover (1995) has pointed out, advertising professionals generally have little time for theory. Hackley (2003d: 319) reported the comments of advertising professionals in top UK and US agencies. One creative professional admitted that 'we hate research', and a senior account planner explained that 'there's an analysis of what a client does, the category of an industry then starting to see what information is missing and what we might need – we also have a group called the Discovery Group and they do ethnographies'. This quote perhaps illustrates the dual character of practitioner research in advertising. It is pragmatic and driven by the particulars of a client's problem, but it also draws on theoretical concepts from the academic world for its operating vocabulary.

Types and Uses of Advertising Research

Agencies place different degrees of emphasis on applying and using research at various stages. Advertising research may be undertaken before, during and after the campaign is devised and launched.

Initial Research

Initial research will often be undertaken as soon as the client's brief is received. It will establish basic parameters of knowledge about the brand, its market, its consumers and competitors, and the way that the brand fits

Table 9.1 Research in the Advertising Development Process.

Stage in the process	Types of research typically undertaken
Client brief	Secondary research into market, business, brand, competitors
Advertising strategy	Primary studies into consumer groups and consumption practices
Creative brief	Anthropological and/or focus group studies of target consumers
Creative development	Focus and/or observational studies of consumer response to creative stimuli
Pre-launch testing	Copy-testing, attitude scaling with finished creative executions
Post-launch testing	Tracking studies, awareness studies, sales response tracking

in with the client's business. All of this work will inform the communications brief, the agency's interpretation of the client brief.

Much of this initial research is likely to rely on secondary data, that is, data already recorded, such as commercial market reports (like Mintel). Professional research organizations produce panel data, for example, that records the purchasing or behaviour of a selected group of consumers over a long time scale. Industry bodies such as JICRAR[2] and OAA[3] in the UK publish data on audience radio listening habits and outdoor poster coverage respectively. Many agencies will also undertake their own primary research in order to understand the client and the business fully.

Creative Research

Creative research will then be undertaken in which the thoughts and behaviour of relevant groups of consumers are assessed in relation to the brand and its categories. The aim will be to generate actionable insights that might form the basis for the creative work. This research will often use **primary** qualitative or first-hand data, such as transcripts of focus or discussion groups, transcripts of in-depth interviews with consumers, or video footage of naturalistic experiments in which consumers are asked to use the product while being observed. This creative research will often be undertaken before writing the creative brief.

BOX 9.3   Research Insights Informing Creative Work

Creative research often uses qualitative data to generate insight into the way consumer groups understand a given brand and its positioning. In a European campaign for VW cars, research found two related insights that drove the advertising for the Polo and Golf ranges.[4] Firstly, the research found that consumers thought they were quite knowledgeable about car prices, but in fact they had very little knowledge about actual pricing structures. Secondly, the research found that consumers had an impression that VW cars were more expensive than other cars in their class. In the case of the new VW small car range, this was incorrect. However, the perception clearly held advantages, since it carried an implication of superior quality. The creative problem was compounded because consumers in Europe and the UK were resistant to advertising that emphasized a price benefit. Not only that but creative staff were bored by a brief that asked them to merely say that 'this price is lower than the others' (called 'a prices brief').

> Few creative awards are won on a prices brief. As a solution
> the agency produced a creative brief that described a need to
> make ads that were telling but off-beat in their quirky humour.
> With humour, the campaign could preach about price without
> alienating or boring consumers. The brief resulted in a campaign
> that ran for over 10 years, based on funny ways to tell consumers
> that they were wrong about VW pricing. Awards were won
> and VW increased its market share substantially. The research
> insight that drove the creative work was derived from
> qualitative data.

Copy-testing and Tracking Studies

Copy-testing prior to campaign launch is carried out in order to try to
predict the likely reaction of consumers to the finished campaign.
Subsequently, after campaign launch, more research will assess the effect
of the campaign against the objectives set for it. These **tracking studies** are
very important for agencies since they constitute a record of the campaign's
evolution and its marketing results. They can provide evidence for clients
that the campaign accomplished the objectives set for it. Case histories
that are written up from successful campaigns provide a learning resource
and, if they are submitted to awards competitions, can be useful PR for
the agency itself.

Methods of Advertising Research

Four sets of contrasting adjectives might help to categorize methods in
advertising research. These are primary/secondary; **qualitative/quantitative;**
formal/scientific; and informal/intuitive. Unfortunately, most research
falls across or between these binaries, but they do offer a useful basis for
discussion. This section offers some examples of the kinds of advertising
research that fall into these categories.

Experimental Research Designs

Advertising has a long tradition of formal-scientific experimental
research. For example, in campaign pre-testing experiments a selected
audience is gathered to watch an ad. The audience presses buttons on
their seat arms to indicate whether they like or dislike particular parts of
the ad. The results are presented in graphical form. In less technologically

enhanced conditions the audience may be given questionnaires to fill out after they have watched the ad, to determine how much or how little they liked it and how much they recalled various components.

This kind of research (as noted above, often known as 'copy-testing') is sometimes conducted according to formulae that dictate the criteria that an ad has to meet in order for the campaign to be launched. If the results are not favourable then the ad may be changed or scrapped. Many creative staff feel that quasi-experimental copy-testing techniques are based on mistaken assumptions about how audiences engage with advertising and therefore miss the point. For many account managers and clients, copy-testing offers a succinct and measurable means of assessing creative executions before the expense of a full campaign launch.

Some experimental advertising research uses biological measures of attention and sensory stimulation. The **psycho-galvanometer tests** measure the activity of sweat glands with carefully placed electrodes and assess the degree of excitement the consumer feels at all times throughout an ad viewing experience. If images in the ad are very uninteresting as judged by the test, they may be changed. The **eye tachistoscope test** tracks the viewer's eye movements across an ad so that the experimenter can judge which bits are the most appealing. They can also see how the eye is drawn through the images. Today the latest trend in biological consumer research involves **magnetic resonance imaging** (MRI) scanners to see which parts of a person's brain are stimulated by particular visual, auditory or other sensual experiences. Since particular parts of the brain can be matched with specific activities and sensations, MRI research holds out the possibility that products and ads could be devised that stimulate predicted responses. It could be argued, though, that such control over consumers is not attainable given the idiosyncracy of consumers and the complexity of the consumer-marketing relation. Furthermore, the brain exhibits plasticity in the sense that different brain regions can support the same physiological function in certain circumstances (such as brain injury), so isolating given activities to specified regions of the brain is extremely difficult.

Survey Research and its Limitations

Formal/scientific primary research into consumer attitudes may be conducted using questionnaire-based attitude surveys. As with experimental designs, these will often be analysed using quantitative methods such as statistical tests of significance. Questionnaire surveys are often most useful where existing knowledge is to be examined in a larger or new audience. For example, if a consumer discussion group revealed that people felt that their music buying was more important to them than their daily newspaper purchase, this could then be tested on a wider scale with a questionnaire survey. For exploring entirely new areas, qualitative research can often be best because the data are not confined to the precise questions that are asked.

There are other potential problems with questionnaire surveys. They often ask people questions upon which the respondent has never been asked to express an opinion before. The scaled questions encourage a response. This process may create a false circumstance in which an attitude is revealed, for example, which does not exist outside the context of a questionnaire survey. A related problem is that people are notoriously forgetful when reporting their own behaviour. If we are asked about typical purchasing behaviour, weekly expenditure, preferred retail outlets or other factual information, we often get it wrong. Finally, the sampling issues associated with survey questionnaires are always difficult to resolve. Statistically, results of surveys cannot be generalized across a wider population unless the sample is randomly generated. In most social studies researchers make do with samples that are representative of the population in which they are interested even though for statistical purists this may mean that the results cannot be **generalized** across the wider population. Rather, the findings tell us only about the small number of people who filled in the questionnaires.

The survey industry is big: political polls, opinion polls and questionnaire-based, market research studies are commissioned daily at great cost. As with all research, questionnaire surveys can only be useful if they are designed carefully to achieve specified outcomes. The interpretation of findings is difficult and must be done in full knowledge of the limitations of these methods.

BOX 9.4   Self-reports as Behavioural Data

While qualitative, research-generated self-reports of feelings and emotions may be sincere, self-reports of actual behaviour can be far less accurate. This was well illustrated in one retail research study in which security cameras were used to monitor shoppers' in-store browsing behaviour. The research aim was to generate insights that might help improve in-store retail design or merchandising techniques. A sign had been erected at the store entrance warning customers that their behaviour might be filmed for research purposes. On exiting from the store researchers approached the consumers to ask them to explain their behaviour. But the exit interviews proved less than informative. When asked why they lingered for so long at one display, or why they moved from display x to display y, most consumers had little recollection of their movements and some insisted that they had not behaved in the way described, even when confronted with the film evidence. We are not very good, as consumers, at remembering our behaviour. We may be better at reflecting on the general emotions that our consumer behaviour reflects.

BOX 9.5   Syndicated Panel Data

Advertising agencies do not always conduct their own survey research and buy the use of secondary data produced by commercial research organizations. Major research companies such as A.C. Neilson and AGB publish syndicated panel data based on continuous surveys of consumers. Studies may investigate trends in, for example, household brand shopping and usage, TV viewing, radio listening or internet usage. The general information contained in these surveys can be useful for advertising professionals to understand the underlying trends and behaviours that are typical in a given product or service category. Nielson internet research, for example, recently claimed that the 10 websites that had most impact on UK consumers were Google, eBay, Amazon, easyJet, Kelkoo, Friends Reunited, Blogger, Napster, Microsoft Outlook and AOL Instant Messenger.[5] Surveys such as this can offer general insights into consumers' preferences and behaviour that can be invaluable in establishing parameters for communication problems.

Apocryphal stories tell us about some of the limitations of questionnaire surveys. Akio Morita's Sony Walkman, the precursor for modern personal stereos (or CD players), is said to have met with adverse market research results, presumably because the consumers questioned could not grasp the concept of walking around with a hi-fi playing in their ears. Sony had a retail network and marketed the Walkman in spite of the bad survey results, to great success. Truly innovative marketing ideas require creative entrepreneurship and teach consumers new consumption concepts. They are beyond the scope of conventional, market research techniques because consumers have nothing with which they can compare a truly innovative concept. The *Reader's Digest* journal once surveyed its huge readership to find out who readers intended to vote for in the US presidential election. Even though the survey population was very large, the result proved wrong because readers of that publication were not **representative** of the wider US voting population.

Quantitative Research

Advertising effectiveness is sometimes tracked using sales figures in relation to the number of target TV spots that the advertisement hits. Statistical techniques such as multivariate analysis can be useful in separating out possible causal variables that might intervene between an advertisement and consumer purchase. Results from experiments can be collated and cross-tabulated, and survey questionnaire results can be statistically analysed for significance. Of course, much of the initial research into the brand category and competitive situation will draw on numerical data to establish items such as brand usage frequency, consumer segment demographics, competitive structure, relative sales volume of the market and so on.

Some agencies use sophisticated, quantitative data analysis techniques, especially when tracking the effectiveness of ad campaigns and trying to establish a statistically significant link between consumer behaviour (for example, purchasing behaviour) and exposures to an ad. It is usually extremely difficult to isolate ad exposure from other possible causal variables. Agencies also use basic quantitative skills in conducting an analysis of their client's business to support the client brief and advertising strategy. Qualitative data-gathering techniques such as discussion groups or in-depth interviews may have a quantitative element, as the transcripts may be subject to content analysis where categories of event are listed and counted. For example, the researcher may want to count the number of times a discussion group mentions 'colour' when discussing a confectionery product's packaging, to see whether the colour of the packaging is closely identified with the brand.

The awareness-interest-desire-action (acronym AIDA) model (see Chapter 2) assumes that consumers will go through a linear, sequential process before purchasing the product. This explains the interest of advertising researchers in intermediate measures of advertising effectiveness such as awareness, interest, degree of liking of an ad (signifying degree of interest in the ad) and, of course, recall. Advertisers are very interested to learn how many exposures to an ad it may take before a consumer can remember their brand or the particular appeal of the ad. The development of **Likert scales** in attitude research seemed to offer a way of quantifying these variables across large numbers of respondent consumers.

For all the intuitive plausibility of measures of recall or positive attitudes towards the ad as predictors of campaign success, no necessary link with consumer purchasing behaviour has been demonstrated. These are states that do not necessarily reflect how the brand personality has been sustained in an ad. We all remember ads that we like or brands that we do not like. We remember ads that we hate for brands that we like. And we forget much advertising, although our weekly purchases often reflect a highly brand-conscious buying mentality.

Qualitative Data and Interpretive Techniques

One senior account planner in a major US agency described how ethnographies were becoming more popular than focus groups: 'The traditional focus group, while it's been very helpful, doesn't always necessarily get you the insights you're going to need because it's very dependent on whether someone can articulate ... and that tends to be rational ... what you really want to get at are more the emotions people have about things rather than the attitudes ... ethnographies (have) become the consumer research of choice these days'.[6]

There is a tendency to use the term 'qualitative research' as if it refers to a commonsense interpretation of naturally occurring social data such as audio recordings of talk or video recordings of behaviour. However, such approaches are more accurately labelled 'interpretive research' because the interpretation of qualitative data is not self-evident: qualitative data are invariably open to a range of interpretations. Qualitative data-gathering methods are largely drawn from traditions of anthropology (especially ethnography) and cultural sociology (Hackley, 2003e) and their theoretical rationale is based on those theoretically driven academic traditions. Popular data-gathering techniques such as participant observation, in-depth interviewing and questionnaire surveys derive from anthropological studies.

BOX 9.6   Qualitative vs Quantitative

One leading London agency has stated in its own literature that the quantitative approach to creative research often 'looks at aggregated data instead of understanding individuals, and judges advertisements against artificial and often irrelevant criteria ... we prefer the flexibility of qualitative research'. This position on advertising research, well-established and formalized in the role of the account planner, is not universally shared in the advertising industry. Many agencies prefer quantitative data as the research basis for planning decisions.

Qualitative research may involve focus or discussion groups, observation studies or in-depth interviews. Sometimes, qualitative advertising research explicitly draws on anthropology for its theoretical foundation. The US agency Ogilvy and Mather has a discovery team of anthropologists who conduct consumer research studies; account planners at DDB Needham Worldwide in New York have conducted **deprivation studies** drawing on anthropological techniques to determine the value and meaning attached to the possession of particular types of consumer goods (Hackley, 2000). As the above quotes attest, agencies have used techniques of ethnography to give their qualitative research greater theoretically-driven insight and hence, they hope, greater intellectual weight with clients. However, what agencies claim as ethnography tends to be based on studies of weeks or months rather than the years typically required of ethnography (Elliott and Jankel-Elliot, 2002).

▶

Some agencies have a relatively informal approach to their qualitative research. They regard qualitative research as 'talking to' consumers (Hackley, 2000) and treat the data of videos, transcripts and audio recordings as stimuli for ideas rather than as empirical evidence to support or reject hypotheses. Publicis Thailand is one agency (see pp. 51–4) which assimilates a commonsense understanding of consumers they call 'street smarts' throughout the advertising development process. Other agencies will have a more explicit, theoretically informed approach to qualitative data interpretation, but most do not. The research skills and sensitivity to nuances of data of experienced planners are relied upon to a great degree, although the interpretations of qualitative research are often hotly debated in the agency account team.

Many agencies have employed trained psychologists for their research expertise in generating insights into consumer reasoning, behaviour and motivation. Consumer psychologists might conduct naturalistic experiments (in a consumption setting) or laboratory experiments measuring attitudes to ad exposures or brand recall. Qualitative research approaches in laboratory settings include **projective techniques** in which a consumer will be given a story-completion task or asked to explain the motivations of a person in a visual consumption setting. The results can generate insights that would not be revealed under more direct forms of interrogation.

Much qualitative/interpretive research focuses on the meaning of consumption, in the hope of generating a fundamental insight that can give the brand personality and the advertising a telling resonance. It does this by

BOX 9.7   Video Data and Qualitative Research

An international qualitative research agency adopted a quasi-anthropological approach in an account with a household cleaning goods manufacturer. They sent a cameraman into a household for two weeks simply filming the housewife doing her cleaning. The video footage makes oddly compelling viewing: after a day or two the presence of the cameraman is forgotten by the householder and the film of the lady unselfconsciously cleaning the kitchen and bathroom reveals the patterns and rituals of product usage in a setting more intimate than any other research method. The detail of how she holds the scouring sponge or the quantities of cleaning fluid she uses and where it is applied are invaluable pieces of information for the brand manufacturer and indeed for the advertiser.

seeking methods to understand the lived experience of the group in question. Studies such as Sherry (1983, 1987, 1991) and Holbrook (1995) have shown how consumers seek and find meaning in their lives from their consumption experiences in ways that are non-trivial and far-reaching. The emphasis on the symbolic meaning of consumption rather than the rational/instrumental utility of consumption underlies much qualitative research.

If consumers' engagement is with the symbolic values portrayed by advertising and marketing, then research techniques are needed which have the subtlety and sensitivity to generate insights that are not necessarily understood fully by the consumers themselves. Ad agencies and marketing organizations need to grasp these elusive insights in order to exploit the underlying motivations for consumer practices.

Informal Research in Advertising

For most people the term 'research' implies formal, quasi-scientific activity conducted according to strict rules and procedures. As we have seen, ad agencies do make great use of formal procedures in their research, but there is also much that is ad hoc and informal. Advertising professionals often rely on intuition and experience in their everyday judgements and many never conduct research that would be recognized as such by an academic social scientist.

Some creative staff when given a brief will try to gain an intuitive understanding of the brand category by watching or taking part in the **consumer practice**. Many would maintain that this is all the research they need. Advertising professionals in general, and creative staff in particular, tend to have a lively interest in the world at large. They are curious about many aspects of human behaviour: after all, a career in advertising is essentially based on practical psychology. How people behave, think and act and what they consume are fascinating questions to an informal social scientist such as an advertising person.

One agency that had the account for children's Lego play bricks set up a Lego playroom in the agency so that creative staff could understand the product from the perspective of a user. They also brought their own children in and watched them playing with the bricks. Another creative spent sometime in a supermarket studying shoppers because he had been given a brief for tea-bags. This kind of informal research will not, of course, tell the agency anything about the market as a whole, but it can act as a powerful source of creative stimulation, sparking ideas and producing novel lines of thinking.

Against Research in Advertising

Advertising is an area in which art and business collide, often with aesthetically striking and commercially fruitful results. Understandably, there are conflicts resulting from the differing values and mindsets associated with each community. Research is a major site of such conflicts: the way it is used, undertaken and interpreted in agencies can place these conflicts in sharp relief. In sociological terms research in agencies can be seen as part of a managerial ideology pushing to impose rational efficiency on administrative fields (Lears, 1994). Research methods can provide measureable criteria with which to judge creative advertising. Regardless of whether measurement in consumer research is valid or useful, it does provide the appearance of rational efficiency, just as work study techniques do in labour-intensive manufacturing. In each area there are those who would argue that the net effect of measurement on output quality or efficiency is negative.

The appearance of rational efficiency is perhaps less important for advertising agencies today than it once was. In the early part of the twentieth century it was considered important for the advertising industry to put its disreputable, snake-oil salesman image behind it and win legitimacy by becoming a rational, bureaucratic field of business. Today, the widespread belief that advertisers are knowledgeable about the psychology of consumption and have skills of hidden persuasion (to borrow Vance Packard's term[7]) is part of the mystique of the advertising business.

For many creative professionals the term 'research' is synonymous with formal methods that are used to test and often veto creative executions. The attitude to research expressed by Toscani in Chapter 8 best captures the creative perspective. Toscani never did any research but produced some of the most striking and effective advertising that the industry has seen.

BOX 9.8   Creatives and Research

Although research is a hugely important part of the advertising and marketing industries, some in the industry think that research can have a bad effect on the standard of advertising. Indeed, many creative professionals in advertising would put it much more strongly than this: many are openly hostile to formal research. They feel that creative inspiration is the basis of successful advertising and they see research as a power tool wielded by those who have little understanding of how or why consumers engage with advertising. The following quote is from a copywriter complaining about research in the New York newsletter of the American Marketing Association: 'Don't tell me that ... [your] ... little questions and statistics can pinpoint the complexity and richness of how people respond to my work' (Kover, 1996: RC9). This quote neatly illustrates the conflicts that can arise when research is conceived as a formalized and method-driven technique that offers definitive findings.

Of course, he took creative risks, but professionals would argue that taking such risks improves the quality of advertising. They feel that over-reliance on research to test creative executions can make advertising neither offensive nor enchanting, simply conservative. Many creative staff believe that inspiration based on an intuitive understanding of consumers is the best way to produce great advertising. Of course, the intuitive understanding of top creative people is built on wide and eclectic interests. It is also based on characteristics such as a capacity for hard work, an acute sense of observation, high intelligence, intellectual flexibility and the ability to work under pressure (McKeil, 1985; Ogilvy, 1963; cited in Wilmshurst and Mackay, 1999).

Promotion agencies often need to invoke research findings because clients are suspicious of creativity that cannot be clearly justified by a well-founded piece of research. Even within the communications industry many professionals place creativity in opposition to advertising effectiveness. In some cases the business case for a creative execution can be supported using statistical or other hard data. Graphs and charts based on numerical data can go a long way to reassuring clients that the pretty advertising pictures are part of a robust and coherent business strategy. Statistically-based research approaches invoke the discourse of science in a field that is often characterized by judgemental or intuitive decision-making. The rhetoric of science has a long history as persuasive advertising copy selling detergent, convenience food or toothpaste. It can be just as valuable to account executives who need to persuade clients that a business decision is based on good evidence and rigorous thinking.

The Account Planning Role and Research

Another reason why research can be a source of conflict is that the consumer is an elusive entity, knowledge of whom confers power in the agency. Whoever can make the most plausible claim that he or she knows and understands the consumer will have the most influential voice in designing advertising strategy. Therefore, the person who has authority over the research and its interpretation wields a great deal of power over the advertising development process. Chapter 4 showed that the account planning role was specifically conceived as taking overall charge of research and, in particular, ensuring that the insights of creative research were assimilated into creative advertising development. It was therefore a politically important role because it would moderate the tension between creative and account management by offering an authoritative voice based on evidence-driven research.

Traditionally, advertising agencies have been organized hierarchically, with the account executive (also called the account manager) in charge. Research would be commissioned by the account executive and he or she would have the major role in interpreting the findings and deciding what

BOX 9.9   Uses of Qualitative Research Insights

There are many examples of products and advertising strategies being developed through qualitative research insights. Disposable nappies (or diapers) were developed from studies which invited young parents into the agency so that their behaviour when changing their babies could be observed. The techniques they used to unwrap, remove and fasten the nappies, and how they interacted with the infant while doing so, were instrumental in informing the design of disposables such as the Huggies brand.

Publicis Thailand hold the account for Nestlé Coffee Mate, a very popular product in Thailand. Staff from the agency observed how consumers use this product in the social context of coffee shops, so that their creative work was informed by an intimate understanding of how consumers use the product within a social setting.

It is said that Toyota executives spent time in California before designing the Lexus in order to observe how affluent consumers used their luxury cars. In these and in many other cases qualitative observation provided practical marketing insights.

the implications might be for advertising strategy and creative executions. In the 1960s a new role emerged that challenged the authority of the account executive by claiming to be the authoritative voice of the consumer in the agency. At a JWT awayday the new discipline was inappropriately labelled 'account planning'.

The account planning role (see Chapter 4) evolved to address some of the difficulties faced by agencies that were trying to formally integrate their research into the creative advertising development process. The success of the discipline has been mixed (Hackley, 2003a, 2003f) but in the agencies which espouse it there tends to be a general acceptance of the value of qualitative insight for guiding creative development. For originators of account planning such as Stephen King at JWT and Stanley Pollitt at BMP (Feldwick, 2000; Pickton and Crosier, 2003; Pollitt, 1979; Steel, 1998), the integration of research into creative advertising development is one of the primary responsibilities of the account planner. The role was also conceived partly to act as a buffer between the account management and creative functions to reduce conflict and promote a better understanding of research within the agency.

Misunderstandings about Research in Advertising

Much misunderstanding about research in advertising occurs because it is not one entity but many. As we have seen, research is conducted for a number of different purposes. First, it is what is done to initially investigate a brand's market category, its role in the client's business and the consumer segments which are current or potential users. Second, it is what account planning staff do to try to generate facts about consumer reality that can give communication a particular resonance. Third, research is what is often done to completed creative work before the campaign is launched, in an effort to predict the likely consumer response. Indeed, in some US agencies research is often regard as being synonymous with copy-testing. Fourth, research is the process of trying to track the response of consumers to the campaign.

The account planning role brings the enigma of research under the remit of one person who is charged to design, conduct, interpret and explain research and its implications for creativity throughout the process. Performing the role successfully demands exceptional interpersonal and research skills from the account planner. It also requires an agency ethos that supports the planning task (Hackley, 2003a). Those advertising professionals dismissive of account planning question whether a specialist account planning discipline is really necessary to perform the tasks described above. In many agencies account management retains control over the use of research and engages the services of a specialist researcher. However, account planning enthusiasts might counter that account management tends to be too close to the client and too dependent on the quantitative notions of research to be able to independently apply the value of consumer insight-driven creativity.

Meaning or Measurement in Advertising Research?

Advertising's Social Character

In Chapter 2 the linear information-processing model of communication (deriving from, for example, Schramm's mass communications research, 1948) was mentioned. Its influence over models of advertising persuasion (Strong, 1925) was discussed. The linear model of communication conceives of advertising as something that acts on individual consumers in social isolation and this assumption has framed much of the research in the field. Some academic researchers (Mick and Buhl, 1992) have argued that this preoccupation with advertising exposure isolated from its social context risks misconstruing the fundamentally social nature of the interaction between consumers and advertising (but also see Scott, 1994a, for comments on Mick and Buhl, 1992a).

For Ritson and Elliott (1999, citing Holbrook, 1995: 93; McCracken, 1987: 123, in support), advertising cannot properly be understood as if it operates in a social vacuum. Advertising, they argue, is actively consumed, reinterpreted and used for purposes of social positioning and identity formation (Buttle, 1994; O'Donohoe, 1994).

Rationality in Advertising

The linear information-processing tradition of advertising theory also emphasizes conscious and rational information-processing. Academic researchers have drawn attention to the symbolic character of advertising communication. For example, McCracken (1986) has alluded to the deeply symbolic character of consumption and argues that this feature has been marginalized in favour of a rational model of how advertising works. For him cultural meaning has a 'mobile quality' (p. 71) and advertising is an 'instrument of meaning transfer' (p. 74). Mick and Buhl (1992: 314) draw critical attention to the tendency for advertising research to regard ads as 'relatively fixed stimuli' and consumers as 'solitary subjects, without identities, who react to ads through linear stages or limited persuasion routes, for the principal purpose of judging brands'.

Economic rationality is not necessarily the driving force of advertising effects. Holbrook and O'Shaughnessy (1988: 400) maintain that humans live 'embedded within a shared system of signs based on public language and other symbolic objects'. Advertising can be seen as a major site of signification, taking consumer cultural meanings, placing them in the context of brand marketing and reflecting them back so that consumers can perform cultural practices symbolically through the consumption of marketed brands. The particular signs that carry meaning in a given context for a given consumer community are difficult for brand advertisers to ascertain unless they can understand the world in the same way as the group of interest.

For Thompson et al. (1989: 433) 'personal understandings are always situated within a network of culturally-shared knowledge, shared beliefs, ideals and taken-for-granted assumptions about the nature of social life'. The implication is that social research cannot fully appreciate personal understandings without also understanding how they interface with the social context in which they are formed. Qualitative research approaches, particularly those drawing on interpretive traditions of social research, offer one way for advertisers to access these meanings.

Studies of the Advertising Development Process

Considering the importance much academic research attributes to advertising there are surprisingly few studies of how advertising is actually developed in agencies. Advertising professionals are, as we have noted, pragmatic and intellectually flexible and tend to intuitively grasp what academics struggle to articulate: namely, that advertising is a form of communication that is ineluctably social and is responded to emotionally by consumers seeking meaning through consumption.

There are some attempts to reveal the ways in which agencies tap into the collective symbolism of consumer culture. Punyairoje et al. (2002) offer an account of advertising development in Thai advertising agencies and

McCracken (1986: 74–6) describes the creative advertising development process in US agencies. Scott (1994a: 468) refers to the 'shared social milieu' upon which advertising professionals depend for the 'learned cultural/textual conventions' (p. 463) that will mobilize meaning in their ads. Scott and McCracken refer to the cultural knowledge underlying advertising interpretation that must be common in order to bind both ad maker and ad watcher in a creatively resonant consummation of advertising development. Hackley (2000, 2002) also refers to the cultural knowledge that presupposes not only the understanding of promotion communications but also the understanding of consumers by communication professionals.

Review Exercises

1. Place yourself in the position of an account planner trying to understand a new brief from a manufacturer of branded disposable nappies (diapers). What sources and kinds of information will be required? What methods will be useful? Explain your choices in terms of the research priorities such a brief demands.
2. Why is research a source of potential conflict in advertising agencies? Form an account team group commissioned with an account for a brand of your choice. Now role-play the planning discussion to pick out the important preliminary issues. In what ways can you see that each account team member (account management, account planning and creative) approach the task with quite different interests at stake?
3. Pick three print ads and conduct copy-test experiments with an audience. Devise scaled questionnaires to asses the strength of feeling subjects have towards various components of the ad. What issues arise? How useful are the findings?
4. Convene a focus/discussion group to explore the issue of ethics in advertising. Use a selection of ethically controversial ads as stimulus material. Write up the main findings. Now write a brief assessment of the main problems and uses of this research technique.
5. Outline how a new brief for a brand of fruit-flavoured alcoholic drink might be better understood through informal and qualitative research.

CASE   Hovis Research Informs the Relaunch Advertising Strategy

Hovis, a 115-year-old brown-bread brand owned by British Bakeries,[8] was suffering declining revenue because of intense downward pressure on price from competition and also from the power of distribution outlets to discount prices. Volume was growing but profit declining. DDB London conducted primary research in the form of questionnaire surveys in order to fully understand why brand equity was diminishing. The brand was seen as out-of-date and **spontaneous brand awareness** was in decline. Qualitative research had previously found that people described a 'Hovis room' as a warm and inviting kitchen. By 2001 they were describing people standing outside the room looking in: people no longer identified with the traditional, old-fashioned positioning of the brand. This kind of research and the thinking it stimulates informed the advertising strategy. It stimulated a new advertising approach that emphasized the health goodness of the bread and eschewed the traditional advertising theme that had played up the bread's northern English heritage. The new campaign was drawn in a cartoon style reminiscent of animated TV shows like 'The Simpsons', to distance it from the old advertising filmed on the cobbled streets of northern England. The relaunch also used new packaging, PR and a supporting website. The brand increased sales while also increasing price. The combination of a radical new advertising approach, new packaging and below-the-line support in the form of PR and a website succeeded in repositioning the brand in a contemporary new light.

Case Exercises

1. List the various research techniques used in the Hovis case. List and then debate the benefits and problems with each technique.
2. In what ways did the Hovis brand research inform the creative approach for the relaunch?
3. Form two groups and choose two brands that (hypothetically) need repositioning in the market because of declining sales and revenue. Each group should write an outline research brief to generate insights as a basis for action. List five research questions that would need to be answered in order to place the strategy on a firm basis of consumer insight.

Further Reading

Ehrenberg, A. and Barnard, N. (1997) 'Advertising and product demand', *Admap* (May): 14–18.

Franzen, G. (1999) 'Brand equity: concept and research', in G. Franzen, *Brands and Advertising: How Advertising Effectiveness Influences Brand Equity*. Henley-on-Thames: Admap.

Hackley, C. (1998) 'Social constructionism and research in marketing and advertising', *Qualitative Market Research: An International Journal* 1(3): 125–31.

Jones, J.P. (1990) 'Advertising: strong force or weak force? Two views an ocean apart', *International Journal of Advertising* 9: 233–46.

Van Raaij, W.F. (1989) 'How consumers react to advertising', *International Journal of Advertising* 8: 261–73.

Wells, W.D. (ed.) (1997) *Measuring Advertising Effectiveness*. Hillsdale, NJ: Lawrence Erlbaum Associates.

Web resource

There is a useful resource based on an Advertising and Consumer Psychology course given by Dr Brian Young of Exeter University at: http://www.ex.ac.uk/Psychology/docs/courses/6036/advertising.html

Notes

1 WARC email newsletter 4 June 2004.

2 JICRAR: Joint Industry Committee on Radio Research.

3 OAA: Outdoor Advertising Association.

4 Source: research interviews at BMP DDB (now DDB London) 1997–9.

5 Reported on the WARC email newsletter 1 January 2004.

6 Qualitative interview kindly granted at Ogilvy New York, 2000.

7 V. Packard (1957) *The Hidden Persuaders*. New York: McKay.

8 Source: research interviews kindly granted at DDB London by Richard Butterworth and Lucy Jameson and case study written up in *DDB London Works*. Henley-on-Thames: WARC and IPA.

Cognitive, Social and Cultural Theories of Advertising and Promotion

Chapter Outline

In this final chapter we will review the major ideas of the book to arrive at an accommodation between the various theoretical perspectives on advertising, which, like theory in other fields of social research, rest on assumptions that are often left implicit. The chapter argues that by making such assumptions explicit, theories of advertising can be sorted into three major categories that focus on different levels of explanation. For our purpose we label these levels the cognitive, the social and the cultural.

The Fascination of Promotional Communication

Part of the fascination of advertising and promotion for practitioners is that they entail solving problems of communication when the main basis of communication, language, is continually adapting to express new kinds of experience and to accommodate new influences. The English language is especially popular in advertising the world over probably because of its flexibility and global familiarity. Of course, advertising's use of imagery and music makes it a richer device of communication than language alone. Indeed, part of advertising's uniqueness as a discourse form derives from its capacity to combine language with music, pictures and substance or medium (Cook, 2001). But language itself carries meaning within its context: there is a medium of transmission (written or aural) and meanings are nuanced through the combination of language with tone, gesture and other aspects of context. Advertising and promotion offer forms of communication that not only set language in any social context with which we are familiar but invent new contexts through novel combinations of imagery, words and, often, music. The possibilities for novelty in advertising communication seem almost limitless. Nevertheless advertising can be seen as a form of discourse (see Chapter 2) since it is an identifiable form of communication that can be described. As a discourse advertising is defined by its conventional forms and styles, even though these are constantly changing.

Advertising and Cultural Knowledge

Advertising and communication agencies produce cultural texts that portray consumption by drawing on social practices and symbols extant in wider, non-consumption culture. For example, at the most simple level, a promotion that pictures people riding on a public bus cannot communicate anything unless viewers of the ad are familiar with the cultural practice of riding on a public bus. Riding on a bus is not merely an act: it is a cultural practice because it is subject to agreed rules that are never actually stated. There are ways of paying one's fare, ways of taking one's seat (or not taking one and standing up), ways of disembarking at the correct stop, even ways of speaking to fellow passengers or to the driver. If one tries to take a bus ride in a strange country with an unfamiliar language the importance of these conventions becomes all too apparent and one can look, and feel, socially inept because one does not know them. Advertisements presuppose the consumer's cultural knowledge of local social practices (Thompson et al., 1994). Consequently it is important for the creators of advertising to share or understand the social milieu of the consumers so that the ads they create will be invested with social significance for the viewer (Bakhtin, 1989; Hackley, 2002, citing Scott, 1994a and b; Iser, 1978).

In portraying everyday activities in rather magnified and glamorized ways advertising and promotion reveal us to ourselves. The ordinary things we do are portrayed in film and photograph, from taking a shower to buying a coffee. No doubt advertising's use of high-quality cinematography and print techniques and elaborate sets, together with its prominence in public space, makes our everyday activities portrayed in this way seem dramatically compelling and loaded with significance. Taking a shave with a Gillette Mach Three wet razor is portrayed as a symbolic statement of social status and material aspiration, and confers a powerful (symbolic) sexual attraction on the shaver. Underlying all advertising communication is the motive of consumption and the implicit message that it is consumption, and not merely its portrayal in advertising, that can make our experience of life more fulfilling. For this communication to work there has to be a shared cultural vocabulary between the makers and consumers of advertising. Advertising and promotional agencies operate at this cultural interface, continually reprocessing cultural meanings to create this communication between brand marketing organizations and consumers.

In communication agencies we have seen that the connection with the consumer is often a site of conflict. In addition, advertising and promotion operate at the intersection of corporate and civic life and attempt to reconcile interests that may be opposed.

We have seen that mass advertising can be a powerful marketing blunderbuss, browbeating consumers into compliance by conditioning through repetition. It also has the flexibility to support many kinds of marketing and business objectives with tailored specificity. It can reflect and magnify social changes and is an important cultural influence. The ways in which advertising and promotion are produced and consumed are constantly changing. There are rapid and far-reaching innovations in technology, media and the organization of agencies. In the future, above-the-line advertising will be seen as one among a range of mediated communications that agencies will be expected to provide. A viable theory of advertising, then, must be able to accommodate this complexity.

What is Advertising Theory For?

Levels of Explanation in Advertising Theory: Cognitive, Social, Cultural

Theoretical explanations in social science rest on assumptions that are not entirely explicit. Social theories based on new research are often adapted from previous studies. Rather than restating the fundamental problem and the historical context of the original research, new research focuses on technical developments or the use of new data. Social science theories, then, can become disconnected from the original, specific context or problem. The marketing field has been particularly prone to this tendency since it has adapted, and often bowdlerized, theoretical and conceptual developments in many other social disciplines, such as economics, psychology and sociology (Foxall, 2000; Gronharg, 2000; Hackley, 2003g; O'Shaughnessy, 1997). Theoretical work in advertising has, as we have seen, similarly adapted work from other fields. Much advertising research draws on assumptions from mass communications research which had, in turn, borrowed ideas such as linearity and the concept of the internal mental state from early research in artificial intelligence and computing. We have also referred to much research into advertising that has drawn on the arts and humanities, for example literary theory (Scott, 1994a, 1994b) and feminism (Stern, 1993), anthropology (Sherry, 1987), ethnography (Ritson and Elliott, 1999), applied linguistics (Cook, 2001), critical theory (Elliott and Ritson, 1997) and so on.

All this diversity begs the question of what theory in advertising is for. In fact, one cannot fairly evaluate a social theory without also understanding the assumptions about the audience for the research and the rightful aims of that research. To accommodate diversity in advertising we will draw on the notion of 'levels of explanation' in social research, which has been used in social psychology education (Stevens, 1996) to integrate differing kinds of theory.[1]

The Cognitive Level of Explanation

Advertising works at a cognitive level in that it influences the individual cognitive functions of perception, memory and attitude. Theories that focus on the cognitive levels of explanation also emphasize rational, conscious consumer thinking. The scope of explanation in such theories extends to the internal mental state of the individual and the assumed connection between those internal states and observed (consumer) behaviour. Copy-testing, experimental research designs and attitude research attempt to isolate the internal mental states that act as causal variables which motivate consumers to act on the advertising they see. This level of explanation offers succinct and measurable results, but its weakness is that it risks distorting the way consumers engage with and understand advertising to fit a set of convenient research methods.

Most importantly, the cognitive level of explanation locates experience in the asocial world of what happens inside our heads. Much cognitive research into advertising has taken the individual consumer as the unit of analysis (Hackley, 2002: 214; Holbrook, 1995: 93, citing McCracken, 1987: 123; Ritson and Elliott, 1999: 261). Unlike computers, humans depend heavily on social interaction for meaning. People born blind who have sight restored in middle age have to learn to perceive structures and images from a jumble of visual, sensory data. In other words, they have to learn how to see. People who are raised in social isolation cannot naturally learn speech and people who live in a culture without mediated communication cannot 'read' advertising. The way that we understand advertising is deeply informed by the cultural understanding we can only acquire in social interaction. The experimental research paradigm that attempts to isolate individual physiological or attitudinal responses to advertising cannot easily capture this dimension.

The Social Level of Explanation

The social level of explanation offers an account of advertising that accommodates its social character. Advertising is not encountered in a social vacuum but in a given social context, and it occupies a place in public discourse. How we think about advertising is strongly influenced by what we hear others say about it. How many times has someone asked you if you have seen this or that ad? As ads become part of social discourse they assume the characteristics of social constructions, in the sense that Berger and Luckman (1966) described. Research and theory that focus on internal mental states (such as memory or attitude) fail to grasp the essentially malleable nature of these states. One's attitude towards an ad is not arrived at in isolation but is constructed in a social context. Social constructionism (see also Burr, 1995; Hackley, 2001) disputes the validity of the internal mental state as a construct and suggests that such states subsist in social discourse. In practical terms, this implies that it not sufficient to measure memory or attitude in experimental laboratories: rather, advertising research needs to look at consumer thinking and behaviour in its normal social context, in interaction.

It is hugely significant that advertising agency professionals understand this intuitively. But politically, many agencies still struggle to justify this form of understanding to clients and account managers who are concerned with measuring consumer attitudes to advertising. This fundamental difference of mentality is the central issue in advertising and promotional management (Hackley, 2003d), but many existing research approaches perpetuate the differences instead of providing possibilities for reconciliation.

The Cultural Level of Explanation

We have seen that advertising can be regarded as a form of cultural text. It takes the symbolic meanings and practices of non-consumer culture and recreates them in juxtaposition with marketed brands to suggest contrived brand values and to portray a brand personality. For advertising to be construed in this way there needs to be a symbolic aspect to the way consumers engage with advertising. We must understand advertising in terms that transfer symbolic meanings from our broader cultural experience to advertised brands (Belk, 1988; Mick and Buhl, 1992). This level of analysis broadens a socially constructed notion of advertising to accommodate the wider cultural influences that are the preconditions for local social discourse.

At this level of analysis power is an inevitable part of the picture. Brand marketing corporations have the economic and political power to impose contrived meanings upon cultural practices. Brand advertising, cleverly designed and expensively produced and exposed, can work to normalize particular social practices (such as cigarette smoking, alcohol drinking for females, fast-food consumption for children) and invest these practices with symbolic values such as personal independence, power and coolness. In this way advertising can be seen to operate as an ideology (Eagleton, 1991) or, indeed, the 'super-ideology' of our time (Elliott and Ritson, 1997).

An exposition of advertising as ideology lies beyond the scope of this book. It is worth pointing out, though, that an intellectually viable appraisal of how advertising works is incomplete without an understanding of advertising's ideological power to render consumption practices normal and everyday in an infinite variety of appealing portrayals, to invest these practices with rich cultural significance and to place the interests of brand marketing organizations in the forefront of social life. If marketing as a whole can be seen as a vast semiotic vehicle constituting experiences and identities (Brownlie et al., 1999, Hackley, 2003g) then advertising is its engine, providing a continuous stream of new images, ideas and portrayals of consumption in juxtaposition with marketed brands.

Advertising Theory and Advertising Practice

This book has drawn on many examples from advertising to illustrate how advertising agencies create advertising. It has offered an appraisal of contemporary brand advertising that accommodates the rapidly changing communications and marketing environment within which advertising operates. Recent developments in advertising practice emphasize the brand personality that is portrayed through advertising on all media forms. This planning perspective changes the tone of advertising from salesmanship in print to one far more abstract and opaque. The meaning of advertisements is increasingly understood not at an explicit, rational level but at the level of the abstract and symbolic, reflecting the planning that informs the advertising.

The cliché that half of advertising expenditure is wasted because it is directed at non-consumers is contradicted by the understanding that the strength of a brand's personality is reflected by the significance it has to those who do not consume it as well as to those who do. Popular brands attain their status as cultural icons by acquiring meaning that reaches far beyond the physical act of consumption. Brands such as Mercedes-Benz and Rolex have powerful meaning for millions of consumers who will never own either. Their only direct knowledge of the brand is through advertising and communication. The presence of a brand in the public consciousness is in itself a powerful marketing device.

Even though advertising practice is a pragmatic and commonsense affair it can, nevertheless, be better understood in terms of a cultural theoretical perspective. Advertising theories tend to fall into one of the three categories outlined above. Each is defined by the scope of its explanation and the implicit assumptions under which it operates. It is hoped that this book has contributed to a better understanding of advertising practice. In drawing attention to the various levels of theoretical explanation of advertising, this book also attempts to point to viable directions for theoretical work in advertising, promotion and marketing communication.

Harrison Troughton Wunderman (HTW) of London wished to revitalize the 70-year-old financial services brand M & G Investments. Branding in financial services tended to be indistinct, with low-impact, jargon-ridden ads. Consumers found it difficult to distinguish the leading brands from each other and were irritated by hyperbole and oversell. To make matters worse, consumer confidence in financial services had been weakened by scandal: Enron, the collapse of Equitable Life and the overselling of high-risk products in the UK mortgage market.

Potential financial services consumers are easy to identify through demographic and income analysis. What was needed in this case was a more penetrating segmentation variable based on insight rather than measurement. HTW's planning revealed a potential target group of 'affluent silvers' who wanted the truth about financial services and were prepared to look carefully for the right home for their investment funds. Qualitative research had shown that this over-45 age group took investments seriously but were sceptical about financial services advertising. The M&G brand was seen as having strong integrity and durability, two crucial values expected in financial services companies.

The newly defined target group required detailed information and straight-talking copy. HTW's 'brand response' advertising campaign entailed full page ads in the UK national press between January 2002 and March 2003. The ads offered jargon-free explanations of esoteric, financial services products, with the M&B brand mentioned almost incidentally near the end of the ad. Images of media personalities who, research revealed, were highly regarded for their understated expertise were used to signify the values that affluent silvers sought. The 1960s England soccer hero Bobby Moore was used rather than David Beckham; the laid-back TV comic Tommy Cooper was featured rather than more radical comedic characters.

The media schedule moved away from the typical financial services ad in the 'money' section of papers by using outdoor sites and colour sections. The brand response campaign was followed with product-specific ads aimed at the consumer and the intermediaries who sold them. Direct mail shots included a teabag to encourage the investor to drink a cup of tea while making a carefully considered decision on which brand of savings product to buy.

The campaign attracted trade awards and increased direct sales by 19% when the market as a whole had shrunk by 30%. Consumer brand awareness for M&G was raised to the highest level in the market. HTW's planning had driven creative executions that were radically different to typical advertising in the financial services sector.

Case Exercises

1. To what extent might hierarchy-of-effects theories of persuasion explain the success of HTW's M&G campaign? Can other theoretical traditions offer more penetrating insight into the way the campaign worked?

2. The campaign increased M&G's revenue in a declining market. Research revealed that brand awareness for M&G improved substantially. Can these two events be connected? Given that brand awareness in financial services tends to be weak, could this have been a significant factor that fed through to M&G's bottom line? If so, how did HTW accomplish this improvement in brand awareness?

3. HTW's research resulted in a new way of segmenting financial services consumers, based not on objective measurements such as income or demographics but on insight into the way consumers understand and interact with financial services marketing. This insight not only drove targeting but also informed creative tactics. Think of four other product or service categories with which you are familiar. Suggest the most useful segmentation variables that you can for these categories. Discuss whether lifestyle and attitude insights might generate more powerful means of segmentation in these cases.

Notes

1 There is a useful conceptualization of the kinds of advertising theory in Percy et al., 2001: 22.

2 This case vignette is based on an award winning submission to the APG Creative Planning Awards, 2003, original case by Malcom Peters of Harrison Troughton Wunderman, London. Adapted with permission.

References

Aaker, D., Batra, R. and Myers, J. (1992) *Advertising Management*. 4th edn. Englewood Cliffs, NJ: Prentice-Hall.

Ambler, T. (1996) 'Can alcohol misuse be reduced by banning advertising?', *International Journal of Advertising* 15(2): 167–74.

Ambler, T. (1998) 'Myths about the mind: time to end some popular beliefs about how advertising works', *International Journal of Advertising* 17(4): 501–9.

Amis, J., Slack, T. and Berrett, T. (1999) 'Sport sponsorship as distinctive competence', *European Journal of Marketing* 33(3/4): 250–72.

Ayer, A.J. (1936) *Language, Truth and Logic*. London: Victor Gollancz, reprinted by Penguin Books, 1990.

Bagozzi, R., Tybout, A.M., Craig, C.S. and Sternthal, B. (1979) 'The construct validity of the tripartite classification of attitudes', *Journal of Marketing Research* 16 (February): 88–95.

Bakhtin, M. (1989) 'Discourse in life and discourse in art (concerning sociological poetics)', in R. Davis and R. Schleifler (eds), *Contemporary Literary Criticism*. New York: Longman, pp. 392–410.

Banister, L. (1997) 'Global brands, local contexts', *Admap* (October): 28–30.

Barnard, N. and Ehrenberg, A. (1997) 'Advertising: strongly persuasive or nudging?', *Journal of Advertising Research* 37(1): 21–31.

Barry, T.E. and Howard, D.J. (1990) 'A review and critique of the hierarchy of effects in advertising', *International Journal of Advertising* 9: 121–35.

Barthes, R. (2000) *Mythologies*. London: Vintage. (Translation Jonathan Cape 1972).

Belch, G. and Belch, M. (2002) *Advertising and Promotion: An Integrated Marketing Communications Perspective*. 6th edn. New York: McGraw Hill.

Belk, R. (1988) 'Possessions and the extended self', *Journal of Consumer Research* 15(2): 139–168.

Berger, P.L. and Luckman, T. (1966) *The Social Construction of Reality*. London: Penguin.

Billig, M. (1987) *Arguing and Thinking: A Rhetorical Approach to Social Psychology*. Cambridge: Cambridge University Press.

Billig, M. (1991) *Ideology and Opinions*. London: Sage.

Brownlie, D., Saren, M., Wensley, R. and Whittington, D. (eds) (1999), *Rethinking Marketing: Towards Critical Marketing Accountings*. London: Sage.

Bullmore, J. (1988) *Behind the Scenes in Advertising*. 2nd edn. Henley-onThames: Admap.

Burr, V. (1995) *An Introduction to Social Constructionism*. London: Routledge.

Burrell, G. and Morgan, G. (1979) *Sociological Paradigms and Organisational Analysis*. London: Heinemann.

Butterfield, L. (ed.) (1999) *Excellence in Advertising: The IPA Guide to Best Practice*. London: Butterworth-Heinemann.

Buttle, F. (1994) 'Marketing communications theory – what do the texts teach our students?', *International Journal of Advertising* 14: 297–313.

Calfee, J.E. and Scherage, C. (1994) 'The influence of advertising on alcohol consumption: a literature review and an econometric analysis of four European nations', *International Journal of Advertising* 13(4): 287–310.

Cook, G. (2001) *The Discourse of Advertising*. London: Routledge.

Cook, W.A. and Kover, A.J. (1998) 'Research and the meaning of advertising effectiveness: mutual misunderstandings', in W.D. Wells (ed.), *Measuring Advertising Effectiveness*. Hillsdale, NJ: Lawrence Erlbaum Associates, pp. 13–20.

Croft, R. (1999) 'Audience and environment: measurement and media', in P.J. Kitchen (ed.), *Marketing Communications, Principles and Practice*. London: Thomson Learning, pp. 111–34.

Crosier, K. (1999) 'Advertising', in P.J. Kitchen (ed.), *Marketing Communications: Principles and Practice*. London: Thomson Learning, pp. 264–88.

Danesi, M. (1994) *Messages and Meanings: An Introduction to Semiotics*. Toronto: Canadian Scholar's Press.

d'Astous, A. and Seguin, N. (1999) 'Consumer reactions to product placement strategies in television sponsorship', *European Journal of Marketing* 33(9/10): 896–910.

DDB London Works, introduced by Richard Butterworth and Lucy Jameson (2003) Henley-on-Thames: WARC and IPA.

De Pelsmacker, P., Geuens, M. and Van den Bergh, J. (2004) *Marketing Communications: A European Perspective*. 2nd edn. London: Financial Times/Prentice Hall.

De Saussure, F. (1974) *Course in General Linguistics*. London: Collins.

Dermody, J. (1999) 'CPM/HEM models of information processing', in P.J. Kitchen (ed.), *Marketing Communications – Principles and Practice*. London: Thomson Learning, pp. 156–71.

Eagleton, T. (1991) *Ideology*. London: Verso.

Easterby-Smith, M., Thorpe, R. and Lowe, A. (2002) *Management Research: An Introduction*. London: Sage.

Eco, U. (1976) *A Theory of Semiotics*. Bloomington, IN: Indiana University Press.

Eco, U. (1984) *Semiotics and Philosophy of Language*. London: Macmillan.

Edwards, D. and Potter, J. (1992) *Discursive Psychology*. London: Sage.

Ehrenberg, A. and Barnard, N. (1997) 'Advertising and product demand', *Admap* (May): 14–18.

Ehrenberg, A., Barnard, N., Kennedy, R. and Bloom, H. (2002) 'Brand advertising and creative publicity', *Journal of Advertising Research* 42(4): 7–18.

Elliott, R. (1998) 'A model of emotion-driven choice', *Journal of Marketing Management* 14: 95–108.

Elliott, R. and Beckmann, S. (eds) (2000) *Interpretive Consumer Research: Paradigms, Methodologies and Applications*. Copenhagen: Copenhagen Business School Press.

Elliott, R. and Jankel-Elliott, N. (2002) 'Using ethnography in strategic consumer research', *Qualitative Market Research: An International Journal* 6(4): 215–23.

Elliott, R. and Ritson, M. (1997) 'Post-structuralism and the dialectics of advertising: discourse, ideology, resistance', in S. Brown and D. Turley (eds), *Consumer Research: Postcards From the Edge*. London: Routledge, pp. 190–248.

Elliott, R. and Wattanasuwan, K. (1998) 'Brands as symbolic resources for the construction of identity', *International Journal of Advertising* 17(2): 131–44.

Feldwick, P. (ed.) (2002) *Pollitt on Planning*. Account Planning Group, BMP (DDB). Needham. Henley-on-Thames: Admap.

Feldwick, P. (2002) *What is Brand Equity Anyway?* World Advertising Research Centre: Henley-on-Thames.

Fill, C. (2002) *Marketing Communications: Contexts, Strategies and Applications*. 3rd edn. Essex: Prentice Hall.

Forceville, C. (1996) *Pictorial Metaphor in Advertising*. London: Routledge.

Ford, B. (1993) *Television and Sponsorship*. Oxford: Butterworth Heinemann.

Foxall, G.R. (2000) 'The psychological basis of marketing', in M.J. Baker (ed.), *Marketing Theory: A Student Text*. London: Thomson Learning, pp. 86–101.

Franzen, G. (1999) *Brands and Advertising: How Advertising Effectiveness Influences Brand Equity*. Henley-on-Thames: Admap.

Gronharg, K. (2000) 'The sociological basis of marketing', in M.J. Baker (ed.), *Marketing Theory: A Student Text*. London: Thompson Learning.

Hackley, C. (1998) 'Social constructionism and research in marketing and advertising', *Qualitative Market Research: An International Journal* 1(3): 125–31.

Hackley, C. (1999a) 'The communications process and the semiotic boundary', in P.J. Kitchen (ed.), *Marketing Communications: Principles and Practice*. London: Thomson Learning, pp. 135–55.

Hackley, C. (1999b) 'The meanings of ethics in and of advertising', *Business Ethics: A European Review* 8(1): 37–42.

Hackley, C. (2000) 'Silent running: tacit, discursive and psychological aspects of management in a top UK advertising agency', *British Journal of Management* 11(3): 239–54.

Hackley, C. (2001) *Marketing and Social Construction: Exploring the Rhetorics of Marketed Consumption*. London: Routledge.

Hackley, C. (2002) 'The panoptic role of advertising agencies in the production of consumer culture', *Consumption, Markets and Culture* 5(3): 211–29.

Hackley, C. (2003a) 'Account planning: current agency perspectives on an advertising enigma', *Journal of Advertising Research* 43(2): 235–45.

Hackley, C., (2003b) 'Divergent representational practices in advertising and consumer research: some thoughts on integration', special issue on representation in consumer research, *Qualitative Market Research: An International Journal* 6(3): 175–84.

Hackley, C. (2003c) 'IMC and Hollywood: what brand managers need to know', *Admap* (November): 44–7.

Hackley, C. (2003d) 'How divergent beliefs cause account team conflict', *International Journal of Advertising* 22(3): 313–32.

Hackley, C. (2003e) *Doing Research Projects in Marketing, Management and Consumer Research*. London: Routledge.

Hackley, C. (2003f) 'From consumer insight to advertising strategy: the account planner's integrative role in creative advertising development', *Marketing Intelligence and Planning* 21(7): 446–52.

Hackley, C. (2003g) '"We are all customers now" … rhetorical strategy and ideological control in marketing management texts', *Journal of Management Studies* 40(5): 1325–52.

Hackley, C. and Kitchen, P.J. (1999) 'Ethical perspectives on the postmodern communications Leviathan', *Journal of Business Ethics* 20(1): 15–26.

Harrison, S. (1995) *Public Relations: An Introduction*. London: Routledge.

Head, V. (1981) *Sponsorship: The Newest Marketing Skill*. Cambridge, Woodhead-Faulkner in association with the Chartered Institute of Marketing.

Hedges, A. (1997) *Testing to Destruction – A Critical Look at the Uses of Research in Advertising*. London: Institute of Practitioners in Advertising. (1st edn, 1974.)

Hirschman, E. (1986) 'Humanistic inquiry in marketing research: research, philosophy, method and criteria', *Journal of Marketing Research* 23 (August): 237–49.

Holbrook, M. (1995) *Consumer Research: Introspective Essays on the Study of Consumption*. London: Sage.

Holbrook, M. and Hirschman, E. (1982) 'The experiential aspects of consumption: consumer feelings, fantasies and fun', *Journal of Consumer Research* 9 (September): 132–40.

Holbrook, M.B. and O'Shaughnessy, J. (1988) 'On the scientific status of consumer research and the need for an interpretive approach to studying consumption behaviour', *Journal of Consumer Research* 15: 398–403.

Holt, D. (2002) 'Why do brands cause trouble?', *Journal of Consumer Research* 29 (June): 70–90.

Horkheimer, M. and Adorno, T.W. (1944) *The Dialectic of Enlightenment*. New York: Continuum.

Hoy, M., Morrison, M. and Punyapiroje, C. (2000), 'Adver-Thai-sing standardisation: does the Western approach of investigating gender role portrayals transfer to Eastern countries?', *World Communication* 19(1): 52–68.

Iser, W. (1978) *The Act of Reading*. Baltimore, MD: Johns Hopkins University Press.

Jefkins, F. (2000) *Advertising*. Harlow: Pearson Education.

Jones, J.P. (1990) 'Advertising: strong force or weak force? Two views an ocean apart', *International Journal of Advertising* 9: 233–46.

Jones, J.P. (1999) *The Advertising Business*. New York: Sage.

Katz, H. (2003) *The Media Handbook: A Complete Guide to Advertising Media Selection, Planning, Research and Buying*. Hillsdale, NJ: Lawrence Erlbaum Associates.

Katz, E. and Larzarsfeld, P.F. (1955) *Personal Influence*. Glencoe, IL: Free Press.

Klein, N. (2000) *No Logo*. London: Flamingo.

Kitchen, P.J. (ed.) (1999) *Marketing Communications: Principles and Practice*. London: Thompson.

Kitchen, P.J. and Hackley, C. (1999) 'Ethical perspectives on the postmodern communications leviathan', *Journal of Business Ethics* 20(1): 15–26.

Kochan, N. (1997) *The World's Greatest Brands*. New York: New York University Press.

Kover, A.J. (1995) 'Copywriters' implicit theories of communication: an exploration', *Journal of Consumer Research* 21 (March): 598–611.

Kover, A.J. (1996) 'Why copywriters don't like research – and what kind of research might they accept', *Journal of Advertising Research* 36/2: RC8–12.

Kover, A.J. and Goldberg, S.M. (1995), 'The games copywriters play: conflict, quasi-control: a new proposal', *Journal of Advertising Research* 35(4): 52–68.

Larzarsfeld, P.F. (1941) 'Remarks on administrative and critical communications research', *Studies in Philosophy and Science* 9: 3–16.

Lasswell, H.D. (1948) 'The structure and function of communication in society', in L. Bryson (ed.), *The Communication of Ideas*. New York: Harper.

Lavidge, R.J. and Steiner, G.A. (1961) 'A model for predictive measurements of advertising effectiveness', *Journal of Marketing* 24 (October): 59–62.

Lears, J. (1994) *Fables of Abundance: A Cultural History of Advertising in America*. New York: Basic Books.

Leiss, W., Kline, S. and Jhally, S. (1997) *Social Communication in Advertising: Persons, Products and Images of Well-Being*. London: Routledge.

Lemle, R. and Mishkind, M. (1989) 'Alcohol and masculinity', *Journal of Substance Abuse Treatment* 6: 213–22.

Levitt, T. (1983) 'The globalisation of market', *Harvard Business Review* (April/May): 92–107.

Lutz, R.J. (1977) 'An experimental investigation of causal relations among cognitions: affect and behavioural intention', *Journal of Consumer Research* 3 (March): 197–208.

McCracken, G. (1986) 'Culture and consumption: a theoretical account of the structure and movement of the cultural meaning of consumer goods', *Journal of Consumer Research* 13(1): 71–84.

McCracken, G. (1987) 'Advertising – meaning or information?', in M. Wallendorf and P. Anderson (eds), *Advances in Consumer Research*, vol. 14. Provo, UT: Association for Consumer Research, pp. 121–4.

McCracken, G. (1990) *Culture and Consumption: New Approaches to the Symbolic Character of Consumer Goods and Activities*. Bloomington, IN; Indiana University Press.

McFall, L. (2004) *Advertising: A Cultural Economy*. London: Sage.

McKeil, J. (1985) *The Creative Mystique*. London: John Wiley and Sons.

Macklin, M.C. and Carlson, L. (eds) (1999) *Advertising to Children: Concepts and Controversies*. Thousand Oaks, CA: Sage.

Manchanda, R.V., Dahl, D.W. and Frankenberger, K.D. (2003) 'Does it pay to shock? Reactions to shocking and nonshocking advertising content among university students', *Journal of Advertising Research* 43(3): 268–79.

Marchand, R. (1985) *Advertising and the American Dream: Making Way for Modernity 1920–1940*. Bakeley, CA: University of California Press.

Marchand, R. (1998) *Creating the Corporate Soul: The Rise of Public Relations and Corporate Imagery in American Big Business*. Los Angeles, CA: University of California Press.

McLuhan, M. (1964) 'Keeping upset with the Joneses', in *Understanding Media*. London: Routledge and Kegan Paul, pp. 226–33.

Meenaghan, T. (1991), 'Sponsorship: legitimising the medium', *European Journal of Marketing* 25(11): 5–10.

Meenaghan, T. and Shipley, D. (1999) 'Media affecting sponsorship', *European Journal of Marketing* 33(3/4): 328–47.

Melewar, T.C. (2003) 'Determinants of the corporate identity construct: a review of literature', *Journal of Marketing Communications* 9(4): 195–220.

Melewar, T.C. and Wooldridge, A. (2001) 'The dynamics of corporate identity: a review of a process model, *Journal of Communication Management* 5(4): 327–40.

Mick, D.G. and Buhl, K. (1992) 'A meaning based model of advertising', *Journal of Consumer Research* 19 (December): 317–38.

Motion, J., Leitch, S. and Brodie, R. (2003) 'Equity in co-branded identity – the case of Adidas and the All Blacks', *European Journal of Marketing* 37(7/8): 1080–94.

Mulder, N. (1996) *Inside Thai Society: Interpretations of Everyday Life*. Amsterdam: The Pepin Press.

Nava, M., Blake A., MacRury, I. and Richards, B. (eds) *Buy This Book*. London: Routledge.

Nelson, J.P. and Young, D.J. (2001) 'Do advertising bans work? An international comparison', *International Journal of Advertising* 20: 273–96.

Nightingale, D.J. and Cromby, J. (eds) (1999) *Social Constructionist Psychology: A Critical Analysis of Theory and Practice*. Buckingham: Open University Press.

O'Donohoe, S. (1994) 'Advertising uses and gratifications', *European Journal of Marketing* 28(8/9): 52–75.

O'Donohoe, S. (1997) 'Raiding the postmodern pantry – advertising intertextuality and the young adult audience', *European Journal of Marketing* 31(3,4): 234–53.

O'Shaughnessy, J. (1997) 'Temerarious directions for marketing', *European Journal of Marketing* 31(9/10): 677–705.

Ogilvy, D. (1963) *Confessions of an Advertising Man*. New York: Atheneum.

Ogilvy, D. (1983) *Ogilvy on Advertising*. 2nd edn. London: Multimedia Books.

Osborn, A. (1963) *Applied Imagination – Principles and Procedures of Creative Problem Solving*. New York: Charles Scribner's Sons.

Packard, V. (1957) *The Hidden Persuaders*. New York: McKay.

Pateman, T. (1980) 'How to do things with images; an essay on the pragmatics of advertising', in T. Pateman (ed.) *Language, Truth and Politics*. East Sussex: Jean Stroud, pp. 215–37.

Pateman, T. (1983) 'How is understanding an advertisement possible?', in H. Davis and P. Walton (eds), *Language, Image, Media*. Oxford: Blackwell. pp. 187–204.

Peirce, C.S. (1958) *Collected Papers*. Cambridge, MA: Harvard University Press.

Percy, L., Rossiter, J.R. and Elliott, R. (2001) *Strategic Advertising Management*. Oxford: Oxford University Press.

Pickton, D. and Broderick, A. (2000) *Integrated Marketing Communications*. London: Pearson Education.

Pickton, D. and Crosier, K. (2003) 'Marketing intelligence and planning', *Account Planning*, special issue, 21(7): 410–15.

Pollay, R.W. (1986) 'The distorted mirror – reflections on the unintended consequences of advertising', *Journal of Marketing* 50 (April): 18–36.

Pollitt, S. (1979) 'How I started account planning in agencies', *Campaign* (20 April): 29–30.

Potter, J. and Wetherell, M. (1987) *Discourse and Social Psychology: Beyond Attitudes and Behaviour*. London: Sage.

Punyapiroje, C., Morrison, M. and Hoy, M. (2002) 'A nation under the influence: the creative strategy process for advertising in Thailand', *Journal of Current Issues and Research in Advertising* 24(2): 51–65.

Richards, B., MacRury, I. and Botterill, J. (2000) *The Dynamics of Advertising*. London: Routledge.

Ritson, M. and Elliott, R. (1999) 'The social uses of advertising: an ethnographic study of adolescent advertising audiences', *Journal of Consumer Research* 26(3): 260–77.

Ritzer, G. (2000) *The McDonaldization of Society*. New Century edn. Thousand Oaks, CA: Pine Forge Press and Sage.

Rosch, E. (1977) 'Human categorization', in N. Warren (ed.), *Advances in Cross Cultural Psychology*, Vol. 1. New York: Academic Press, pp. 1–49.

Rossiter, J.R., Percy, L. and Donovan, R.J. (1991) 'A better advertising planning grid', *Journal of Advertising Research* (October–November): 11–12.

Russell, C.A. (1998) 'Towards a framework of product placement: theoretical propositions', *Advances in Consumer Research* 25: 357–62.

Sawchuck, K. (1995) 'Semiotics, cybernetics and the ecstasy of marketing communication', in D. Kellner (ed.), *Baudrillard: A Critical Reader*. Oxford: Blackwell. pp. 89–116.

Schlosser, E. (2001) *Fast Food Nation: The Dark Side of the All-American Meal*. London: Harper Collins.

Schor, J. (1998) *The Overspent American: Upscaling, Downshifting and the New Consumer*. New York: Basic Books.

Schramm, W. (1948) *Mass Communication*. Urbana, IL: University of Illinois Press.

Schroeder, J.E. (2002) *Visual Consumption*. London: Routledge.

Schroeder, J.E. (2004) 'Visual consumption in an image economy', in K. Ekstrom and H. Brembeck (eds), *Elusive Consumption*. Stockholm: Berg.

Scott, L. (1994a) 'The bridge from text to mind: adapting reader-response theory to consumer research', *Journal of Consumer Research* 21: 461–80.

Scott, L. (1994b) 'Images in advertising: the need for a theory of visual rhetoric', *Journal of Consumer Research* 21: 252–73.

Shankar, A. and Horton, B. (1999) 'Ambient media – advertising's new media opportunity?', *International Journal of Advertising* 18(3): 305–21.

Sherer, P.M. (1995) 'Selling the sizzle: Thai advertising crackles with creativity as industry continues to grow', *The Asian Wall Street Journal Weekly* 1: 6–7.

Sherry, J.E. (1983) 'Gift giving in anthropological perspective', *Journal of Consumer Research* 10, (September): 157–68.

Sherry, J.F. (1987) 'Advertising as cultural system', in J. Umiker-Sebeok (ed.), *Marketing and Semiotics*. Berlin: Mouton, pp. 441–62.

Sherry, J.F. (1991) ''Postmodern alternatives – the interpretive turn in consumer research', in T.S. Robertson and H.H. Kasserjian (eds), *Handbook of Consumer Behaviour*. Englewood Cliffs, NJ: Prentice-Hall, pp. 548–91.

Shimp, T.A. (1997) *Advertising, Promotion and Supplemental Aspects of Integrated Marketing Communications*. 4th edn. Orlando, Florida and Fort Worth, Texas: Dryden Press.

Schultz, D.E., Martin, D. and Brown W.P. (1987) *Strategic Advertising Campaigns*. 2nd edn. Lincolnwood, IL: NTC Business Books.

Schultz, D.E., Tannenbaum, S.I. and Lauterborn, R.F. (1993) *Integrated Marketing Communications*. Lincolnwood, IL: NTC Publishing Group.

Schultz, D. and Kitchen, P. (1997) 'Integrated marketing communications in US advertising agencies: an exploratory study', *Journal of Advertising Research* (September/October): 7–18.

Sperber, D. and Wilson, D. (1986) *Relevance: Communication and Cognition*. Oxford: Blackwell.

Steel, J. (1998) *Truth, Lies and Advertising: The Art of Account Planning*. New York: John Wiley and Sons.

Stern, B.B. (1993) 'Feminist literary criticism and the deconstruction of ads: a postmodern view of advertising and consumer responses', *Journal of Consumer Research* 19: 556–66.

Stern, B.B., (ed.) (1998) *Representing Consumers: Voices, Views and Visions*. London: Routledge.

Stevens, R. (1996) 'Ten ways of distinguishing between theories in social psychology' and 'Trimodal theory as a model for interrelating perspectives in psychology', in R. Sapsford (ed.), *Issues for Social Psychology*. Milton Keynes: Open University, 45–66; 77–84.

Strong, E.K. (1925) *The Psychology of Selling and Advertising*. New York: McGraw-Hill.

Supharp, S. (1993) *Thai Culture and Society: Values, Family, Religion and Tradition*. 8th edn. Bangkok: Thai Watanapanich (in Thai).

Szmigin, I. (2003) *Understanding the Consumer*. London: Sage.

Tanaka, K. (1994) *Advertising Language: A Pragmatic Approach to Advertisements in Britain and Japan*. London: Routledge.

Thompson, C.J., Locander, W. and Pollio, H. (1989) 'Putting consumer experience back into consumer research: the philosophy and method of existential phenomenology', *Journal of Consumer Research* 17: 133–47.

Thompson, C., Pollio, H. and Locander, W. (1994) 'The spoken and the unspoken: a hermeneutic approach to the understanding the cultural viewpoints that underlie consumers expressed meanings', *Journal of Consumer Research* 21: 431–53.

Tirakhunkovit, V. (1980) 'Why Thais do not like Thai products', *Monthly Business Journal* (February): 22–9.

Tiwsakul, R., Hackley, C. and Szmigin, I. (2004) 'Explicit, non-integrated product placement in British television programmes: an empirical study', *International Journal of Advertising* (in press).

Umiker-Sebeok, J. (ed.) (1997) *Marketing and Semiotics*. Amsterdam: Mouton de Gruyter.

Usunier, J.-C. (1993) *International Marketing – A Cultural Approach*. New York: Prentice-Hall.

Vakratsas, D. and Ambler, T. (1999) 'How advertising works: what do we really know?', *Journal of Marketing* 63 (January): 26–43.

van Raaij, W.F. (1989) 'How consumers react to advertising', *International Journal of Advertising* 8: 261–73.

van Raaij, W.F. (1998) 'Interactive communication: consumer power and initiative', *Journal of Marketing Communications* 4(1): 1–8.

Van Riel, C. (1995) *Principles of Corporate Communication*. London: Prentice-Hall.

Varey, R.J. (2000) *Corporate Communication Management; A Relationship Perspective*. London: Routledge.

Varey, R.J. (2002) *Marketing Communication: Principles and Practice*. London: Routledge.

Vaughn, R. (1986) 'How advertising works – a planning model revisited', *Journal of Advertising Research* (Feb-March): 57–66.

Veblen, T. ([1899] 1970) *The Theory of the Leisure Class*. London: Unwin Books.

Webley, P., Burgoyne, C.B., Lea, S.E.G. and Young, B.M. (2001) *The Economic Psychology of Everyday Life*. Hove: Psychology Press.

Wells, W.D. (1975) 'Psychographics: a critical review', *Journal of Marketing Research* 12 (May): 196–213.

Wells, W.D. (ed.) (1997) *Measuring Advertising Effectiveness*. Hillsdale, NJ: Lawrence Erlbaum Associates.

Wernick, A. (1991) *Promotional Culture – Advertising, Ideology and Symbolic Expression*. London and Newbury Park, CA: Sage.

West, D. (1993) 'Cross-national creative personalities, processes and agency philosophies', *Journal of Advertising Research* 33(5): 53–62.

West, D. and Ford, J. (2001) 'Advertising agency philosophies and employee risk taking', *Journal of Advertising* 30(1) (Spring): 77–91.

Williamson, J. (1978) *The Semiotics of Advertising*. London: Sage.

Wilmshurst, J. and Mackay, A. (1999) *The Fundamentals of Advertising*. 2nd edn. Oxford: Butterworth Heinemann.

Wilmshurst, J. and Mackay, A. (2000) *The Fundamentals of Advertising*. Oxford: Butterworth-Heinemann in association with ISBA.

World Health Organization (WHO) (1988) *Alcohol and the Mass Media*. Copenhagen, WHO.

Yeshin, T. (2000) *Integrated Marketing Communications*. Oxford: Butterworth-Heinemann.

Young, M. (1995) 'Getting legless, falling down pissy-arsed drunk', *Journal of Gender Studies* 4(1): 47–61.

Glossary

Above-the-line, below-the-line, through-the-line: Terms that originate from the UK system of ad agency remuneration (now largely defunct). If a medium generated commission payment to the agency, it was regarded as above-the-line. Above-the-line media included mainstream advertising on press, cinema, commercial radio and TV. Below-the-line media generated no agency commission and included sales promotion, public relations and direct mail. Through-the-line campaigns utilized combinations of above and below-the-line media.

Account manager: The role responsible for client liaison and general business management of an account.

Account planner: The account team role responsible for research and strategy.

ACORN: A Classification of Residential Neighbourhoods: a form of geodemographic segmentation which categorizes consumers on the basis of the residential neighbourhood where they live (further details on www.caci.co.uk).

Ambient media: Promotional messages inserted into traditionally non-promotional spaces in the consumer environment, such as the back of car parking tickets, farmer's fields, the sides of buildings, and printed on toilet tissue.

Audience: The number of people or households exposed to a given communication in a specified time period.

Awareness: The extent to which consumers have heard of or seen and recall a brand or a particular promotion, often measured by surveys.

Client brief/advertising strategy/creative brief: Internal agency documentation charting and guiding the development of communication.

Connote, connotation: A term referring to the subsidiary or secondary meanings that may subsist in a given sign and which depend upon the cultural knowledge and interpretive preference of the viewer. For example, a picture of a motor vehicle in a promotion may demonstrate its comfort, performance and elegance. A particular brand of vehicle pictured in a given lifestyle setting may carry other connotations, just as a BMW Mini connotes movies, Britain, the swinging 1960s, rally-car performance and fun for those familiar with the Mini's cultural heritage.

Consequentialist, consequentialism: The doctrine that the ethical status of acts should be judged according to the actual or possible consequences. In other words, if an advertisement may have good consequences, it is judged ethically acceptable. Many charities and public-service campaigns that try to shock people into driving more safely, drinking less alcohol and so on are allowed to do so based on these implicit grounds.

Consumer communities: Consumer groups whose only commonality is their mutual interest in a particular set of consumption values or practices. Some advertising agencies use the phrase 'brand communities' to indicate that heterogeneous social groups who share only a mutual interest in a particular brand can be defined as a group on this basis. The 'values' that are integral to the brand are, implicitly, shared by the group. An example might be the Manchester United supporter's club, a widely diverse group in terms of age, sex, ethnicity, nationality and social status, which is united only in their interest in the soccer club (and its merchandise).

Consumer practice: Consumer behaviour implies that consumers 'behave' according to rules while consumer practice implies that consumers' motivations are more complex and their actions volitional. Consumer 'practice' carries a symbolic value in that it can serve purposes of social positioning and identity formation. For example, from a consumer behaviour perspective a brand might be purchased because the repetitious advertising has created a conditioned response, but from a consumer practice perspective purchasing a particular brand might carry symbolic value for that consumer.

Copy-testing: A quasi-experimental group of research approaches usually conducted to test creative executions before campaign launch. Copy-testing measures attitudes towards an advertisement and its different visual or other components.

Copy-testing: A term covering various forms of pre-campaign testing of advertising. In many versions quasi-experimental techniques are used to assess the audience response to particular elements of a creative execution.

Cost-per-thousand: The cost per thousand consumers reached through a given medium, e.g. website banner ad, direct mail shot, TV ad.

Covert communication: Covert communication in advertising occurs where the absence of a clearly designated communication source facilitates meanings that are hinted, suggested or implied.

Creative hotshops/boutiques: It is common in the marketing communications field for successful professionals to break away from their employing agency to form new partnerships known as creative hotshops or boutiques. They are normally small partnerships of experienced professionals who seek a more responsive and rewarding environment than a large agency can offer.

Database mining software: Data mining entails using large databases of customer information to generate new segments to target with direct marketing initiatives. Software packages such as Viper can be useful in allowing marketing analysts to create contact lists of consumers from larger customer databases grouped according to any given criterion.

Deontological, deontology: The doctrine that acts should be judged on their intrinsic rightness or wrongness regardless of consequences. For example, many consumers objected to Benetton ads on the grounds that they were offensive: this is implicitly a deontological, ethical position.

Deprivation studies: A technique used in anthropological studies that requires research participants to forego an item for a period of time and to record their feelings about its absence in a diary. The feelings of deprivation endured (and expressed) can be a measure of the importance and role of the item in the person's life. One such study conducted for a global audio equipment manufacturer examined the role of audio equipment in peoples' lives by getting a panel of consumers to do without their audio equipment for a month.

Discourse: Anything that can be described in words: a category of social text that entails accepted or conventional communicative practices.

DRTV: Direct-response television.

Embedded marketing: Marketing initiatives presented in the context of entertainment vehicles such as movies, TV shows or sponsored media events. The key element of embedded marketing is that the audience is not necessarily explicitly aware that the brand exposure is a paid-for promotion.

Ethics: The study of the good life, including the exploration of questions of what good conduct is conducive to living the good life.

Eye tachistoscope test: A technique of advertising research in which a camera device tracks the movement of a viewer's eye over a creative execution.

Frame of reference: One way in which we see and understand the world is by comparing new experiences with old ones stored in our memory. Our vocabulary of stored cultural representations can be seen as a frame of reference which informs and limits our interpretation of new experiences.

Full-service agency: An increasingly rare breed of agency that purports to offer the full range of communications services to clients. In practice most agencies rely to a greater or lesser degree on sub-contracting of specialist services.

Generalization: Many traditions of advertising research seek findings in the form of simple factual propositions that can hold true for entire populations.

Geodemographics: A technique of consumer segmentation which combines demographic with geographical information.

Glocalization: A coined word referring to the managerial application of local criteria to marketing policy while retaining global themes and values. In marketing communication it might refer to allowing local agencies some licence to design creative tactics that make sense to local people within a controlled set of global brand values represented by particular logos or visual themes.

Guerrilla marketing: Tactics can include placing paid individuals in bars to engage customers in seemingly spontaneous conversation about an alcohol brand, marketers entering internet chatroom conversations under the guise of consumers, illegal fly-posting and graffiti campaigns.

Hierarchy-of-effects theories: Theories of persuasive communication that conceive of a passive and indifferent consumer who must be persuaded to buy the brand by the accumulated effect of a number of ad exposures.

High involvement: Consumers' purchase experience can be categorized as 'high-involvement' if it represents a purchase of such importance that it requires a high order of processing, including for example an information search and evaluation of alternatives. Purchases such as a house, car or family holiday might be characterized thus. Many purchases that take a lower proportion of disposable income are thought to be more spontaneous and subject to a lower order of rational processing (i.e. low-involvement). This binary construct loses its explanatory effectiveness when purchases have a powerful, symbolic value for consumers. The motive behind such purchases lies beyond the reach of the processing metaphor.

Integrated Marketing Communications (IMC): A management initiative to link and coordinate brand communications through all media channels in order to generate a **synergy** effect. IMC is often only partially achieved because of functional divisions within organizations between, say, public relations, advertising, personal selling and corporate communications.

Integrated solutions: Clients seeking solutions to their marketing and communication problems may require communications strategies that cut across the traditional demarcations of the communications mix of channels. Integrated solutions do not merely use differing channels, but co-ordinate them so that they act in a mutually reinforcing way.

Interpretive community: A group that shares certain cultural reference points and therefore a sense of meaning in some situations. For example, inter-textual references in ads to scenes from Hollywood movies or to sports events will be most quickly understood by, respectively, movie buffs and sports fans.

Intertextuality: A characteristic of discourses whereby they adapt, copy or refer to other discourses, e.g. where ads refer to movies, or movies refer to brands.

Likert scales: The original form of attitude measurement scale; usually in the form of a five-item response scale ranging from 'strongly negative' to 'strongly positive'.

Linear information processing theories of communication: Theories (or models) that draw an analogy between human and machine information processing. Humans are assumed to process sensory data in a linear sequence. Also known as Consumer Information Processing (CIP).

Magnetic resonance imaging (MRI): A medical technique for scanning the brain also used in consumer research.

Managerialist: Management and business research that is influenced by the assumptions and values of business managers as opposed to that produced mainly for an audience of policy makers, business ethicists or social scientists (adjective, managerial).

Media channels/media vehicles: The term 'media channels' normally refers to the various media that can carry promotional communication, such as TV, radio, cinema theatres, outdoor and press. Word-of-mouth is usually regarded as a non-mediated channel even though it may be utilized deliberately in marketing campaigns. A media vehicle may be a specific newspaper or TV station.

Media planner: A specialist whose responsibility it is to see that a given campaign reaches the largest number of targeted consumers possible within the allocated budget. The media reach of a campaign refers to the size of the audience.

Media-neutral planning: Agencies have historically been biased towards mass advertising in their media planning, partly because mass media advertising tended to earn the most money for agencies under the commission-based remuneration system. As the commission system is breaking down in favour of a billing system of remuneration, agencies are more willing to choose between media on an objective appraisal of their relative effectiveness for the campaign in hand.

'New' media: Technological development and cost reductions have made possible promotional media such as SMS text messaging, email, DVD ROMS, internet, and WAP-enabled and G3 mobile telephony.

Operant conditioning: In behavioural psychology operant conditioning changes behaviour in response to repeated stimuli administered by an operator. Advertisements can be conceived of as stimuli which, if repeated often enough, might change consumer behaviour. One flaw in this hypothesis might be that behavioural conditioning demands a closely controlled learning environment while the advertising exposure of an individual consumer cannot easily be controlled.

Ostensive communication: Communication which is explicit and has an identifiable source, usually contrasted with communication that is implied or hinted.

Panel data: Various marketing research organizations (e.g. AGB, Neilson) compile longitudinal market and consumer research data that they then sell to interested parties. Panel data can include weekly measures of grocery purchasing behaviour, TV viewing or radio listening, each of which are based on a panel of consumers statistically extrapolated to reflect the possible behaviour of whole populations.

Peer group: We refer closely to the views and values of people in our immediate social circle when we form new views. These people form our peer group and they can be influential in our own consumption and other choices.

Penetration: The percentage of a market that is reached by a given medium or an individual promotional communication.

Perception matrix: A spatial technique of conceptualizing brand positioning using two axes based on contrasting polar opposites. For example, in a perceptual map of the positioning of beer brands, the two axes could be dark-light and strong-weak. The axes/are drawn to form a cross and the various beer brands plotted on a scale.

Polysemy: The capacity of a social text such as an ad to have multiple meanings. The meanings inferred will depend on such things as the cultural context of interpretation and the interpretive strategy of the reader.

POS: Point-of-sale can refer to sales promotions at the cash till of a store or to any in-store promotion such as free sample stalls and LCD screen advertising.

Positioning: A key marketing concept indicating the values or ideas that are associated with a given brand. For example, the Nestlé Kit Kat chocolate confection is positioned (in the UK) as an excuse to have a break (that is, a rest) from work; the Marlborough cigarette brand is associated (through the image of the Marlboro cowboy) with individualism and toughness (see also pp. 73–5).

Positivistic: A term borrowed from the philosophy of logical positivism (Ayer, 1936) but referring in management and business research to approaches that model their methods and assumptions on those of natural science. One common form of positivistic research seeks to test hypotheses across large populations in order to generalize findings.

Primary research: The generation of new data. Contrasts with secondary research, which refers to the use of data already in existence.

Product placement: The practice of placing branded products or services in TV, radio, movie or other forms of entertainment.

Projective techniques: A psychological technique used in qualitative consumer research. It can take the form of a story-completion or picture-completion task. It originated in the psychiatric technique of asking a respondent to interpret Rorschach ink blots.

Promotional mix: The combination of differing promotional devices used to promote a brand or service. The term 'communications mix' is often used to indicate the differing communication channels that are deployed to reach the targeted audience.

Psycho-galvanometer tests: Tests carried out by a machine that measures the stimulation of the central nervous system by measuring the activity of sweat glands, thereby indicating the degree of interest a viewer has in a creative execution.

Psychographics: A lifestyles and attitudes-based approach to consumer segmentation. Many advertising agencies have devised their own categorisation system.

Qualitative: Adjective describing non-numerical research to seek insight into the quality of a group or person's experience of a given phenomenon.

Quantitative: Adjective describing research that generates numerical data.

Reach: The number of individuals or households within a target audience reached by a given promotional communication. Often expressed as a percentage.

Representational practices: A term common in cultural studies simply meaning ways of communicating. The term implies that truth in the world has an element of subjectivity so that, for example, advertising researchers may understand the social world in quite incompatible terms, such as when consumer research is cast in qualitative or quantitative terms. The word 'practice' is important in this phrase since it implies that communication is not confined to meaning-transfer but also fulfils social strategies (see Edwards and Potter, 1992; Potter and Wetherell, 1987). In some agencies quantitative data are regarded as more authoritative as grounds for argument than qualitative data.

Representative: Adjective describing a sample which, for research purposes, is assumed to have the same characteristics as the whole population of interest.

Segmentation: Conventional wisdom in marketing management holds that marketing resources are most effectively deployed if they are aimed at a clearly defined market segment, a group of existing or potential sales prospects.

Semiology: The study of linguistic signs. Associated with the work of Ferdinand de Saussure.

Semiotics: The study of all signs and their meaning in communication.

Signification: Used in this book to indicate the passive communication implicit in marketing signs of all kinds. For example, the 'swoosh' design, indicating the Nike brand and deployed on a huge variety of media, is probably one of the most widely recognized signs in all contemporary culture. The 'swoosh' carries a complex of contrived meanings deriving from Nike promotional activity, including sporting excellence, winning, 'street' style, etc.

Socio-economic group: An approach to classifying groups of individuals based on the occupation of the main household wage earner. Devised by the UK civil service in the late 1940s and still used in audience analysis.

Split-run studies: A technique of measuring advertising effect by comparing two differing executions in demographically similar regions.

Spontaneous brand awareness: Brand awareness is often tested using prompted and unprompted survey measures. Consumers might be asked to list the brands in a given category that they are aware of (unprompted). They might then have a list of brands read to them and are asked to indicate which they have heard of or seen in the last week (prompted).

Sub-culture: A sociological term referring to the way some people seek identity and realization in non-mainstream, group activities. The term has become associated with illicit activities such as street fighting gangs or punk rockers, but might equally apply to any group whose values, activities and social practices lie outside mainstream and establishment culture.

Sub-text: Texts that subsist beneath the main text, in other words, implied meanings additional or subordinate to the primary meaning of a text.

Synergy: A coined word indicating the mutually reinforcing promotional effect of portraying a brand in a similar style on two or more media channels.

Targeting: The task of reaching the chosen segment of consumers by placing creative executions on carefully chosen media channels.

TGI: Target Group Index. An audience and market research agency (www.bmrb-tgi.co.uk).

Tracking studies: Research studies which track the effect of a campaign after launch against the objectives set for it.

Traffic controller: An administrative role within agencies responsible for keeping track of the progress of different accounts.

Viral marketing: Originally confined to internet-based techniques of generating publicity (the establishment of Hotmail was the model for viral marketing), it is now sometimes conflated with guerrilla marketing tactics to include any attempt to contrive apparently spontaneous WOM publicity.

WOM: Word-of-mouth (promotion).

Index

Please note that page references to boxes, case studies and tables are in **bold** print.